In a Field of Static

Black Feminism on the Edge

A series edited by Jennifer C. Nash and Samantha Pinto

In a Field of Static

Missed Encounters with Black Feminist Theorizing

James Bliss

DUKE UNIVERSITY PRESS DURHAM AND LONDON 2026

Designed by Matthew Tauch
Typeset in Garamond Premier Pro by Westchester Publishing Services

Library of Congress Cataloging-in-Publication Data
Names: Bliss, James, [date] author
Title: In a field of static : missed encounters with Black Feminist theorizing / James Bliss.
Other titles: Missed encounters with Black Feminist theorizing | Black feminism on the edge
Description: Durham : Duke University Press, 2026. | Series: Black feminism on the edge | Includes bibliographical references and index.
Identifiers: LCCN 2026013515 (print)
LCCN 2026013516 (ebook)
ISBN 9781478039167 paperback
ISBN 9781478034223 hardcover
ISBN 9781478062806 ebook
Subjects: LCSH: Feminist theory | African American feminists | Queer theory | Critical theory | Feminist criticism
Classification: LCC HQ1190 .B5725 2026 (print)
LCC HQ1190 (ebook) | DDC 305.4201—dc23/eng/20260330
LC record available at https://lccn.loc.gov/2026013515
LC ebook record available at https://lccn.loc.gov/2026013516

Contents

Introduction

In a Field of Static

> And so my idea was to try to generate a discourse, or a vocabulary that would not just make it desirable, but would necessitate that black women be in the conversation. And that is a theoretical conversation about any number of things but one of the things is certainly the feminist project. I had to write a piece called "Interstices . . ." for a feminist conference at Barnard College in 1982. I was supposed to talk about black women, the sexuality of black women. And I thought, you know what, before I can get to the subject of the sexuality of black women I didn't see a vocabulary that would make it possible to entertain the sexuality of black women in any way that was other than traumatic. Before you could have a conversation about sexuality of black women you had to clear the static, clear the field of static.
>
> **Hortense Spillers, "Whatcha Gonna Do?," 300–301**

The conversation is always caught in a field of static.

Marking the twentieth anniversary of her essay "Mama's Baby, Papa's Maybe: An American Grammar Book," Hortense Spillers described the discursive static she was writing within and against in the first decade of the institutional life of Black feminist theorizing. By the 1980s, Spillers was one of dozens of Black feminist scholars announcing and analyzing the work of their contemporaries, building new traditions of Black feminist criticism, designing curricula and courses, mentoring students, and rediscovering the work of previous generations of Black women writers. All of this work took place within and against contexts hostile to the project of Black feminism. "What happens is that the forces that are really hostile to black life, to black people, are always operating," Spillers warned, "the forces of opposition are so forceful and so powerful and they're always pushing against us, they always want to enforce forgetfulness." Black feminist theorizing emerged from within that context of "psychological violence, epistemic violence, [and] intellectual violence," and the conversations we might have are always swimming against the tide of a forced forgetfulness.[1] From one angle, Spillers's "field of static" emerges from the forced and forceful forgetting of the Blackness peculiar to the figure of the Black woman, the figure that conditions the subjectivity of all social subjects, and the forced and forceful forgetting of the Blackness internal to all living. That static conditions every conversation about Black women—in the flesh or on the page; as social subjects, sentient objects, or discursive figures—even, or especially, within the fields of inquiry that were made possible by Black feminism and Black feminist theorizing.[2]

In a Field of Static argues that the debates that have shaped contemporary feminist and queer cultural studies have been missed encounters with Black feminist theorizing. It reads between Black feminist theorizing and feminist and queer cultural studies to understand how our attempts to escape the discursive static of antiblackness fall apart from within. The four chapters that follow each engage in some conflict, turn, debate, or disagreement that has informed the present shape of feminist and queer cultural studies (and, in a necessary way, the interdisciplinary humanities and social sciences more generally). Audre Lorde's public falling out with Mary Daly, feminist theory's arguments about intersectionality and assemblage theory, queer theory's debates over negativity and futurity, and the transnational and diasporic turns in feminist and queer studies, each demonstrates how our debates, misunderstandings, and missed encounters have drawn the horizons of our political and conceptual imaginations, and how we might imagine different horizons.

Within my treatment of those conflicts, I am particularly interested in the conceptual stakes of relationality, subjectivity, negativity, and belonging. These concepts are central to the work of feminist and queer studies as a privileged place-name for the attempt to think the relationship between power, meaning, and being—that is, the interplay of generative and repressive deployments of power, the production and reproduction of meaning, and the status of subjectivity and the terrain of ontology. These concepts lead us toward the question of the invention of the Human as a privileged genre of being and toward a critique of the Human. In *Engendering Blackness*, Patrice Douglass offers a provisional definition of the Human as "the modern philosophical and scientific social construction of a being that is actionable and willful because it is not a slave or an animal."[3] The constructedness of this figure, and the nature and stakes of its construction, has been a recurring theme across the long itinerary of Black political and social theory, as well as Black artistic and political practice. The most radical critiques of the Human—in its historical and contemporary outline, its ontological and political expressions—have been pursued under the heading of Black feminism. Black feminist theorizing, then, names a kind of speculative practice and an art of invention or inventiveness, an apocalyptic poiēsis within a field of static—the world of indeterminacy produced between Blackness and antiblackness. Across this project, as different chapters hold focus on particular conceptual problems, the indeterminacy of Blackness and antiblackness recurs as a guiding idea.

The past decades have seen a resurgence of academic, aesthetic, and activist discourses, often explicitly feminist and queer, confronting antiblackness. These discourses have been some of the most vital and energizing critiques of contemporary racial capitalism. They give shape to the mess we find ourselves in. Within the academy, they also represent a desire to build intellectual and political communities worthy of our most radical dreams of freedom. To be sure, the academy is a fraught and inhospitable site for building community, and scholarship is only one vehicle for cultivating a collective political imagination.[4] We all well know our employers are not our comrades. But we use the spaces available to us to cultivate discourses that might sustain the open revolt we hold in our hearts. Within these discourses confronting antiblackness is a tradition of Black feminist theorizing that cuts to the center of the historical, political, and ontological figures of the Human and the Slave—and, further, the systems, structures, and institutions that emerged in the wake of these figures. From these figures, an entire world emerged. Black feminist theorizing is one name for the desire to write a new world from the indeterminate position of the enslaved.

The current renaissance of feminist and queer Black studies scholarship is not new. A Black feminist invention and inventiveness has burst onto the American scene before. In different times and places, Black women have announced when and where they would enter the national conversation. Much of the Black feminist scholarship produced between the 1970s and the 2000s, that began from the rediscovery of those earlier expressions of Black women's cultural production, now awaits a similar rediscovery. More than that, many of that literature's most radical, innovative, and counterintuitive interventions have been forgotten, simplified, prettied, and appropriated. In her afterword to *Conjuring: Black Women, Fiction, and Literary Tradition*, Hortense Spillers noted the emerging status of "the community of Black women writing in the United States" as a "vivid new fact of national life."[5] But she warned against taking this vivid new fact for granted. A literary tradition "arises not only because there are writers there to make it, but also because there is a strategic audience of heightened consciousness prepared to read and interpret the work as such." Traditions are not, "like objects of nature, here to stay, but survive as *created social events* only to the extent that an audience cares to intersect them."[6] This insight spoke to a moment when much of the work of a recently dubbed "Black feminist criticism" was recovering and recuperating the works of "lost" Black women writers like Zora Neale Hurston, Dorothy West, Nella Larsen, and Jessie Fauset, as well as discovering and producing first readings of emerging writers like Gayl Jones, Toni Morrison, Paule Marshall, Toni Cade Bambara, and Alice Walker. Spillers's insight holds new meaning today as much of this Black feminist criticism is itself long lost, out of print, and understudied, and a burgeoning field of inquiry is once again recovering and reimagining Black feminist theorizing itself. Part of this work of recovery is to recover Black feminism from its own academic reception. That is, tracing how an emerging Black feminist criticism was filtered through field formations that at once relied on and resisted Black feminism.

In a Field of Static is interested in the material lives of ideas and discourses, and it proceeds from a practice of close or symptomatic reading. It is situated in the academy, in academic discourses, but it is also about how we make sense of the world, how we act on or within the world, and how our practices for making sense and making change get disrupted from within. The project is interested in the internal limits of our creative and critical practices (the indeterminacy of the field of static), how those limits shape how we relate or fail to relate to our world and its objects (which is to say that there are only ever different kinds of missed encounters), and, finally, how often those limits become externalized as figures of Blackness, and especially the Blackness of Black women. As the epilogue argues, Black feminist theorizing is not immune to this relationship to indeterminacy, but Black feminism opens a space for a creative or critical or political practice to be elaborated through indeterminacy, heterogeneity, promiscuity, incoherence, incompleteness, and impossibility.

This introduction will (1) begin to articulate the titular figures of the project; (2) lay out some of the interventions I understand the project to be making in the overlapping fields of Black studies, gender and sexuality studies, cultural studies, and critical theory; (3) describe the practices of reading I deploy across the text; (4) and briefly summarize the arguments of each chapter. Along the way, it will begin to articulate the stakes of something called *Black feminist theorizing* in relation to the itinerary of Hortense Spillers, and in relation to the concept-metaphor of *indeterminacy*. My engagement with Spillers cuts across all of the chapters that follow, as does the figure of indeterminacy as an essential element of Black feminist theorizing.

A FIELD OF STATIC

The figures in my title, *In a Field of Static: Missed Encounters with Black Feminist Theorizing*, shorthand the constellations of desires that animate this work. The figure of a "field of static" is a recurring image from the work of Hortense Spillers. In the preface to her *Black, White, and in Color*, Spillers says of her long essay "All the Things You Could Be by Now, If Sigmund Freud's Wife Was Your Mother," "[It] does not offer a 'solution,' . . . but, rather, finds and circumlocutes certain static in a field of force." "Doing so," she adds, "may be preferable, after all, to the false certainty of solutions."[7] Here, static is simultaneously that which stands in the way of an object of study and an object in its own right. We learn about the object through the outline of the distortions that make it available to us. In the essay on eating in the diaspora that introduces the volume, Spillers describes her "Interstices: A Small Drama of Words" as "a provisional reading of the sexuality *concept* as discursive static in the field of black women's historicity."[8] Again, the object of study is figured through the metaphor of static, a stuttering disruption in a field of stuttering disruptions. In the conversation, marking the twentieth anniversary of the publication of "Mama's Baby, Papa's Maybe," that serves as the epigraph to this chapter, Spillers emphasizes the moment of "Interstices" within her theoretical itinerary. Spillers would go on to describe her work across the 1980s as a contribution to a larger, collective project of cultivating a theoretical and conceptual apparatus that might allow Black women to "actually be in battle."[9]

But let's step back a moment, to the occasion of "Interstices." In the essay that opens *Black, White, and in Color*, Spillers reflects on the 1982 Scholar and Feminist Conference at Barnard College, where she first presented "Interstices." "Whatever the truth was about black women and sexuality would be, for all of thirty minutes or so, entirely in my hands! And

I knew impeccably well what one must do: *Tell* something about 'sexual experience' that would roughly equate with the suspect positioning of the 'native informant' to an audience of other cultural nuance."[10] This impetus toward, and anxiety around, *telling* touches something central in Spillers's critical practice. The Spillersian text always seems to be protecting itself, and Spillers herself remains something of a mysterious figure. The challenge and often the thrill of reading Spillers is that her text insists on this distance. It is a style that remains private in public.

Though well known as a stylist, Spillers's work has rarely been read as if it were, itself, literary. In the recollection of her former student Nick Davis, "People sometimes say to me, 'Hortense, why can't you just express these ideas more simply? Why do you have to use all these difficult words?' And the answer is, because that's the version of the fucking thought that I had, and those are the words that mean what I am trying to say."[11] Put differently, it may be that Spillers has a certain reverent irreverence toward the "difficulty" of her writing, and toward writing as a practice of thought.[12] Spillers never pursued the project of systematizing her concepts into a larger architecture (or, such a project has never appeared bearing her signature). And it is *to her credit* that she never did this. So many intellectual projects founder at the attempt to turn a provocative essay into a coherent book.[13] If she had chosen to settle the meanings of these ideas, they'd become problems costumed as solutions. Spillers's text is simultaneously critical, theoretical, and literary. Her theorizing is a literary act.[14] So why have so many critics in her wake, and I don't mind including myself here, grasped at her world of concepts as if it aspired to simply *represent* the lifeworld? Why has such a literary practice been read so literally?

Instead of showing or telling, her paper at Barnard became, in her words, "a provisional reading of the sexuality *concept* as discursive static in the field of black women's historicity. This view of the question, then, shifted the topic from the genre of the public (im)personal confession, with its links to the traditions and habits of pathos and sentimentality, to an examination of a field of discursive objects and events."[15] Around the occasion of the Barnard conference, Spillers seems to imagine the left turn toward discursivity as a way to short-circuit the choice between "the public (im)personal confession" and finding herself saying nothing, or having nothing to say. In what she *does* say at Barnard, Spillers turns our attention away from the things that might be said about Black women's sexuality and toward the discursive world that Black women's sexuality finds itself in. "Whatever my mother, niece, and I might say and do about our sexuality,"

Spillers writes, "remains an unarticulated nuance in various forms of public discourse as though we were figments of the great invisible empire of womankind." This is the beginning of Spillers's formulation of invisibility and hypervisibility as two forms of the same conundrum. And it is here that we find the best-known passage of "Interstices": "With the virtually sole exception of Calvin Hernton's *Sex and Racism in America* and less than a handful of very recent texts by black feminist and lesbian writers, black women are the beached whales of the sexual universe, unvoiced, misseen, not doing, awaiting *their* verb. Their sexual experiences are depicted, but not often by them, and if and when by the subject herself, often in the guise of vocal music, often in the self-contained accent and sheer romance of the blues."[16] The "beached whale" of the sexual universe—the image borders on the psychedelic. What type of universe is sexuality? What is the difference between an ocean and a land mass in that universe? What leads whales from the safety of the ocean to suffocating under their own weight on the shores of the sexual universe? Why has this image been treated with an almost sociological seriousness, as if it were self-evidently referencing reality? Let's belabor this point a bit more. What does it mean for this whale to be unvoiced? Or misseen? Why is it that a beached whale is awaiting a verb? What is it about a beached whale that *needs* a verb?[17]

The litany of concepts emerging from Spillers's body of work has beckoned generations of critics: ungendering, the pornotrope, flesh and a hieroglyphics of the flesh, the zero degree of social conceptualization, *being for* the captor, psychoanalytics, the socionom, the intramural, and the "beached whale" of Black women's sexuality. These concepts have an esoteric quality, like riddles or shibboleths. We may imagine we've pinned one down, or we grasp at another critic's interpretation, and the meaning is fixed, for a moment at least, in the citational sediment of academic practice.[18] It is the singular strangeness of her metaphor that calls out to us. In her essay "Strange Bedfellows: Black Feminism and Antipornography Feminism," Jennifer Nash puts Spillers's image in a list with concept-metaphors from Darlene Clark Hine and Evelyn Brooks Higginbotham. Nash writes, "For black feminists, terms like the 'culture of dissemblance,' the 'beached whale' of black female sexuality, and the 'politics of silence' have provided frameworks for considering how black women strategically avoid describing their own sexuality as a way of guarding against 'over-exposure.'"[19] The weirdness of Spillers's formulation is stripped in a way that presumes something knowable about both Spillers's metaphor, its referent, and her project as a theorist.

The indeterminacy of Spillers's meaning touches at the fuzzy boundary between theory and literature, which I also take up across chapter 2, where I consider the overlapping itineraries of Spillers's figure of the interstice and Kimberlé Crenshaw's figure of the intersection. Spillers's work has been central to a genealogy of work by Black feminist critics, and about Black women's invention and inventiveness, possessing a conceptual lexicon that is singular and resistant to systematization. Further, her work almost never simply "responds to" or "builds from" the work of her predecessors or her contemporaries.[20] If Spillers saw her project as "clearing a field of static," she was not replacing that static with something more clear—nothing like "the false certainty of solutions."[21] And so the present project approaches its subjects within these irreducible fields of static. This book is about finding new ways of relating to and within the indeterminacies of our fields of static.

The recent history of Black studies, in its imprecise and overlapping relationship to Black feminist and queer studies, has offered many species of indeterminacy. Consider the wayward, the monstrous, the ensemble, the (black) fantastic, the utopian, the beyond, the ecstatic, and the afterlife of slavery. Or errancy, grotesquerie, creative destruction, funk, emancipation, abolition, and apocalypse. Then there's excess, exorbitance, extravagance, anarchy, insurgency, fugitivity, maroonage, and the underground and undercommon. We also have figures like poiēsis, plasticity, thingliness, quiet, and the otherwise. There is Blacksound and (brown) jouissance, magic, madness, aliveness, (afro)fabulation, disorder, counterlife, mu, terror, and the end of the world. All of these figures can be, or can become, markers of indeterminacy *and* strategies for containing the indeterminate. They close off potential lines of flight in order to pursue others. To the extent that *static* is another name for indeterminacy, another way of domesticating it, I turn to it for the ways it resists wrestling indeterminacy into a specific prescription for critical practice.[22] The traditions of Black feminist theorizing that I read in this text don't have all of the answers, but the questions they pose and the questions they make possible aim at the foundations of a world worth reinventing.

In different ways, these figures reflect back the excess and incoherence of a racialized world, the "structuring irrationality" of antiblackness.[23] They also indicate the ambiguity and ineffability of Blackness itself. Figures of the indeterminate may have special purchase within Black studies because the field's object of study is, itself, indeterminate. Put it this way: Is the "black" in antiblackness the same as the "black" in Blackness? Or in

Black Study, Black feminism, or Black feminist theorizing? Does Blackness name some kind of positive content, or does it name an absence? If it names an absence, is it a foundational absence? In her study of Afro-Indigenous performance in Mexico, Anita González asks, "Is blackness a skin color, cultural persistence, a sense of marginality or, perhaps, a distance from notions of modernity?"[24] These questions can only have provisional answers, answers that allow an argument to be elaborated, a text to be written, a work of art to be created, a community or a collectivity to cohere, or a political project to be pursued. I add "static" to the field's figures of indeterminacy because I want to mark the contingency of my answers to these questions—they are the answers that enable *this project*.

At the same time, I take these questions to be essential to any study of the relations between power, meaning, and being—which I take to be the throughline that connects the best work of Black studies, feminist and queer theory, cultural studies, and critical theory. In the opening pages of *Disturbing the Peace*, Bryan Wagner summarizes the predicament at the heart of Black cultural studies. "Africa and its diaspora are older than blackness," Wagner writes, and "blackness does not come from Africa. Rather, Africa and its diaspora become black during a particular stage in their history." In the world that invented Africa as Black, "blackness indicates . . . existence without standing in the modern world system."[25] Blackness problematizes the guiding assumptions of cultural studies because Blackness enters discourse "not as a shared culture but as a condition of statelessness."[26] In Wagner's formulation, Blackness is an effect of antiblackness, the historical residuum of the racialization of slavery. Those beings marked by Blackness live in a shared (though not undifferentiated) relationship to antiblackness.

In this formulation, where Blackness emerges from antiblackness, the latter term imprecisely names a system of domination on the basis of continually invented and reinvented perceptions of "race." The paradox of this formulation is that it requires a prior Blackness, a Blackness that only comes into being through antiblackness. One way to resolve this contradiction is to place Blackness into a historical or anthropological sequence of successive regimes of creating in- and out-groups. In these accounts, Blackness is the form of non-belonging that succeeds the figure of the infidel or barbarian. It emerges from the specific historical and geopolitical conjunctures of the previous millennium (the emergence of capitalism, the changing value of labor following centuries of plague, the complex of sugar cultivation and plantation slavery that spread across the Mediterranean world, the consolidation of the Russian and Ottoman Empires, the loss of old trade routes and the search for new ones, the incipient consolidation of nation-states in Europe, and so forth). To my mind, although those accounts are significant as works of history or anthropology, they do not resolve the paradoxical relationship between Blackness and antiblackness.[27]

Within the text that follows, *antiblackness* is one name for the tactics, methods, strategies, and impulses that have been mobilized to push away the indeterminacy, incoherence, incompleteness, negativity, deathliness, and excess internal to life, living, or aliveness. Antiblackness writes that disavowal onto the surfaces of the body and has built a world from that species division, of those who live as Humans within the fantasy of coherence and those made to live otherwise. The critique of antiblackness can also be a critique of this figuration of the Human, can also aim at a world without the forms of coherence the Human so desperately chases. The counterintuitive privilege of racialization, then, is being excluded from the Human and so having access to the fullness of humanity.[28] And then, for that privilege, being rendered open to violence without limit: "From the incoherence of black death, America generates the coherence of white life."[29] Recent theorists of antiblackness have called this genre of being a type of deathliness, marked by the impossibility of relationality.[30] This tendency is organized in part around an encounter and engagement with the forms of social and civic death that coalesce around Blackness. And, further, the forms of lethal state and state-sanctioned violence disproportionately experienced by Black people. As we will see in chapter 1, it may also be that "death" is our ready-made language for a space bereft of the possibility of relation—that we experience ourselves as dead insofar as we experience ourselves beyond the reach of the socially structuring fantasy of the intersubjective. *Blackness* is one name for a crisis internal to relationality.

There is a split, here, between Blackness as one condition or aspect of African and African diasporic life across the long duration of modernity and Blackness as the indeterminacy internal to living. It may also be that the positive content of Blackness is the form of living that emerges *through* a violence without limit, or a humanity without foundation, fabricated in and as a no-place within and outside of the Human. In a given context, to *be* Black is to represent indeterminacy for others (and, potentially, for the other within oneself). The symptoms that appear across the different field formations in the following chapters—second-wave lesbian feminism, assemblage theory, queer negativity, queer futurity, transnational feminism, and diasporic queer studies, among others—represent different missed encounters with Blackness as one name for the indeterminacy, excess, and incoherence within life itself. The field of static, then, is both the discursive static produced by antiblackness, and the enabling impossibility internal to the collective enterprise of Black Study.

AND A MISSED ENCOUNTER

Spillers was reticent to participate in the conference where she delivered "Interstices." The 1982 Scholar and Feminist Conference at Barnard took on "The Politics of Sexuality." The uproar around the conference is well known as a node in the history of the feminist sex wars. In a 2011 essay, Spillers described receiving a call from Carole Vance inviting her to present at the conference. In the kitchen of her faculty house at Haverford College, Spillers recalled being "chary of phone calls like the one I perceived this to be." Black women in the academy "were talking among ourselves about our token position at feminist conferences and how we should refuse to cooperate in it." On the other end of the call, Vance "seemed implicitly aware of the fragile moment that the movement had entered, but in her own courteous way did not seem prepared to take no for an answer."[31] Vance's invitation may have struck Spillers as the beginning of a missed encounter. At the time of Vance's call, the most famous missed encounter of that moment was unfolding between Audre Lorde and Mary Daly, though, as we will see in chapter 1, their conflict took on its historical importance over a longer span of time.

The occasion of the Barnard conference seems to have provoked a special constellation of anxieties for Spillers. The conference organizers produced a special volume for the occasion of the conference, called *Diary of a Conference on Sexuality*. It collected the meeting notes of the planning committee, formatted as diary entries, and snippets from the participants, some of which were formatted in the style of personal ads. The document was playful and iconoclastic, and it also became a site of controversy. Spillers's statement in the *Diary* reads as follows:

> It is every teacher's nightmare—an analogy on every writer's dream of death: Suppose I got up there and forgot everything, or worse, could think of nothing to say? What would happen? In preparing my piece for

> "The Scholar and Feminist IX" conference, I imagined just that, and every time I did I read another paragraph or stalked another book, or jumped up from whereever [*sic*] I sat or lay and scribbled another note. Fragments shored against a possible ruin is what it is! Truly, we strive as much in the name of a "good name" as we do for our ownselves. Here's hoping. When I read this again, in a different context, under other lights, my "twenty minutes," a perfect solitude before 10,000 others, in effect, will be over, or nearly. I won't know until then. . . . [32]

The nightmare of standing on stage, or at the lectern, and your words have left you. Tasked with saying something about Black women's sexuality, would she suddenly turn aphasic? Around the occasion of "Interstices," Spillers seems to describe two different but related anxieties. First, that she will be on the unwelcome end of a missed encounter with white feminists, of the sort that had become a known issue among Black women in the academy. Second, she seems afraid of her own missed encounter with herself, or with the subject of Black women's sexuality—however it might intersect with her own sense of herself as a Black woman.

The debates, fights, misunderstandings, and missed encounters that shaped feminist and queer studies have drawn the horizons of our political and conceptual imaginations. These intellectual and institutional histories live with us in the present, long after what were once pitched battles have faded into the archive. This book reads these old histories in new ways, drawing out lessons from the archive of Black feminist theorizing. It is not interested in exploring "missed encounters" in the hope of, instead, having "true" or "authentic" encounters with Black feminism. I first began thinking about these questions through the figure of the missed encounter when I was introduced to Herman Rapaport's intellectual history of deconstruction in the United States, *The Theory Mess*. In it, Rapaport traces the academic and intellectual career of deconstruction as a winding network of missed encounters. Rapaport's guiding concept-metaphor is the Derridean figure of the *faux bond*: "My working thesis is the idea that over the past thirty years critical theory has obeyed the principle of the *faux bond*: the false bond, no show, failed encounter, or missed interlocution that creates some kind of linkage, despite itself."[33] For Rapaport, "the *faux bond* . . . resembles two ships passing in the night. They may miss. But even so, they come into proximity. It's the two ships together we are talking about, the missing of an encounter whose meeting place was at least staged and whose conditions were at least partially realized."[34]

In the present text, I argue that different missed encounters with Black feminism have created the linkages and the meeting places that we otherwise call feminist and queer theory, critical cultural studies, and critical theory; that we also call the various disciplines of the university; and that we might call intellectual life, as such.

For what it's worth, Rapaport has an inchoate sense of this. By way of opening his intellectual history of deconstruction, he turns to Ann duCille's "The Occult of True Black Womanhood," with an eye toward her most famous passage: "Much of the newfound interest in African American women that seems to honor the field of black feminist studies actually demeans it by treating it not like a discipline with a history and a body of rigorous scholarship and distinguished scholars underpinning it, but like an anybody-can-play pick-up game performed on a wide-open, untrammeled field. Often the object of the game seems to be to reinvent the intellectual wheel: to boldly go where in fact others have gone before, to flood the field with supposedly new 'new scholarship' that evinces little or no sense of the discipline's genealogy."[35] It is duCille's account of literary criticism's missed encounters with Black feminist theorizing that sets Rapaport's study in motion. Or, rather, it is Rapaport's missed encounter with Ann duCille that sets his book in motion. Immediately he writes, "What bothers duCille and what should bother us is a certain failed encounter with African-American studies, *if not black feminism*, when critics ignore disciplinarity, history, and intellectual genealogy and write whatever comes to mind."[36] Here we have the *faux bond* of displacing Black feminist studies for African American studies, as though the former were reducible to the latter. In his study of "deconstruction in eclipse," Black feminism is eclipsed. It is in this spirit, of a book on failed encounters with deconstruction that begins with a missed encounter with Black feminism—the everyday tragicomedy of being undone by one's own intentions—that I turn to the figure of the missed encounter.

This book is not so much interested in asserting what a "correct" encounter with the texts or traditions of Black feminism might consist in. Rather, it is interested in reading the symptoms of the encounters that *do* happen. My argument is not that some encounters with Black feminism are pathological and others are not. It is that every encounter carries within it something pathological. When I say pathological, I don't mean in the sense of being bad, broken, or defective. I mean, precisely, that all encounters, and all experiences of intersubjectivity, are mediated by the unconscious and so cannot be given anything like a complete or coherent accounting. In an encounter with Blackness, with what will be called a buried subjectivity, with a crisis internal to subjectivity, or with a subjectivity under erasure, the pathology internal to relationality can operate in still more peculiar ways. Ultimately, I read the symptoms of these encounters to ask what they make possible (or fail to make possible), and to ask if there might be different encounters that make different things possible.

Around when I began this project, practitioners in the field were talking about a "post–Black feminist era."[37] It was an era during which the debates produced by, and in some sense productive of, Black feminist theorizing had been "folded into the cultural imperatives and interpretive strategies of a new millennium in which black women and *their* literature" were "no longer in vogue in the academy or anywhere else."[38] The short, happy life of Black feminist theory had come and gone. In 2007, Farah Jasmine Griffin noted that Black feminist theorizing had been, since the 1990s, "one of the most intellectually exciting and fruitful developments in American literary criticism," but that it was experiencing "a backlash from both the left and the right."[39] The Right's rage over "political correctness" and multiculturalism was metastasizing into open fascism. The Left, moving beyond the polarizing radicalisms of the past, saw in Black feminism retrograde attachments to identity and essence. Further, the pipeline of graduate training was in crisis. Institutional antipathy and other formal and informal barriers to more widespread training prevented broader groups of scholars from engaging meaningfully with Black feminist theorizing.[40] The wholesale abandonment of the intellectual mission of the university, through which we now live and work, began with assaults on Black feminist theorizing.

In the 1990s, when Cultural Studies was ascendant and the interventions of poststructuralism were taken for granted, Black feminism seemed to signal whatever was "other" to Theory. Carole Boyce Davies wrote that "many scholars in the academy participate in the devaluing of Black women who are writers and theorists by not recognizing them or engaging their ideas" via citational absence and restricted access to modes of publication and distribution as well as larger structures of intelligibility within the academy, preventing Black feminist theorizing from being recognized *as theory*.[41] In order to elaborate Black feminism in this sense, the present text produces an archive and genealogy of Black feminist theorizing that reads both broadly and deeply within the tradition. Throughout, my emphasis is on those elements of Black feminist theorizing that have historically been occluded from scholarly study. Historically, Black feminism's structural critiques of the apparatus within which academic work (or "knowledge production") takes place have been recodified as different resistances to theory—where "theory" itself is reduced to a handful of poststructuralist projects.

Here, we might return again, unhappily, to a debate over "theory" and "practice" that, on Deborah McDowell's reading, was "often racialized and gendered," as Black feminist thought, "with precious few exceptions, [was] constructed as 'practice' or 'politics,' the negative obverse of 'theory.'"[42] In the late twentieth-century theoretical moment, Euro-American theorists sought to exorcise their racial demons through scattered engagements with Black women's literatures.[43] As a discourse, Black feminist interventions were not typically seen as interventions that might orient a theoretical practice. Moreover, in the wake of Barbara Christian's "The Race for Theory," the methodological gap between practical criticism and theoretical criticism became a proxy for the presumed political distance between different critical practitioners, and the abstraction or negativity of theoretical criticism was read as a species of political quietism, obscurantism, or elitism. Rather than read Black feminism as an expression of concreteness, or as an insistence on the agential capacity of the self-contained subject, its body and consciousness, my analysis elaborates elements of the negative and the irrelational, the insovereign, abstract, and nonpractical.

AND BLACK FEMINIST THEORIZING

At the same time, I insist that Black feminism is irreducible to this archive of the negative, and irreducible to any archive and any genealogy. The book resists a narrow conceptual definition of Black feminism that would treat the field as separate or separable from the more "universal" concerns of cultural studies and critical theory. If Black feminism is repressed in and among the identity knowledges, it isn't solely some truth or fact of "the Black woman" that is repressed and that must, or might, be recovered. Repressed are the questions that Black feminist theorizing makes possible, and that are repressed so that field formations can become coherent to themselves. Black feminist theorizing can be read here as a genre of Black invention—where the Black female, femme, feminine, mater, and maternal operate as synecdochic figures for a species of poiēsis. The critical task here is to approach the subject of Black feminism not as a known or knowable object but as a generative capacity, as an absent core that produces questions toward the foundations of subjectivity in the afterlife of slavery. The work is to inhabit a field of static and explore its potential for the practice of thought. The work of recovery is never the end of the story. It is never about restoring some missing content, but about discovering what questions are made possible when we allow our critical and theoretical work to be elaborated by, or in some other relation to, Black feminist theorizing.

When "Interstices" was published in *Pleasure and Danger: Exploring Female Sexuality*, Spillers's research agenda was laden with possibility. She described herself as at work "on a critical theory of black women's writing, a critical perspective on the rhetoric of the African-American sermon, and a long piece of fiction."[44] As the decade progressed, she would stop describing herself as a writer of fiction (the draft of her novel now resides among her papers at Brown University), and her work on the African American sermon, the subject of her doctoral dissertation, also disappeared from her academic biographies for decades. Her "critical theory of black women's writing" would become a project called "In the Flesh: A Situation for Feminist Inquiry." By 1993, "In the Flesh" was "forthcoming," but in the years that followed, its title was replaced by brief, shifting descriptions of the project. In 1996, the project had split into "a collection of essays and a monograph on women in slavery and its implications for feminist critique."[45] The collection became *Black, White, and in Color*, a primer for Black feminist theorizing, and by the time it was released in the spring of 2003, Spillers was "at work on a new project called 'The Idea of Black Culture.'"[46] The gift of Spillers's published work lives alongside the dream of all the work she promised but didn't publish.

Black feminist theorizing may be one name for the space between a gift and the dream of something more. It may live in the space between what is possible to say, what can be written, and an inarticulate and illegible excess, an indeterminate and impossible account of unfreedom and its others. The space between what is and what might be is also the space of desire, of demand. In "The Race for Theory," Spillers's contemporary, the late Barbara Christian, described another experience of the demands made of Black feminist literary critics. "Some of us are continually harassed to invent wholesale theories regardless of the complexity of the literature we study," she wrote. "I, for one, am tired of being asked to produce a black feminist literary theory as if I were a mechanical man."[47] For Christian, the *theorizing* of people of color—"and I intentionally use the verb rather than the noun," she added, parenthetically—occurred "in forms quite different from the Western form of abstract logic." This theorizing could be narrative, could take the form of "riddles and proverbs," or could appear "in the play of language." The "grace and pleasure" of this play of language gestured toward a theoretical practice "in the form of the hieroglyph," something "both sensual and abstract, both beautiful and communicative."[48] Responding to the institutional pressures of her moment, as Theory became a common currency in university English departments, with unequal effects for women of color critics, Christian understood the conceptual language and stylistic conventions of Theory to be inapposite to these other forms of theorizing.[49]

Though both critics theorized, in the sense that both engaged in speculative practices on the relation between power, meaning, and being, Spillers and Christian had different *orientations* toward the act of producing a critical theory of Black women's writing. Spillers promised such a volume for over a decade. Christian maintained that with so few working experts in Black women's literature, it would be "presumptuous . . . to invent a theory of how we *ought* to read."[50] Ultimately, neither ever produced such a work. Moreover, although there was a powerful desire (and individual and institutional demands) to produce general theories of Black women's expressive cultures, no single-authored work is understood to have produced such a theory—not by Spillers or Christian, not by Claudia Tate, Nellie McKay, Cheryl Wall, or Hazel Carby, nor by Barbara Smith, Akasha Hull, Shirley Anne Williams, Hortense Thornton, Deborah McDowell, Valerie Smith, Mae Henderson, Sandra Adell, Carole Boyce Davies, Mary Helen Washington, Ann duCille, Abena Busia, Michele Wallace, Wahneema Lubiano, Eleanor Traylor, Joyce Ann Joyce, Trudier Harris, Frances Smith Foster, VèVè Clark, June Jordan, or bell hooks. As a field of study, there are many dozens of works with different names for the indeterminacy that Spillers intended to call "In the Flesh" and that Christian identified in the figure of the hieroglyph. But Black feminist theorizing is irreducible to one figure. By the time the moment of Theory faded into the era of Cultural Studies, producing a theory of Black women's writing lost its urgency. By and large, the chapters that follow live between the moment of Theory and the time of Cultural Studies, though in the current crisis state of the academic humanities, neither theory nor cultural studies enjoys pride of place. The chapters that follow offer different perspectives on how we lost theory *and* cultural studies as orienting ideas and gained perpetual crisis. It may be that the crisis implied by Black feminist theorizing has been generalized across the speculative humanities.

This book is not a theory of Black feminist theorizing. In this book, Black feminism names a necessarily heterogenous and heteroglot assemblage of interventions that are resistant to systemization—not, or not only, or not reducible to, an academic (inter)discipline or party program. It names discourses, archives, genealogies, and communities of practitioners (past, present, and future). What interests me in bringing together a diffuse group of authors and texts is not a shared set of avowed theoretical positions or methodological or epistemological assumptions. What I refer to as Black feminist theorizing is, perhaps, a shared insistence that "there is not a subject that you can speak about in the modern world where you will not have to talk about African women and new world African women."[51] If Blackness is a genre of living marked by its vulnerability to violence without limit, but also a living with access to those forms of experience prohibited and disavowed in the pursuit of a fictive coherence, in the name of a form of living called the Human, Black feminist theorizing may be a theorizing of or from the experience of being made to embody indeterminacy, of having indeterminacy written onto and read from the surfaces of the body, of remaking the skin from the site where intimacy and alienation cohabitate into a marker of one's proximity to violence and violation—dynamics that, by now, implicate *all* subjects, that speak to any experience of human being.[52]

The thread that connects Black feminist theorists within this study is their capacity to open up new fields of thought at "the nexus of violence and sexuality," the indeterminate space of Blackness.[53] If Blackness emerges at this nexus of violence and sexuality, it is not only because of the ways violence and sexuality figure into the historical emergence of Blackness. Rather, it is the indeterminacy of violence and sexuality, their porous borders, their fundamental ineffability, that bind them to Blackness, generally, and the Blackness of Black women, especially. Similar continuums connect force and violence, sensation and sexuality, and Human and Black. Over several centuries, and within a matrix of changing and emerging social institutions, the varieties of indeterminate human experience settled around the idea that indeterminacy, excess, and incoherence could be written onto and read from the surfaces of the body, which is one angle of the story of the racialization of slavery.

Theorizing from the vantage of a Black feminist theorizing is also an argument about the persistence of slavery as a structuring force in the contemporary world. This book resists an approach that engages with slavery as a bounded historical event, albeit one that might survive as an inheritance or legacy or source of accumulated disadvantages. I am interested in thinking slavery following Jared Sexton's provocation: "But what if slavery does not die, as it were, because it is immortal, but rather because it is non-mortal, because it has *never* lived, at least not in the psychic life of power? What if the source of slavery's longevity is not its resilience in the face of opposition, but the obscurity of its existence? Not the accumulation of its political capital, but the illegibility of its grammar?"[54] Here, "slavery" is freighted with both its historical materiality (the history of slavery and its racialization) and the gravitational pull of its discursivity (its life in and as discourse). In a paper given at the English Institute in 1987, Spillers articulated the overlap in the material and discursive lives of slavery. "As concretely material as the 'institution' was, as a natural historical sequence and as a scene of pulverization and murder," she argued, "'slavery,' for all that, remains one of the most textualized and discursive fields of practice that we could posit as a structure for attention."[55] As much as slavery reshaped the physical world, political and economic systems, and the material lives of individuals, the institution was also *lived* in discourse. Spillers continues:

> In a very real sense, a full century and a half "after the fact," "slavery" is *primarily* discursive, as we search vainly for a point of absolute and indisputable origin, for a moment of plenitude that would restore us to the real, rich "thing" itself before discourse touched it. In that regard, "slavery" becomes the great "test case" around which, for its Afro-American readers, the circle of mystery is recircumscribed time and again. This realization is stunning: as many times as we reopen slavery's closure, we are hurtled rapidly forward into the dizzying motions of a symbolic enterprise, and it becomes increasingly clear that the cultural synthesis we call "slavery" was never homogeneous in its practices and conception, nor unitary in the faces it has yielded.[56]

In this formulation, slavery lives and is lived in discourse, in the ways meaning is written onto and read from the surfaces of the body, in the ways these meanings circulate across the time and space of the premodern, modern, and postmodern. Black feminist theorizing is one name for a practice of reading the discursive lives of slavery—not only the ways they circumscribe our political imaginations and underwrite sociality and social institutions, but their presence in and as the literary.

In this context, in which "slavery's critical agency in Western self-conceptualization . . . is nothing short of foundational" and "the quintessential 'slave' is *not* a male, but a female," we might rethink how Black feminism interacts with other claims toward understanding social relations in their totality.[57] Across this study, the structural position of the Black woman is not (yet another) particular position; it is what Slavoj Žižek has called a *universal singularity*, "a kind of direct short circuit between the singular and the universal, bypassing the particular."[58] "The Black woman" is an abstraction that Black women in the world live in relation to in myriad ways; it is one name for the experience of being made to represent indeterminacy, excess, incoherence, and deathliness for the world around you. It may also be a "structural position of non-communicability in the face of all other positions."[59] Ultimately, this is to say, following the Combahee River Collective, that "if Black women were free, it would mean that everyone else would have to be free since our freedom would necessitate the destruction of all the systems of oppression."[60] Put differently, any politics that is not invested in a feminist Black radicalism is not invested in freedom *as such*. In our missed encounters with Black feminism, we reinvest in our own unfreedoms. In some way, our anxieties over Black feminist theorizing are anxieties over our own ambivalence toward freedom.[61] Across the field formations emerging from critical cultural studies, the question that avoids being asked is, what do we want, what do we keep wanting, in place of this wild freedom?

What would it mean to want a Black freedom more than the freedoms of slave owners, capitalists, subjects, and sovereigns? In a recent work, Sara Clarke Kaplan looks to the figure of "the Black reproductive"—"the constellation of national discourses, state policies, and individual practices through which Black reproductive acts, capacities, and labor have been imagined and administered in the United States for some 350 years"—as the point of departure for imagining a "Black feminist politics of freedom."[62] For Kaplan, "the generative potential of Black freedom" resides in "aporetic instances of the contingent and ephemeral, the unsustainable and the ruptural, the still-not-achieved yet not-quite-impossible."[63] It may also be that we don't know what it would mean to be free. We may know that the liberal tradition's account of liberty is vouchsafed by antiblackness, but we lack language for articulating different species of unfreedom or for imagining a free world, a Blackened world, and what we might be within one.[64]

AND A PRACTICE OF READING

> The adopted procedure for this essay is neither fish nor fowl and, as such, breathes in the impure air of literary interpretation, verging on social theory. It assumes for the moment a sort of critically illegitimate stance—the literary text *does* point outside itself—in the primary interest of leading the reader back inside the universe of the apparently self-contained artifact.
>
> —HORTENSE SPILLERS, *BLACK, WHITE, AND IN COLOR*, 131

Reading slavery in this way demands a critical procedure that can think through what Spillers called "the (il)logic of the 'symptom.'" It demands a symptomatic reading practice attuned to how "an 'inside' materializes in an 'outside' as a specified break in a kinetic relay of movement."[65] For Spillers, "slavery . . . offers an analogous spectacle of successive displacements" to the Freudian symptom, where the task of the critic is "to hear its stutter more clearly."[66] Methodologically, *In a Field of Static* is a metacommentary on field formation and a study of the necessary absences around which these formations in critical cultural studies cohere. By and large, rather than attempting broad surveys of different discourses, my critique proceeds by way of close readings of individual authors emblematic of discursive formations, if not unproblematically representative of them. This close reading across the intellectual itineraries of the authors opens space for symptomatic readings, attuned to different forms of "discursive static" that are produced by missed and anxious encounters with Black feminism.[67] Part of this work, then, is an exploration of the psychic life of field formation. Working in a productive tension between methods associated with historical materialism, deconstruction, and psychoanalysis, my critical operation is an experiment in thinking *with* Black feminist theorizing. It is a speculative practice *enabled* by Black feminism rather than an attempt to systematize or instrumentalize Black feminism as a practice of reading.

What Spillers called breathing the impure air of literary interpretation verging on social theory was already becoming, by the mid-1980s, emblematic of a growing genre of literary and cultural criticism called Theory. Compared to earlier, practical criticisms, this criticism could be inventive, or irresponsible, in its treatment of the literary work of art, aspiring itself to be a literary act.[68] There was considerable acrimony; this new theoretical-qua-literary criticism generated several new star critics and many more detractors and imitators. It also shaped the emergence of a field of practice called Cultural Studies, that combined interpretation and social theory within the terrain of the interdisciplinary. The whole short, happy life of Cultural Studies would be the topic of another book (though I cover some of it here in chapter 4), but it represented both the generalization and politicization of Theory. Theory opened a space for the different varieties of academic practice, which had once understood themselves as narrowly interested in the production of knowledge, to become creative, inventive practices. Building from this, the model of Cultural Studies opened a space for different forms of academic practice to understand themselves as political interventions. If every act of knowledge production was implicated in relations and operations of power, then the act of producing knowledge might *intervene* in larger relations and operations of power.[69] The desires called Cultural Studies may have failed to generate a historical bloc, but they opened a space for the practice of reading I pursue in this book, a practice that is interested in what becomes possible in the indistinction between the theoretical and the literary.[70]

If we expand the ambit of the theoretical, we allow other sets of concerns within the work of literature to announce themselves. For instance, "124 was spiteful" is an argument; it theorizes.[71] So do lines like "come into the / Black / and live."[72] The literary's arguments can only be made by rejecting or letting go of closure, of letting go of the presumption that arguments must (or can) close down on themselves. There is also something literary in the text of theory—some part of the idea that can only be expressed through beauty, terror, joy, or anguish.

There are openings in the text of theory that are properly literary, and there are other openings in the text of theory that make space for anxieties of one kind or another: the anxiety that the argument cannot be made (at all), or cannot be made by me (whoever "me" happens to be), or cannot be made by me now as I'm writing it (maybe it needs to be made by someone smarter or someone who can see or read or write better). There are openings in the text of theory that make space for these anxieties, and there are openings that make space for silence, for the undecidable or unknowable. All of these the text of theory shares with the literary text. The challenge is in the balance we allow between these forms of discourse. The challenge is not to allow the openness of the text to be an alibi for fear—fear that the thought we mean to express, the argument we mean to make, takes us somewhere we don't want to go. And so we settle for beauty, ambiguity, or sentimentality. We settle for an easy and pleasing beauty, to protect us from the fearful no-places our arguments may take us.

In a Field of Static works between genres, reading history, criticism, prose, and poetry as forms of theorizing. This practice of reading is one inheritance of the deconstruction internal to Black feminist theorizing—a serious attention to the indeterminacy of the literary and the theoretical, the ways that each form of expressive speculation is implicated in the other. In literature, it is taken for granted that there is no transparent relationship between argument and author, that the argument is more *and* less than the author's intention. On the other hand, we understand the text of criticism, philosophy, or theory to collapse the space between intention and argument. In the case of Black literary art, these distinctions have always been in crisis. Often, the interpretation of Black literary art has been caught in a reductive empiricism. In a 1974 response to Sara Blackburn's *New York Times* review of Toni Morrison's *Sula*, Alice Walker wrote that Blackburn, "like only too many reviewers before her, is incapable . . . of experiencing black fiction as art but must read it instead as sociology."[73] This tendency to read Black literature as sociology, to bracket away the indeterminacy of the literary text, has also shaped the reception of Black theorizing, and in particular Black feminist theorizing, which is reduced to metasociological reflections on works of sociology.

Jennifer Nash has identified in recent Black feminist scholarship a formal turn toward "risky" genres, writing inflected by the personal and poetic, or what she terms "beautiful writing." On Nash's analysis, beautiful writing in contemporary Black feminist theory is "the form *required* to develop cartographies of black women's losses," where "loss" encompasses "absence, erasure, what is missed and missing, what is taken or stolen, what is unknown and unknowable."[74] These works belong to hybrid genres, caught between a formal inventiveness that the thought invites, and the institutional demands of journals, presses, and universities. The theorization of a Black feminist invention seems to demand, if not formal *innovation*, then at least forms other than our generic, disciplinary, or received forms of scholarship. These forms, these innovations on reading, remind us that reading, as a critical practice, *does something* to its objects, something more or something other than simply *revealing* the object. Reading is itself a practice of invention.

Along those lines, Black feminist theorizing seems to demand different practices of reading. In her work on the receptions of "intersectionality" in the neoliberal corporate university, Tiffany Lethabo King builds out a distinction between "anxious" and "loving" reading practices. "Lovingly pushing back against post-intersectional theories," she "calls for a less anxious and therefore more loving reading practice that tarries with the potential and future of intersectionality rather than overcoming it in a neoliberal era of disposability."[75] There are two orders of King's distinction. On one hand, she distinguishes between reading practices that tarry with the potential and future of a text against those reading practices that race to find reasons to disengage from a text. The present text endeavors to follow King's advice, and example, on this front. On the other hand, there is the remarkable phrasing of "a less anxious *and therefore more loving* reading practice." The tension here between anxiety and love is one of the central themes of this study. Across the chapters that follow, I read different engagements with the texts and interventions of Black feminist theorizing as "anxious."[76] I am interested in how critical, intellectual, and political anxieties manifest, and what they tell us about what it means to try to think with Black feminist theorizing.

What are the stakes for critique of this distinction between anxiety and love? Is the distinction itself tenable? Surely in our everyday lives, as simultaneously anxious and loving beings, the distinction is more aspirational than actual. In his *Introductory Lectures on Psycho-Analysis*, Sigmund Freud called anxiety the universal currency of the affects. Any feeling might become anxiety and anxiety might become any other feeling.[77] For the work of criticism, anxiety is easy to diagnose but hard to unravel. Though Jacques Lacan is said to have called anxiety the only affect "which does not deceive,"[78] anxiety is both itself and the feelings it translates, transmutes, or exchanges for. An anxious reading is a signpost for the unknowable, for the inaccessible inner life of the critic. But anxiety is also a short circuit between the unconscious and the socionom.[79] In *Black Skin, White Masks*, Frantz Fanon writes that "the Negro is a phobogenic object, a stimulus to anxiety."[80] "What this means," Ronald Judy argues, in a signal reading of Fanon, "is that the black body does not live on the symbolic level in an anti-black world. It is locked in the serious, material values of the real."[81] Elsewhere in the same study, Judy writes that, "in revealing . . . the anomalies of affect responsible for what Fanon comes to call nègro-phobogénèsis, he reveals a pathology that is coterminous with the very symbolic order of modernity, and not just colonialism."[82] This is all to say that critical encounters with Black texts—in the present study, with the texts of a Black feminist theorizing—are freighted with anxieties that precede and exceed both critic and text, that cut across the semantic fields of modernity while also touching our innermost lifeworlds and unconscious minds.

In chapter 3, the relationship between love and anxiety finds expression across the discourses of Black feminist theorizing, queer negativity, and queer futurity. Each reveals, in some way, the overlap between love and anxiety. Love is not a safeguard against anxiety. Fanon is just one theorist of race to argue that negrophobia and negrophilia are both expressions of a stimulus to anxiety. Love is never guaranteed, and love is never a guarantee—of fidelity, exactitude, felicity, reciprocity, care, or goodness. That love can never be guaranteed, that love cannot guarantee, is one reason anxiety is so powerful.[83] A loving reading can be beholden to the same pathologies as an anxious one. A fraught endeavor. We can only pursue a critique without guarantees, where failure (or something worse) is a potential outcome.

AND AN AFFIRMATION

The chapters that follow are organized around different debates, different conflicts that shaped feminist and queer cultural studies, different missed encounters with Black feminism that touch ideas central to a critique of the Human—relationality, subjectivity, negativity, and belonging. The first two chapters are organized around different missed encounters: in one, the missed encounter that unfolded between Audre Lorde and Mary Daly; in the other, the missed encounter between two discourses—intersectionality and assemblage theory. Those chapters are interested in both the immediate stakes of those missed encounters and the ways they live on in academic practice and Black feminist theorizing. The second pair of chapters looks more broadly at field formations, at the ways specific debates or interventions coalesced from missed encounters with Black feminist theorizing: in one, queer theory's competing discourses of negativity and futurity; in the other, the transnational and diasporic turns in feminist and queer cultural studies. In those chapters, I trace the symptomatic presence and absence of Blackness across those field-defining interventions, focusing on how their most important insights might be reimagined in relation to Black feminist theorizing.

The first chapter, "Open Letters, and the Irrelational Erotics of a Black Feminist Negativity," unpacks the racial politics of relationality across the early histories of lesbian feminism and the institutionalization of women's studies as an interdiscipline. Through an extended engagement with the work of Audre Lorde, and with special attention to her missed encounters with Mary Daly, immortalized in her "Open Letter to Mary Daly," I read relationality as a fantasy underwriting the politics of second-wave or sisterhood feminism. Lorde's practice of reading, and her readings of contemporaneous feminists and the whiteness of women's liberation, revealed the ways Black women functioned for feminism, as what made feminist sisterhood possible and feminist politics impossible. Across her work, across the essays and poetry she produced during her missed encounters with Daly, Lorde began to articulate a Blackened mode of relationality, an irrelational erotics that traverses the terrain of a structural impossibility, that explores the fullness of a buried subjectivity, of a subjectivity lived through indeterminacy. The chapter reads contemporary theorizations of relationality in Black studies, especially those informed by the interventions called afropessimism, for their accent on the *impossibility* of relationality. In the failed relation between Lorde and Daly, I find an alternative relation to impossibility that might be called irrelational. The irrelational is relationality touched by impossibility, the erotics of a Black feminist negativity.

The second chapter, "Buried Subjects, and the Lines from Intersectionality to Abolition," begins from the tension internal to Black feminism over its institutionalization and the impossibility of Black feminism as an institutional project. Intersectionality and the critique of intersectionality is one privileged example of this tension. The chapter offers a reading of the spatial politics of Black feminist theorizing to examine those critiques of intersectionality produced under the heading of assemblage theory, and most famously in the work of Jasbir Puar. I argue that these critiques produce intersectionality as a spatial metaphor that locates and fixes compound subjects, a fixing complicit with the work of the national security state. Intervening in these critiques of intersectionality, I trace alternative theorizations of spatiality and subjectivity internal to Kimberlé Crenshaw's work, extending them through Hortense Spillers's theorization of the interstice as the indeterminate nonsite of the Black female subject. In this rereading of Crenshaw through Spillers, I explore how intersectionality belongs not only to a tradition of Black feminist theorizing on particularity and compoundedness but to a tradition of Black feminist theorizing on placelessness, singularity, and absence. Rather than bolster oppressive institutions through liberal models of inclusion, Black feminism names a monstrous potential for a different theorization of freedom from the vantage of a buried subjectivity.

The chapter also takes seriously the irreducible promiscuity of the conceptual languages we use to give substance to, and to make sense of, the knowledge of freedom expressed otherwise through collective struggle. On either end of the popularization of intersectionality, the chapter engages with Crenshaw's earlier contributions to Critical Legal Studies and Critical Race Theory and, more recently, the rise of an abolition feminism as the radical edge of feminist politics. Crenshaw's early work gives context for understanding the history of Black freedom struggle that informed her theorizations of intersectionality. As that theorization was popularized, first in gender and sexuality studies curricula and then in the cultural mainstream, as "intersectionality" became a nominal principle of one of the United States' two political parties, and as the most radical insights of Crenshaw's text were jettisoned, the radical edge of political activism and lay political theorizing moved toward "abolition" to express and to structure an evolving set of political principles. The chapter traces some of this movement from intersectionality to abolition and how each is animated by the problem of imagining the subject of a Black feminist theorizing.

The third chapter, "Hope Against Hope, and the Queer Negativity of a Black Feminist Poiēsis," turns to competing discourses within queer studies, queer negativity and queer futurity, to theorize Blackness as one name for the negativity internal to intersubjectivity, for the fecund absence that generates a Black feminist poiēsis. The queer negativity of Lee Edelman pursued a theorization of queer positionality that aligned it conceptually, if not politically, with the project of afropessimism as one expression of a Black feminist negativity. Meanwhile, the queer futurity articulated by the late José Esteban Muñoz expressed itself through an antiracist politics that, nevertheless, aimed for the radical promise of a relationality prior to antiblackness, what might be the desire for an antiracist antiblackness. Rather than dwell in the moment of that debate, such as it was, the chapter travels prehistories of queer theory in the Black women's writing of the post–Black Power moment and the foundational works of Leo Bersani.

Beginning with a reading of Toni Morrison's 1976 essay "A Slow Walk of Trees (as Grandmother Would Say), Hopeless (as Grandfather Would Say)," the chapter considers the dialectic of hope and hopelessness central to the Black radical tradition, and the ways Morrison finds this dialectic expressed across generations. Morrison's essay troubles an easy formulation of reproductive futurity, even as it dramatizes a familiar tension between pessimism and optimism. The chapter turns to the early works of Beverly Smith and Barbara Smith, twin sisters who cofounded the Combahee River Collective while charting individual paths as writers and activists. Alongside discussions of the published diary writings of the Smith sisters, the chapter pursues an extended engagement with the theoretical itinerary of Leo Bersani, whose foundational work around the antisociality of homosexual desire helped shape the discourses of negativity and futurity in queer studies. Bersani's innovative reading between Freud and Foucault allowed for the theorization of a negativity that shatters subjectivity, but Bersani's project sought redemption in a sociality untouched by antiblackness, which is also to say a desire for a sociality untouched by Blackness. In productive tension with Bersani, Beverly and Barbara Smith theorized the relationships between violence and sexuality from the perspective of a Black feminist theorizing. Turning back to the debate over queer negativity and queer futurity, the chapter reads the intergenerational interlocution between Audre Lorde and Alexis Pauline Gumbs for the beginning of a queer Black feminist theorization of negativity. Returning to Morrison, the chapter closes on Kara Keeling's account of a Black future, as an alternative to both reproductive futurity and queer futurity, and Joy James's formulation of Afrarealism as an orientation that pursues what is generative and sustaining within negativity—a hope against hope, or a hope without hope.

The fourth chapter, "Nowhere, and Notes to Not Belonging," reads the organizing terms of the transnational turn in feminist and queer cultural studies—hegemony, citizenship, and sovereignty—as desires for a belonging that salvages the Human as a shared and shareable form of being. Each term touches some aspect of belonging: hegemony is belonging imbued with agency, citizenship is belonging imbued with rights, and sovereignty is belonging imbued with power. The texts of transnational feminism return, symptomatically, to Blackness and to Black feminism as failures of belonging, and transnational feminism and diasporic queer studies tell stories about power and resistance that avoid the world created from racial slavery. Through readings along the itinerary of Saidiya Hartman, the chapter posits the racialization of slavery, the anoriginary and an-archic invention of Blackness, as the irrelational moment that sets belonging into motion. Enslavement is being without belonging. It might even be a *shared* experience of being without belonging, drawing focus to the indeterminate distance between being in common and belonging. Following Hartman, the chapter posits a feminist Black radicalism, or the indeterminate anarchism of Black feminist theorizing, as one possible name for a politics of collective being without belonging. As an extension of Black feminism, this anarchism holds the promise of a politics that starts nowhere, wants nothing, and threatens everything.

The epilogue turns from theorizing in a field of static to theorizing in a burning house. The Black feminist negativities explored across the book open a space for something to the side of optimism and pessimism. By way of closing, I return to Barbara Smith's "Toward a Black Feminist Criticism" and her Black lesbian reading of Toni Morrison's *Sula*. The scandal of Smith's reading of Morrison set a new mode of Black feminist theorizing into motion. Returning to that scandalous beginning, I meditate on the figure of the burning house offered by Morrison's novel. In the fraught and promiscuous potentiality of that space, the book closes on an affirmation of different names for indeterminacy: a Black feminist anarchism, the impossible inventiveness of Black feminist theorizing, and the nonagential affirmation of the Blackness internal to being.

Part I
Missed Encounters

Chapter One

Open Letters, and the Irrelational Erotics of a Black Feminist Negativity

> Of course, in that time, it was believed, still, that the society could be prettied, quieted, cradled, *sweetened*, if only people talked enough, glared at each other yearningly enough, waited enough.
>
> **Gwendolyn Brooks, *Report from Part One*, 68**

Attendees know well: The Annual Meeting of the Modern Language Association can make for difficult choices. On a Wednesday afternoon just after Christmas 1977, attendees may have found themselves in one of two Chicago hotels, deciding between concurrent panels. On the third floor of the historic Palmer House hotel, in private dining room 9, Elaine Scott and Barbara Smith were moderating a workshop titled "Black Women Writers: Included, Excluded, and Ignored." At the same time, nestled in a corner of the sixth floor, there was a special panel with J. Hillis Miller, Gayatri Chakravorty Spivak, and Paul Bové called "Deconstructive Criticism." Conference programs make strange neighbors.

But if you were at Scott and Smith's workshop, you may have already had the rest of your afternoon planned. You had two hours to make the six-block walk south to the Conrad Hilton. In the Beverly Room, on the third floor, a special session called "Lesbians and Literature: The Transformation of Silence into Language and Action" brought together Judith McDaniel, Adrienne Rich, Mary Daly, and Audre Lorde. It was the first meeting of Daly and Lorde. Sometime later, Lorde would gift Daly a copy of her collection of poems, *The Black Unicorn*. In return, Daly would send Lorde a copy of her *Gyn/Ecology: The Metaethics of Radical Feminism*. After the session there was a cash bar in the foyer.

The conflict that grew between Lorde and Daly, immortalized in Lorde's "Open Letter to Mary Daly," crystallized questions of feminist solidarity across the color line that redound in the present. This chapter is interested in how Lorde's work, within and beyond the "Open Letter," touches on questions of relationality and power, and sexuality and subjectivity, that have shaped the fields of feminist, queer, and Black studies.

COALITION, SISTERHOOD

Audre Lorde has a particular purchase within the psychic life of feminist and queer politics. Legitimately an icon, in the lifeworld of feminist and queer theory Lorde can function as a symbol, a fixed point of reference. Much of Lorde's popularity derives from her well-earned reputation as an advocate of cooperation across difference, of the liberatory potential of relationality. But this Lorde, the Lorde of coalition politics, has taken such pride of place within feminist and queer politics that she has eclipsed the elements of Lorde's work that skew toward the antirelational, to the limits of coalition. In her place is a beatified Lorde, the matron saint of coalition politics, a figure that sutures strained coalitions. When relationality is revealed to be in crisis, Audre Lorde *is* relationality. Lorde was acutely aware of this, anticipating appropriations of her work and likeness in the service of racist political movements. In a journal entry reflecting on the oft-appropriated image of the Rev. Dr. Martin Luther King Jr., Lorde wonders what it will cost her to speak her truth. "What I will have to pay someday for that privilege, and in whose coin? Will those forces which serve non-life in the name of power and profit kill me too, or merely dismember me in the eyes of whoever can use what I do?"[1] This prescient description of her eventual appropriation is one place in her published writings where Lorde thinks out loud about the limits of relationality that obtain for Black women. In this section, I begin to think through the ways Black feminism has theorized occupying a position of such openness to appropriation. I look to places where Lorde has been put to use by non-Black feminists to discipline Black feminist and queer movement. In these moments, I track the function of Audre Lorde in the psychic life of feminist theory and politics. In the next section, I place Lorde's "Open Letter to Mary Daly" within the overlapping contexts of Lorde's career as a poet and theorist, Mary Daly's own path, and the wider dynamics of the feminist movement as it was being incorporated into the American academy. In the final section, I articulate an alternative theorization of relationality available in the work Lorde produced over the same span of years the "Open Letter" was published and republished. The form of relationality we find in these moments of Lorde's work anticipates conversations about the possibility or impossibility of relationality, communicability, and the intersubjective in later critiques of antiblackness.

In the decades following her death with cancer in 1992, white feminists have continued the work begun in earnest during the later years of her life to make Audre Lorde a synecdoche for Black feminism. Lorde's career as author, activist, and theorist—or, in Lorde's famous iteration, "black, lesbian, feminist, mother, poet warrior"—is often made to stand in for Black feminism writ large through a double gesture in which, first, Lorde's life and oeuvre are reduced to a handful of sound bites, and second, Black feminism is constructed as a parochial response to white feminist movement from the 1970s to the 1990s. This "textual and historical erasure or tokenization" of Black feminist theory through the figure of Audre Lorde has been an important disciplinary technique for white feminists impatient with Black feminist critiques and critics.[2] This represents one pole of Lorde's ambivalent living legacy.

In her work on queer Black feminist futurity, Alexis Pauline Gumbs offers another reading of Lorde's continued presence within the precincts of *Black* feminist movement. For Gumbs, "Lorde . . . walks the earth" through continued reference to her written work, particularly her poem "A Litany for Survival," which still "shows up on blogs, at rallies against police brutality, [and] reprised in the section headings of third wave feminist anthologies." This "sacred repetition" is "much of the way that Audre Lorde survives into the present."[3] However, Lorde survives also in quotations such as "Your silence will not protect you," "There is no hierarchy of oppression," "The master's tools will never dismantle the master's house," and "Survival is not an academic skill." To be acquainted with Lorde solely through these phrases can be one's entire engagement with the critical enterprise of Black feminism. But this limited engagement with Lorde offers only a very small glimpse into the project of Black feminism, as well as a misleading glimpse of the breadth and depth of Lorde's work. Lorde's reduction to a series of sound bites has been a central mode through which white feminists weaponized Audre Lorde for use against contemporary practitioners of Black feminist and queer cultural and political work.

In February of 2021, the longtime activist and writer Kenyon Farrow articulated some of these themes in an essay called "Audre Lorde and I Were Once Enemies." Farrow's story goes back to 2004, when he wrote what was—at least for me and my friends—a canonical essay on hip-hop, cultural appropriation, and the conceptual and political distinctions between white supremacy and antiblackness within multiracial activist formations. According to Farrow, "One of the most common responses to my critiques came in the form of weaponizing the words of Audre Lorde against me." Indeed, "in nearly every debate, informal conversation, blog comment or unsolicited remark for many years after the piece was published, I was met with some form of an Audre Lorde quote, used in an attempt to silence or at least 'check' me on my thinking and position." For Farrow, these fragments of Lorde's thought were weaponized in a context where multiracial coalition politics were not *pursued*, but *taken for granted*. And taken for granted in a way that insisted on Black participation while policing Black political desires and erasing anything of the universal-singular internal to Blackness. After several years estranged from Lorde's work, Farrow returned to her. He built new relationships to her work, and to the fragments that had been weaponized across so many forums "to tell [him] to politely shut the fuck up."

In *The Queer Art of Failure*, Jack Halberstam turned to an archive of the unserious to chase "the chance to be frivolous, promiscuous, and irrelevant," to find something other than the serious, disciplinary knowledges of the academic publishing machine.[4] When I first began writing this chapter, I caught inspiration from an episode that was both serious and unserious, a sort of insipid repetition of everyday violences. It was an anonymous blog post, meant to intervene on what was not yet called "cancel culture," aimed at Black women bloggers who wielded a frightening power to "take down" any well-meaning person who ran afoul of them.[5] It came and it went. Unless you were living on Tumblr in the winter of 2012, you missed all of it. Today, the page only exists in the archives of the Wayback Machine. *Feminist X*, as it was called, was a minor intervention within the larger life of feminist media in the middle period of Web 2.0.

The *Feminist X* "statement" indexed many of the concerns of its historical moment, as the continuing Great Recession abutted the rise of progressive and feminist online media outlets (which were yet to be consolidated out of existence). The authors introduced themselves as "a group of established feminist activists, educators, writers, bloggers and lecturers," united by concerns over "take-down culture" within the larger culture of feminist politics. In point of fact, they were most immediately concerned with the treatment of a white male feminist who had made a name for himself in the blogosphere as a wounded soul. He taught transgressive courses with feminist themes at a community college outside of Los Angeles, admitted to some unsavory behaviors (all in the past, of course), and tried his best to make feminism *sexy*. For his feminist contemporaries, he was a mascot for how feminism could rehabilitate men who, too, had been damaged by patriarchy. For others, he had a troubling knack for chasing headlines, for pursuing an especially ambitious publishing itinerary, and for reliving his more colorful escapades repeatedly across the outlets he pursued.[6] For a certain class of white professional feminists, he was emblematic of one of the chief ambitions of feminist movement: the positive transformation of white men.[7] To a degree, the *Feminist X* "statement" was white women protecting white men from Black women.

The anonymity of *Feminist X* is analytically useful because it doesn't especially matter who they imagined they were defending or who they imagined they were speaking as.[8] Effectively, they attempted to speak as a pre-racial (rather than post- or multiracial) iteration of feminism, from the position of a naturalized and prepolitical Humanity. In other words, they sought a redemptive antiblackness.

Their statement concludes, "Audre Lorde famously said, 'Your silence will not protect you.' Within the feminist movement, we must all remember that our silence—or the silencing of others—will never produce radical social change." This clumsy invocation of Lorde's essay, "The Transformation of Silence into Language and Action," works against both the letter and spirit of Lorde's text: It shifts from Lorde's silence to "the silencing of others," and it transforms a call for white women to work to overcome their own destructive racism into a call for Black women to comport themselves in ways more agreeable to white feminists. In the fantasy of *Feminist X*, not only are Black women at fault for preventing "radical social change," but they have also, in doing so, turned against the principles put forth by their Black feminist foremothers. The solution, in this case, is to follow Lorde's lead and fall in line with the dictates of "the feminist movement." In their analysis, Lorde is the cudgel with which unruly Black women might have their antisocial behaviors corrected.

But this invocation, with its symptomatic distortions of Lorde's text, opens the door to an exploration of one of the more noteworthy conflicts of relation in feminism's second wave—that between Lorde and the radical feminist theologian and social philosopher Mary Daly. The history of the conflict between Lorde and Daly is of interest here both because it is a direct predecessor of the contemporary conflicts I have outlined (extending outward in all directions of feminist politics and theory) and because it highlights a tradition of Black feminist theorizing on the limits of relationality. Through a series of critiques of Daly, Lorde would articulate an understanding of the singularity of Black women's suffering and begin to outline, sometimes performatively, a mode of Black feminist theorizing along the edges of the antirelational, what I will call the irrelational.[9]

READING AUDRE LORDE READING

> A core of the conversations we never had
> lies in the distance
> between your wants and mine
> a piece of each
> buried beneath the wall that separates
> our sameness
>
> —AUDRE LORDE, "SISTER, MORNING IS A TIME FOR MIRACLES,"
> IN *THE COLLECTED POEMS OF AUDRE LORDE*, 347

The story of Audre Lorde's letter to Mary Daly is split across the original, mostly private exchange of letters, and the versions of Lorde's letter that were published during the 1980s. The latter have shaped the field of feminist theory and the lifeworld of the feminist classroom up through the present. In important ways, Lorde's "Open Letter to Mary Daly" exists independently of both Lorde and Daly. In her critical account of how Daly features in the historiography of feminist theory, Kathryn Telling identifies the "Open Letter" as a major landmark in the stories feminist theory tells about itself. "The eloquence, poignancy and, arguably, timeliness of that letter means that it is known to almost every Western feminist as a crucial marker in feminist movement away from the white-centric, essentialist, radical feminism of the 1970s."[10] In this context, Audre Lorde and Mary Daly came to function as place-names for different feminist discourses. They also represent our investments in defending or defeating those discourses. Our investments in those discourses have eclipsed the missed encounters at the heart of the original exchange, the encounters Lorde's "Open Letter" simultaneously describes and embodies.

After meeting at the MLA Conference in December 1977, Lorde and Daly initiated an exchange of books. Lorde sent Daly her recent *The Black Unicorn*, and Daly eventually sent Lorde a copy of her *Gyn/Ecology: The Metaethics of Radical Feminism*. Lorde sent what would become her open letter to Daly on 6 May 1979, sending it also to mutual friends Adrienne Rich and Michelle Cliff.[11] In a preface to a later edition of *Gyn/Ecology*, Mary Daly describes meeting briefly with Lorde during the summer of 1979 at a poetry reading in Boston. "I told her that I would like to discuss her letter in person so that we would have an adequate opportunity to understand each other in dialogue, and I suggested places where we might meet for such a discussion."[12]

Daly wrote a letter back to Lorde on 22 September 1979. Among other things, Daly's letter suggested that the two meet privately during an upcoming conference on the work of Simone de Beauvoir, *The Second Sex*—Thirty Years Later: A Commemorative Conference on Feminist Theory.[13] The two met at the conference on 28 September. In the "New Intergalactic Introduction" to the 1990 edition of *Gyn/Ecology*, Daly described "an hour-or-so-long meeting" during which "we discussed my book and her response." She went on, "I explained my positions clearly, or so I thought. . . . Apparently Lorde was not satisfied, although she did not indicate this at the time."[14] In Alexis De Veaux's biography of Lorde, she describes the setting and Lorde's experience of the meeting: "At NYU, Lorde and Mary Daly met in a private space beyond earshot of the public. Their meeting proved comparatively trivial. Although Lorde was more willing than Daly to risk a public confrontation between them, Daly was wary of even a private one. Lorde found the moment 'disappointing' because she hadn't expected Daly 'to be so out of emotional touch with herself.'"[15]

The particulars of this correspondence, Daly's response, and their private meeting at the conference are significant elements of Lorde's critical performance and the larger reception of both Lorde's and Daly's work. At one level, the story of Audre Lorde and Mary Daly, of Lorde's open letter and the ways Daly did and did not respond, is the story of a missed encounter that touches both the structural dynamics of antiblackness and the everyday ways people are opaque to themselves, and the ways that opacity becomes emotional illiteracy or self-righteousness. Put differently, their story—both the story of the original exchange of letters and the story of the open letter—is about relationality and the stakes and racial politics of feminist theory.

In the time and place of its arrival, Mary Daly's *Gyn/Ecology* was an important intervention for a feminist reading public that was still being fitfully incorporated into the academy. As feminist theory was consolidated as an academic project, space disappeared for Daly, her work, and the wider reading community of Sister-Hags and Spinsters who had so energetically received her work. The reviews of *Gyn/Ecology* from the feminist press reflected an enthusiastic identification with Daly's feminist mysticism. "*Gyn/Ecology* is written to us, for us, from our experience, about us, the untamed, the Hags," Susanna J. Sturgis wrote in *Off Our Backs*. "This wonderful, brilliant, amazing Hysterical book," she adds, "spins itself beyond the words that Mary Daly wrote. It is a creation, the work of a revolutionary feminist; it is a vision of strength and integrity of sisterhood."[16] Writing in *Sinister Wisdom*, Susan Leigh Star called *Gyn/Ecology* "the total confluence of method and content, of the personal and the historical, of the reach for change and the unflinching examination of suffering, that I have come to know as feminism." Put simply, "Where this book is, there is feminism."[17] In form and content, Daly's work in *Gyn/Ecology* was an invitation into an ecstatic, transcendent, galaxy-spanning feminist re-invention of feminine life, living, and being.[18]

The story Daly tells in *Gyn/Ecology* follows a three-act narrative arc: a space of pre-patriarchal female plenitude is disrupted by a global religion of terror that feeds from the suffering of women, and then, by identifying the lies and illusions of global patriarchy, Daly's global community of Hags, Harpies, Crones, and other Voyagers can Spin and Weave a new form of living. The book's First Passage traces the mythohistorical origins of woman-hate. "*Patriarchy is itself the prevailing religion of the entire planet*," she writes, "and its essential meaning is necrophilia." This necrophilia is "not in the sense of love for actual corpses, but of love for those victimized into a state of living death."[19] In the Second Passage, Daly conducts a global tour of patriarchy's lust for violence—witch burnings in Europe, widow burning in India, foot-binding in China, genital mutilation in Africa, gynecology and psychotherapy in the United States, and the medical violences of the Nazi Holocaust. Having journeyed across this blood-soaked history, the Third Passage turns to the spooking (the exorcism of patriarchy), sparking (the flame of female friendship), and spinning (bringing into Be-ing new cosmic tapestries) of a Radical Feminism. The political and imaginative project of *Gyn/Ecology* obtains in reconnecting with the mythohistoric Goddess as a figure of an integrated female energy (in Daly's parlance, *gynergy*).

Audre Lorde's biographer, Alexis De Veaux, describes *Gyn/Ecology* as "a highly original, dense meditation, synthesizing philosophy, literary criticism, history, poetry, and feminist rhetoric."[20] The wide ambit and aperture of Daly's analysis, her formal experimentation, and her paradigmatic analysis spoke to a feminist readership that extended beyond the university. Daly's mysticism, her purported essentialism, her polemicizing, and her style of argumentation would all become targets of a feminist theory increasingly monopolized by the languages of the academy.[21] As feminism became institutionalized as a curricular object, the wildness of popular and para-academic feminisms became a problem to be disciplined. In 1979, Susan Leigh Star could write, "Where this book is, there is feminism." By the 1990s, the stories feminist theory told about itself had changed radically.[22] Once a central figure in feminist theory, Mary Daly became an anachronism and an embarrassment.[23]

Lorde's critique revolved around what she saw as the selective eurocentrism of the text, a eurocentrism that ignored non-Western women in some instances, and misrepresented non-Western women in others. Presenting first a history of patriarchal myths and a re-discovery of the power of female Goddess figures, *Gyn/Ecology*'s First Passage dealt solely with the European tradition, leading Lorde to the conclusion that "Mary has made a conscious decision to narrow her scope and to deal only with the ecology of western-european women." However, the Second Passage turned its attention to non-Western cultural practices—among them, "Chinese footbinding," "Indian *Suttee*" ("widow-burning"), and "African Genital Mutilation." From these chapters, Lorde was dismayed that non-European women appeared in Daly's text "only as victims and preyers upon each other."[24] "I find the relics of my history," Lorde would write in a poem the same year, "fossilized into a prison."[25] Finally, Lorde took issue with the use of her poetry as an epigraph to the chapter on "African genital mutilation." "I felt," Lorde wrote, "that you had in fact misused my words, utilized them only to testify against myself as a woman of color."[26]

In one passage, Lorde poses a series of questions to Daly: "So the question arises in my mind, Mary, do you ever really read the work of black women? Did you ever read my words, or did you merely finger through them for quotations which you thought valuably support an already-conceived idea concerning some old and distorted connection between us? This is not a rhetorical question."[27] These questions find a place between Lorde's earlier concern that her critiques would be overshadowed and distorted because "the history of white women who are unable to hear black women's words, or to maintain dialogue with us, is long and discouraging," and her later statement that "beyond sisterhood is still racism."[28] "Racism," then, is that which "distorts" the "connection" that might otherwise exist between Lorde and Daly as lesbians and feminists, and as women under patriarchy.

The form of the letter, and its appearance in different feminist anthologies and then in Lorde's *Sister Outsider*, made Lorde's and Daly's lives into an allegory for the politics of feminist sisterhood across the color line. In this construction, Lorde and Daly were both living, imperfect persons *and* representations of structural positions. The force of Lorde's critique emerges from this collapse of the personal and the structural, where individuals become representations of social dynamics. The piece's popularity and staying power in the feminist classroom speaks to the power of this dramatic conflict. But the same force that popularized the "Open Letter" also points toward its limits. The individualizing attention on Daly, as Lorde well understood, allowed her to function as a scapegoat for the antiblackness that structures all social relationships.

Sometime after their disappointing meeting of 28 September 1979, Lorde decided to open the letter "to the community of women." The now-opened letter was first published in 1980 in *Top Ranking: A Collection of Articles on Racism and Classism in the Lesbian Community*, published by a small Brooklyn press and largely unavailable today. It was published again in the pathbreaking women-of-color feminist anthology *This Bridge Called My Back: Writings by Radical Women of Color*. Finally, it was published in 1984 in Lorde's own *Sister Outsider: Essays and Speeches*. By this last republication in 1984, the letter had two additional opening paragraphs and a preface that read, "The following letter was written to Mary Daly, author of *Gyn/Ecology*, on May 6, 1979. Four months later, having received no reply, I open it to the community of women."[29]

It is this version, from *Sister Outsider*, that most circulated in feminist classrooms, and the new note that begins the piece was central to how the piece, the figure of Audre Lorde as a figure of Black feminism, and the figure of Mary Daly as a stand-in for white feminism, were received in the emerging institutional space of a feminist academy. Lorde's critiques of *Gyn/Ecology* were subordinated to the more salacious question, *Why didn't Mary Daly ever respond?* In the classroom and around the seminar table, students could explore their own anxieties through these figures.

The Black feminist icon taking on the racist white feminist. In the 1980s it might have been called trashing, taking out the trash. Later, it might have been dubbed a call out, Audre Lorde called out Mary Daly. More recently, we might hastily say Mary Daly found herself canceled. Mobilized as a feminist parable, the story of Lorde and Daly became a container for non-Black people to hold our anxieties about encountering the anger, rage, or righteousness of Black women.

After Mary Daly died in 2010, Lorde's letter and Daly's response to it were a piece of the legacy that feminist scholars reckoned with. One feminist religious studies scholar offered a characteristic story. Written as "A Letter to Mary Daly," she describes her first encounter with Lorde's letter in graduate school. "As a feminist scholar of religion, I read Lorde's words carefully. I felt indicted. For me, the open letter was a cautionary tale." She described the lessons she took from Lorde, about cultivating careful practices of citation, taking seriously the work of scholars of color, and incorporating an analysis of racism into the different parts of her work. She would go on to teach the "Open Letter to Mary Daly" in her classes for decades.

> For a long time, perhaps too long, I took a certain comfort in teaching Lorde's open letter. The "facts" that Lorde supplies—that you did not respond to her most especially—enabled me to offer a rather stark argument for how to read her text. What did it mean to make this letter public? How long is long enough? And for my students, the real question was how could you, Mary, have never responded? This was the most upsetting thing. And in these discussions, your presumed "lack" of the notion that you had never responded fueled a kind of energy and confidence. We often agreed that you were wrong not to engage with Lorde. And so it went for so many years.

In the classroom, "An Open Letter to Mary Daly" becomes a kind of inoculation against racism. Mary Daly becomes a totem for the wrong kind of feminism and the wrong kind of feminist. This scholar, writing to Daly after her passing, also reckons with the distant intimacies of the academic lifeworld. The ways we attach ourselves to the person we imagine behind the texts we read and assign. In that way, Daly's failure to respond to Lorde becomes a personal betrayal. But it isn't clear if it is the racial politics of Daly's text, or Audre Lorde's critique of it, that sets Daly outside the loving circle of feminist scholarship. In this particular eulogy to Daly, the scholar takes a different lesson from the entire affair. She continues,

And now I suspect that you knew this would indeed be the case. It was not until Lorde's death that you yourself allowed even some of your closest colleagues to know that in fact you had responded. Reading the account in Alexis De Veaux's biography of Lorde, it seems that there was a small circle of feminist colleagues of yours who did know (especially Adrienne Rich) and that you all decided to keep this knowledge to yourselves. My sense is that you decided it best to let Lorde have this one. What an astonishing thing to do. You kept silent in a way that I can only marvel at, especially now so long after you made this decision.[30]

Having been sacrificed to appease feminists of color, Mary Daly could be posthumously reclaimed as a feminist martyr. In this account, Daly gave up her reputation so that Lorde's critique of racism could be heard by the community of feminists. "As a prolific writer and speaker, Mary, I am still struck by your silence. And without you here to tell us why you never went public with your response, we can only speculate. It is such a powerful statement, an ambiguous but deeply respectful gesture, a nod to Lorde's critique. You let it stand for all of these years in her voice. You gave her the last word—a gift."[31]

An obituary can be forgiven for sentimentality, but this characterization of history is a common one—that Daly went decades without commenting on Audre Lorde's letter, and that Daly may have only discussed it with a few colleagues, but otherwise suffered in silence. Or, less generously, that Daly and her wounded pride disappeared into the shadows, unwilling to change and unwilling to grow.[32] In these formulations, Daly offers a potential model for students and practitioners in the field of feminist theory—a model of how or how not to respond to criticism.

In her reflections on the legacies of Mary Daly, written for the critical Festschrift *Feminist Interpretations of Mary Daly*, Amber Katherine aims right for the question at the heart of the matter. "Still, I have wondered, *why* didn't Daly respond?" Indeed, she continues, "This is also what my students most want to know after reading Lorde's letter. They move with vacuous speed to the conclusion that Daly was 'just racist,' a conclusion that at once presumes an understanding of Lorde's letter, dismisses historical understandings of Daly's decision, and situates them on the other side of racism. Likewise, I think, many feminist scholars, stepping around the ad hominem, have interpreted Daly's decision not to respond in kind as an admission of *Gyn/Ecology*'s inherent flaws."[33] Katherine's essay goes on to excavate the historical, intellectual, and political contexts that shaped

Daly's decision not to respond "in kind" to Lorde. Daly's decision, Katherine contends, ultimately harmed her own project ("Her work has suffered and fallen short of its radical potential").[34] Looking outward, Katherine suggests that the more important question is not why Daly failed to respond to Lorde's letter, but why didn't the larger community of radical feminists?[35] But even Katherine's at once critical and sympathetic reading of Daly is oriented around the problem of Daly's response.

When *Gyn/Ecology* was republished by Beacon in 1990, Daly contributed a "New Intergalactic Introduction" that commented on Lorde's letter and its reception in "academentia." "I was acutely aware," she writes of *Gyn/Ecology*, "that I had not done or written everything. I had not written the Last Word. . . . Rather, I had set free this book, this Thunderbird, in the hope that its Call would be Heard."[36] With *Gyn/Ecology*, she "looked forward to the profusion of New Creation," which she "believed could emerge from women of all races, cultures, classes—from all over this planet—speaking/Be-Speaking out of our various and vital heritages." But, she cautioned, "explosions of Diversity do not happen without conflict."[37] The primary conflict concerning Daly was Lorde's "Open Letter."

Daly's commentary on her interactions with Audre Lorde, and with the response from the community of feminists in the academy, is marked by the frustrations of speaking at once as an individual and as a position, of adjudicating an interpersonal conflict that is also a structural antagonism. And so Daly writes of her regret and then reaches for justifications. She is accountable and then defensive. As a person, she may, in her words, "regret any pain that unintended omissions may have caused others, particularly women of color, as well as myself." She may also be sincere when she says that "the writing of *Gyn/Ecology* was for me an act of Biophilic Bonding with women of all races and classes, under the varying oppressions of patriarchy."[38] But, as an individual, she does not know how to bear the weight of the *position* she is made to represent, so she is immediately back on defense. "Clearly, women who have a sincere interest in understanding and discussing this book have an obligation to read not only the statements of critics but also the book itself, and to *think* about it."[39] To *engage* with Mary Daly would mean to see the ways "each subject reoccurs differently everywhere."[40]

Daly was acutely aware of the ways she was remade as a symbol of a particular kind of pathology, as a way of inoculating the larger project of a particular type of feminism. She correctly understood this as a type of violence, and as an expression of Rage. "Rage," she writes, "can be displaced. In reaction to the Absolutely Righteous Rage of women of color against racism, some women retreat into passivity, hostility, and guilt, often displacing energy into targeting scapegoats."[41] Two years later, the "New Intergalactic Introduction" to *Gyn/Ecology* reappeared in the Third Spiral Galaxy of Daly's intellectual autobiography, *Outercourse: The Be-Dazzling Voyage*. In it, Daly appends a footnote that reads: "[Lorde's 'Open Letter'] has been assigned as required reading by not a few professors in academentia to students in classes where *Gyn/Ecology* itself has not been assigned, or a mere handful of pages of this book have been required reading. This kind of selectivity is irresponsible. It imposes a condition of self-righteous ignorance upon students, often within the setting of 'Women's Studies.' This is, in my view, a worst case [*sic*] scenario of pseudoscholarship. It is, even if 'well-intentioned,' divisive, destructive. It functions, at least subliminally, as a self-protective statement about the purity and political correctness of the professor."[42] Daly realized and resented that she had been made to stand in for the racism of white women. What was harder for her to name was that she had also been made into a symbol of a feminist past that feminists sought to leave behind. As Clare Hemmings observes in *Why Stories Matter*, these are one and the same symbol. In the story of feminist theory, racism is sutured to a past that is always being transcended. Daly's racism was adjoined to her mysticism and essentialism. Lorde's critique was instrumentalized in this production of a feminist future beyond essentialism, a feminist theory that, not incidentally, could be incorporated into the academy without the same types of acrimony that so notoriously marked Daly's career at Boston College.[43]

All of the Sturm und Drang around the legacies of Lorde and Daly, all of the hand-wringing within the feminist academy, orients itself around the opening lines of the 1984 publication of the "Open Letter." The addition of the prefatory note, not present in either of the first two publications, places retroactive significance on the month of September 1979 ("four months later"), the month when, in fact, Lorde both received a letter in response and spoke privately with Daly in New York. What does it mean for feminist theory that Daly's responses were never received as responses?[44] On one hand, the posthumous figure of Audre Lorde was appropriated as a representative of modes of feminist theory and politics about which the living Lorde was much more ambivalent. On the other, Daly was rejected as a relic of an outmoded feminism. For different reasons, in different directions, they were deployed to guarantee the coherence of the project of feminist theory.

What other meanings might emerge from Lorde and Daly's missed encounter at the Simone de Beauvoir conference in September of 1979? How else might we read their missed encounter?

The month of September 1979 stands out elsewhere in Lorde's work. In *The Cancer Journals*, first published in 1980, Lorde combines poetry, prose, and her personal journal entries in a series of reflections on her experience of her first early cancer scare, her later diagnosis with breast cancer, and her recovery from a modified radical mastectomy. Among the journal entries, arranged chronologically in the introductory essay, is an entry for "9/79." It is the only entry in the book not to also include a day along with the month and year. The entry reads:

> There is no room around me in which to be still, to examine and explore what pain is mine alone—no device to separate my struggle within from fury at the outside world's viciousness, the stupid brutal lack of consciousness or concern that passes for the way things are. The arrogant blindness of comfortable white women. What is this work all for? What does it matter whether I ever speak again or not? I try. The blood of black women sloshes from coast to coast and Daly says race is of no concern to women. So that means we are either immortal or born to die and no note taken, un-women.[45]

We are left uncertain over the date of the entry, unsure whether it is before or after Lorde's meeting with Daly. The meeting De Veaux calls "comparatively trivial." The meeting where Daly felt she had explained her positions clearly, only to discover later that Lorde was not satisfied by their conversation. The meeting that disappointed Lorde because Daly was "so out of emotional touch with herself." The larger context of that meeting, the conference at which Lorde gave a paper that would come to be called "The Master's Tools Will Never Dismantle the Master's House," hangs over the entry as well. Daly is one of many comfortable white women, blinded by arrogance. They are an extension of the larger world and its "viciousness," its "stupid brutal lack of consciousness."

Lorde cannot find space, in this iteration of feminist sisterhood, for Black women and their suffering, their desires to be still, to be alive, to have space to reflect, to be able to hold their pain and their longing. They are either immortal or born to die, no note taken. To be so marked by death is less to be un-made as women than to be made as un-women. The imbrication of gendered Blackness with death here marks a situation where relationality is not *in* crisis, but *is* crisis. Further, it is the crisis from which relationality emerges. The Black un-woman—the Black woman ungendered, to borrow from Hortense Spillers—exists as the condition of possibility for the figure of "the woman," the woman gendered *as woman*.

In the years that followed their meeting in September of 1979, Lorde would perform versions of their crisis of relationality in her remarks on Daly and the status of the "Open Letter." Her claim in 1984 that she received "no reply" from Daly troubles how we might understand relationality across the color line. In a 1982 interview for *Off Our Backs*, conducted after a poetry reading in Washington, D.C., Lorde was asked about her "Open Letter." In a section of the interview titled "The Faces of Racism," Lorraine Sorrel asked if Daly had responded to the letter published in *This Bridge Called My Back*: "Was there a resolution in any form to that?"

"No, it was not resolved," Lorde responded, "I had no response that had any satisfaction to it. Mary Daly and I feel very differently about the function of racism in our lives. I suspect that this is an area that Mary is not able to deal with personally and so, therefore, it affects her theoretical work. We talked. If I had had a response, I don't think I would have made the letter open."[46] *We talked. We talked but it was not a response. If our talking had been a response, the letter would have remained private.* Lorde's answer is both a negation and a caveat ("I don't think I would have . . .") that suggests something more beneath the surface.

Sorrel pressed gently for more. "I respect the privacy of any response from Mary Daly, but it is a public matter, too, and that's why I'm asking." Lorde replied at some length:

> It is a public matter. That's why I made the letter public. I hoped that the questions would resound and continue to be asked. One of the ways of silencing, or of simply not dealing with things, is not responding. It doesn't make the asking any less valid; it doesn't even make it any less useful. That was a very useful letter. It freed me in one way: it helped to focus my rage. There was both anger and real pain involved in that interchange because Mary's work had given me something. Mary is not my enemy, but she speaks with many of the voices of my enemies. Before I attempt to destroy her, I need first of all to be very sure I'm using energies to destroy my real enemies. It's very easy for us to attack the hated in each other because we are more vulnerable to each other. God knows, no one's perfect, right? I just wish that Mary was not a racist.[47]

In these two answers, Lorde performs something at the edges of the relational and the antirelational. She dictates to her interlocutor the conditions of the exchange. Lorde leaves for herself the power to decide what does or does not constitute a response. In effect, she repurposes the letter. The Lorde who wrote the letter sought connection; the Lorde who opened the letter did not.

In place of the connection she once sought with Daly, the letter becomes a lens for focusing her rage. Daly stops being the woman whose work had given her something. She becomes one embodiment of the voices of her enemies. As such, those parts of Daly that speak with the voices of Lorde's enemies become enemies to be destroyed. It is easier to attack one another because being in community means we are vulnerable to each other. When they met in 1979, Lorde experienced her vulnerability to Mary Daly. Daly made her feel alone, unheard, un-woman, like the blood of Black women didn't mean anything for a feminist sisterhood. We are more vulnerable to each other. The intersubjective—relationality—is one name for the experience of being vulnerable to one another. After September of 1979, Lorde closed herself off to Daly. After this interview, Lorde would append to the letter the preface that has haunted and shaped feminist theory.

No one's perfect, right? I just wish that Mary was not a racist. Lorde is signifying here.[48] Rather, this is a moment when Lorde is reading Mary Daly. In *Paris Is Burning*, drag legend Dorian Corey defines reading as "the *real* art form of insult."[49] It is a practice of using one's verbal prowess and power of observation to perform an interpretation of an adversary. It is meant to force them into an undesired encounter with their self, unvarnished and on public display. Lorde leaves behind all of the niceties of academic debate or literary disagreement. She simply wishes that Mary was not a racist. Her comment encapsulates what so many students take away from the "Open Letter." Mary Daly, whoever she might be, is racist—that's too bad for her. Reading reaches for the part of relationality that makes us most vulnerable to each other, for whatever there is internal to relationality that *is* a crisis.

In her "Open Letter," this crisis of relationality is also what Lorde calls "the history of white women who are unable to hear black women's words." It is the crisis that Lorde refracts through her performance of being unable to hear Mary Daly. It is also the crisis of relationality that Hortense Spillers calls the "structure of unreality that the black woman must confront." A structure that "originates in the historical moment when language ceases to speak, the historical moment at which hierarchies of power (even the ones to which *some* women belong) simply runs out of terms because the empowered meets in the black female the veritable nemesis of degree and difference."[50] In this formulation, the Black woman is a figure that undoes differentiation; it is the perpetual sameness against which difference announces itself. Immortal, and therefore the background that makes mortality, the border of life and death, meaningful. Born to die and no note taken, and therefore the static out of which bios and biography emerge.

And yet, Daly's work had given something to Lorde. Lorde wrote to Daly seeking connection. She sent copies of the letter to Michelle Cliff and Adrienne Rich. She wrote the letter as an expression of sisterhood. The failure of the exchange ultimately helped to shape a new iteration of feminist theory. But it also held a great pain for Lorde. De Veaux's biography describes Lorde's hurt following the Beauvoir conference, which had included the meeting with Daly and the acrimony of the conference organizers and attendees following her presentation of "The Master's Tools." "Having met with Daly on principle," De Veaux writes, "Lorde felt that she'd done what she had to do, and there was no further reason to expose herself to what she'd seen in Daly's face as they talked."[51] Whatever Lorde saw in Daly's face is left unexplained in De Veaux's account. In her hurt and rage, "Mary Daly the person . . . ceased to exist." And so Lorde never said more about her exchange with Daly, adding the preface that Daly had never replied long after their falling out.

Elsewhere in Lorde's writing, there are suggestions of a deeper pain and longing involved with her missed encounter with Mary Daly. Sometime in 1979, she wrote a poem titled "Sister, Morning Is a Time for Miracles," which would be included in her 1982 collection, *Chosen Poems: Old and New*.[52] The poem does not name Daly, but the poem theorizes the vexed form of relationality Lorde was processing in the "Open Letter" and across the early years of the letter's reception. In the poem, the speaker awakes in the early morning reaching toward a distant friend, a sister feminist on the other side of an unnamed conflict.

> A core of the conversations we never had
> lies in the distance
> between your wants and mine
> a piece of each buried beneath the wall that separates
> our sameness
> a talisman of birth

hidden at the root of your mother's spirit
my mother's furies.[53]

The two women are marked by a difference larded with the ambivalent magic of race. Daly seems present in the feminist mysticism of Lorde's choices of objects. One mother's spirit, the other's furies, and then the figure of a "runic stone" that speaks to her in the space "between sleeping and waking." Lorde may also be describing the letter and its demand—if we follow the Lacan who said that every demand is a demand for love—when she writes that "what is asked for is often destroyed / by the very words that seek it." The gesture that sought to connect with Daly is precisely what closed them off from each other.

Lorde's hurt reaches out to her distant friend, or once-friend. "And I call you secret names of praise and fire / that sound like your birthright / but are not the names of a friend / while you hide behind 100 excuses." And again, seeing a friend "encased like a half-stoned peach / in the rigid act of your healing."[54] The poem's voice speaks with hurt and rage about someone, like Daly, who is out of touch with herself emotionally, someone who has "Mary's rigidities, her self-protections, her tendency to see all criticisms as onslaught, as pure attack," as Adrienne Rich described it in a letter to Lorde.[55]

The poem is also a work of mourning and a theorization of loss. In its fourth stanza, the poem becomes "a memorial to the conversations we won't be having / to laughter shared and important / as the selves we helped make real," and then also "to the dead / revelations we buried still-born / in the refuse of fear and silence."[56] This mourning is for the relationship Lorde sees, after the meeting in September of 1979, as unsalvageable. But it is also for the generative political potential of feminist sisterhood that moments of her work continued to believe in unfailingly. In her biography of Lorde, Alexis De Veaux describes her as "insecure and intensely jealous" of the relationship shared by Adrienne Rich and Mary Daly. "Lorde's love-hate-competitive relationships with white women informed an unresolved anger toward them and raised deeper questions unresolved by her theory of the 'creative uses of difference' as to why she'd chosen them as lovers, allies, or enemies."[57] Lorde's poem speaks to the intense and contradictory matrix of affects and motivations that shaped her relationships with white women, as sister friends and sister comrades, the way her path collided, briefly, with Mary Daly, and the decisions she made to open her letter, to publish and republish and augment the letter.

In the feminist classroom, Lorde's "Open Letter to Mary Daly" has been read only too clearly. As if a pure expression of a straightforward desire to move feminism beyond the parochial white supremacy of certain radical feminists. But Lorde's text and the lifeworld around it offer no such purity. In the final passage of "Morning Is a Time for Miracles," the "I" of Lorde's poem laments,

> Once I thought when I opened my eyes we would move
> into a freer and more open country
> where the sun could illuminate our different desires
> and the fresh air do us honor for who we were.[58]

This optimism is a near relation to what Gwendolyn Brooks said of the party years of the 1940s. "Of course, in that time, it was believed, still, that the society could be prettied, quieted, cradled, *sweetened,* if only people talked enough, glared at each other yearningly enough, waited enough."[59] We might greet the dawn with our eyes wide open, we might bare our souls and open our hearts and talk all night long. That other country, a new day in a new world, still slips our grasp. We never seem to reach the redemptive relationality that guides so much of our politics, from radical to reactionary.[60]

Perhaps, though, that was always too much to ask of a letter, to ask of one another, to ask of our art, our theorizing, our classrooms, and our individual and institutional projects. With her letter to Mary Daly, Lorde was hoping for connection but there was something in the way. There's always something in the way. In chapter 3, we will see how Leo Bersani traced the something within intersubjectivity that gets in the way of relationality. For Bersani, gay desire was a privileged way to experience the impossibility internal to relation. But besides experiencing that impossibility, in the ways that all subjects must, Lorde also *embodies* the something in the way of relationality. For the world around her, she *is* that impossibility. The Blackness that marks Lorde is the nonrelation internal to relation. At the end of Lorde's poem, she aches for some short circuit of this nonrelation within relation:

> but just once
> in the possibilities of this too-early morning
> I wanted you

to talk
not as a healer
but as a lonely woman
talking to a friend.[61]

THE IRRELATIONAL EROTICS OF A BLACK FEMINIST NEGATIVITY

> I want to write rage but all that comes is sadness. We have been sad long enough to make this earth either weep or grow fertile. I am an anachronism, a sport, like the bee that was never meant to fly. Science said so. I am not supposed to exist. I carry death around in my body like a condemnation. But I do live. The bee flies. There must be some way to integrate death into living, neither ignoring it nor giving in to it.
>
> —AUDRE LORDE, *CANCER JOURNALS*, 13

Elsewhere, there are moments in Audre Lorde's work that help elaborate what remains generative in the space of the nonrelational. In this section, I examine the resonances between Lorde's theorizing on relationality and contemporary work around the interventions called afropessimism, or, contemporary critiques of Blackness and antiblackness. I also want to take seriously a tendency within Black feminist critiques of afropessimism to challenge how gender and the sexual are elaborated within that formation. Along the way, I engage with Lorde's *Cancer Journals* and her descriptions of the stakes of living and dying in an antiblack world.

In the months before the 1977 MLA meeting in Chicago, Lorde had her first breast biopsy. The growth that had been detected was benign. She went into the panel on "The Transformation of Silence into Language and Action" with a new sense of her mortality, with a new awareness that another growth might appear later, that might not be benign, that she might become sick, and that she might die. On Labor Day of the next year, she discovered a lump in her right breast that another biopsy revealed to be malignant. On 22 September 1978, she underwent a modified radical mastectomy of her right breast. The essays collected in *The Cancer Journals* detail different moments in her experience before, during, and after her diagnosis. They include the paper she presented at the MLA alongside Adrienne Rich, Judith McDaniel, and Mary Daly.

Throughout, Lorde incorporates entries from her personal journals. On many pages, Lorde faces different forms of pain, different species of overwhelm, as she encounters the limits of human existence with a new intimacy. "The enormity of our task, to turn the world around," she writes on 16 April 1979, "it feels like turning my life around, inside out."[62] For Lorde, the changes she faced after surgery felt as large as the political task that sat before her, to turn the world around, "the only thing in the world worth the effort of starting."[63] "If," she continues, "I can look directly at my life and my death without flinching I know there is nothing they can ever do to me again." There are moments in *The Cancer Journals* when Lorde seems to pair an unflinching paradigmatic analysis with unflinching self-analysis. But, even in light of the power she sees in an unflinching analysis, she sees the limits of her reach. "I must be content to see how really little I can do and still do it with an open heart."[64] What might it mean for our practice—practices of critique, politics, art, or living—to find contentment in how really little we can do? And to pursue our different forms of practice with open hearts?[65] In the previous section, we saw how Lorde closed herself off in some ways to remain open in others.

That exchange, the missed encounter between Audre Lorde and Mary Daly, might be read in an afropessimist register as an instance of what Frank Wilderson has called "noncommunicability." That is, a moment fitting Wilderson's description of afropessimism as a theory of Black positionality where "the meaning of Blackness" is understood as "a structural position of noncommunicability in the face of all other positions."[66] In this case, Lorde is performing and drawing attention to something noncommunicable in her relationship with Mary Daly. But Lorde's text pursues this critique of Daly, of the voices of Lorde's enemies caught within Daly's voice, in the name of building multiracial feminist community. By way of closing, I want to take seriously the tension between these aspects of Lorde's project—between the politics of pessimism and the politics of hope, between its shades of the antirelational and its bent toward the utopian. The latter aspects of Lorde's work are at the center of scholarship on Lorde and scholarship pursued in her name. Reading the pessimist dimension of Lorde's text opens a space in the tradition of Black feminist theorizing for imagining the *irrelational.* Or, the challenge of theorizing a relationality that moves through registers of impossibility—psychic, ontological, epistemological—to experience a relationality *touched by impossibility.* The touch of the impossible might also be the irrelational erotics of a Black feminist negativity.

In the wake of Wilderson's interventions, his focus on questions of relationality and the stakes of the capacity for communication, recent work in Black studies has endeavored to outline the limits of relationality, or the limited ways that relationality has been theorized—and especially the ways relationality gets taken for granted. This work, much of which is pursued through Black feminist and queer frameworks, has sought a critique of relationality—in the precise sense of elaborating what relationality consists of, and how our investments in particular understandings of the relational shape and are shaped by other desires.

Wilderson, of course, pursues this critique within the larger ensemble of interventions he calls afropessimism.[67] In *Red, White and Black: Cinema and the Structure of US Antagonisms,* Wilderson referred to several scholars as afropessimists, and this act of naming, this attempt to delineate a field formation that Wilderson saw as incipient across the history and present of Black Study, became a rather massive point of contention. In a vexing way, afropessimism circulated around the academy as an identity marker, often an unwelcome one. Somehow, the moniker was thornier to take on than other common academic place-names; much worse to be miscategorized as an afropessimist than a deconstructionist, Lacanian, feminist, or poststructuralist. Over a decade later, the disquiet over the term remains. All this to say, the argument here does not rely on the several scholars I read below "being" afropessimists. Besides Wilderson, they may simply be practitioners in the interdisciplinary humanities who take afropessimism seriously, who think *with* these still-emerging researches. In my own attempts to think with these discourses, I hope to trace some of the pathways relationality takes within the texts of afropessimism, with an eye toward the ways relationality touches aporias within the unfolding elaboration of afropessimism.

"The meaning of Blackness" that Wilderson explores as a "structural position of noncommunicability" is "noncommunicable" because, he argues, "Blackness is predicated on modalities of accumulation and fungibility, not exploitation and alienation."[68] For Wilderson, these are discrepant "grammars of suffering," different ways for subjects (and sentient objects) to be positioned in the world.[69] This discrepancy between ways of being positioned in the world "marks a difference between capacities for speech."[70] The capacity for speech might also be understood as a question of what cultural, social, ideological, political, and psychic infrastructures are required for expressions to be imbued with meaning. If afropessimism owes something to the structuralisms of the last century, it is this concern with the relationship between power, force, and the creation of meaning.

Power and force create the conditions of possibility for the production and reproduction of meaning. The place, time, and medium of exchange, of communication and relation, are all shaped by relations of force. And the relations of force that kickstart modernity are the relations of a newly global and newly racialized system of slavery. This new world seems to begin with the trans-Saharan trade of the latter half of the first millennium CE, spreading eastward across the Indian Ocean and northwest through the Mediterranean world. That path through the Mediterranean saw increasingly racialized forms of slavery and increasingly capitalist forms of production reinforcing one another until they spilled into the Atlantic world, becoming the settler colonial societies of the past five hundred years.[71] In a relatively brief span of history, new forms of sociality and new forms of being appeared which would consolidate themselves as the first versions of a globalized humanity. In an essay preceding his elaborations of afropessimism, Wilderson poses the problem of "seeing slavery," in this historic and global context, "as a structuring relation that constitutes the paradigm of human interaction."[72] "The slave overdetermines Human relationality," he writes, "because without the slave there would be no foundation for Human exchange. In other words, humanity can only occur at the place and in the time where the slave is not; but the slave . . . must be present (whether figuratively or literally) if humanity is to experience its time and place imbued with coherence."[73] Time and place, temporality and geography, are the necessary contexts for meaning to circulate as meaning. But temporality and geography only become coherent when there is a constitutive outside. At different moments and in different human societies, there have been many constitutive outsides that imbued time and place with coherence. One argument of afropessimism is that, for the global human society we call modernity, that constitutive outside is Blackness.

Modernity's interiors are those times and places imbued with coherence, and modernity's subjects can imagine themselves as coherent in a range of ways—as citizens and consumers, as rights-bearing and legal subjects, as natives and settlers, as workers and capitalists, as men and women, as white and nonwhite, as straight and gay, as cis and trans, et cetera—but that coherence is always vouchsafed by the incoherence beyond. "The only way Humanity can maintain both its corporeal and libidinal integrity," Wilderson claims, "is through the various strategies through which Blackness is the abyss into which Humanness can never fall."[74] All these forms of coherence and integrity may be illusory, but these illusions are the world's very infrastructures of meaning (thus Wilderson's recurring use of "grammar" as a guiding metaphor). Within these infrastructures, "Human relationality is defined in absolute opposition to Blackness," and "for the Black to become Human, relationality itself, as defined and constituted by the march of Modernity, would have to be destroyed."[75] For the reader, this is less a prescription than an invitation—Wilderson does not offer a ten-point program to ending relationality, but we are invited to imagine what this destruction might be.

Within the terms of Wilderson's discourse, this is a destruction unencumbered by any specific vision of what might come next. It is an invitation to a dance with death as a form of pure invention. In her own work, Audre Lorde imagined a similar relationship between destruction and invention. In 1981, Lorde delivered "The Uses of Anger" as the keynote address at the annual meeting of the National Women's Studies Association. Lorde used the settings of an emerging feminist academy to comment on recurring dynamics between herself and white feminist women.[76] "I speak out of direct and particular anger at an academic conference," she begins, "and a white woman says, 'Tell me how you feel but don't say it too harshly or I cannot hear you.' But is it my manner that keeps her from hearing, or the threat of a message that her life may change?"[77] In Lorde's example, both the speaking I and the white woman are moved by particular kinds of self-knowledge, by forms of recognition and misrecognition. The white woman recognizes that there are acts of speech that can exist without her hearing them, but she misrecognizes what it is that breaks that act of communication. Lorde knows that what is standing in the way of that act of communication is not the tone or timbre of the message, the emotional disposition of the person speaking, but the threat that the white woman's life might change. It is not anger, but a resistance to anger, Lorde argues, that sits in the way of an encounter with Blackness that might change white life, or what an antiblack world has imagined life to be. The question remains, though, whether the resistance is internal to that woman; that is, if the white woman is trying to preserve what she imagines her life to be, or if what keeps her from hearing is something internal to life itself.

Lorde here is making a case for an authentically multiracial feminist sisterhood, for relationality within a crisis of relationality. In this formulation, anger is something like the stuff of relationality. It is the content of the intersubjective. And so "anger expressed and translated into action in the service of our vision and our future is a liberating and strengthening act of clarification," because "it is in the painful process of this translation that we identify who are our allies with whom we have grave differences, and who are our genuine enemies." Anger is part of a process of discernment. Lorde recognizes discernment as an affective practice. In her famous line, "Anger is loaded with information and energy," anger is, at once, a way of knowing and something to know, a form of knowledge and the experience of knowing.[78] Anger is a work of translation and transformation that occurs between women. But Lorde, nevertheless, does not take the potential outcomes of any encounter with anger for granted.

For most work in the humanities—to say nothing of projects extending outside the academy—relationality is an a priori, it is taken for granted. Academic discourses tend to see it everywhere, even where it isn't, and it is also taken to be self-evident and self-evidently *good*. We bristle against the possibility of its impossibility. For Tyrone Palmer, relationality is a problem precisely because it crowds out all alternatives. In Palmer's formulation, Blackness is "the limit case of relation(ality)," where the latter term "indexes a self-evident logic of transcendence in which all things are connected." Much of the Western tradition, leading up to Palmer's case study on contemporary affect theory, naturalizes "relation(ality) as the inevitable order of things." Effectively, Palmer is asking, what if relationality is not a priori? How might a place be made in theory for what lies beyond relationality? And what possibilities are foreclosed by the assumption of a universal relationality? Palmer echoes Wilderson both when he refers to relationality as "the capacity for communicability," and when he makes a case for intensifying, rather than minimizing or mystifying, antagonism.[79]

Palmer links his theorizations on Blackness and relationality to the work of Zakiyyah Iman Jackson. "Yet throughout this constant appeal to the power of relation(ality) and its 'prior'-ness—its status as presubjective, prepersonal, prediscursive, and so on—there is little recognition of the essential fact that"—and here he quotes Jackson's essay "Theorizing in a Void"—"the ongoing production and nullification of black mater is the condition of possibility for relation and the dialectics of the Subject."[80] When Palmer calls this an "essential fact," he introduces an interesting tension between his text and Jackson's. Jackson's essay challenges the status of empiricism and positivism, the very ways of seeing that make the world after the "scientific revolution" meaningful. In a reading that builds from the work of Sylvia Wynter, Jackson points to the ways the mythological status of racial Blackness has been "produced under the guise of empirical scientific fact, or positivism," and she challenges a "representationalism bestowed with scientific authority or acting in accordance with the ideology of scientific naturalism."[81] Palmer's "essential fact," then, would have to be underpinned by a different type of certainty. Here, the text is more vulnerable than its rhetoric suggests. It is a moment when the text is grasping for a certainty that its political project demands but that its analytic apparatus cannot allow for.

Palmer's attention to affect theory is informative here. The language of the text reveals conflicts of feeling that the argument otherwise belies. For Palmer, this might also be an instance of what he terms "Black affect." He writes,

> Blackness yields a mode of feeling that intensifies one's outsideness to the World, a felt antagonism to the World. This antagonism functions as the genesis of a Black desire for the End of the World in all of its manifestations, a desire for the end of worlding. This destructive impulse that threatens the stability of the social, this relentless negativity that portends its upheaval, is the driving force of Black affect. How one contends with this force takes various forms, be they sublimation, repression, resignation, passivity, or an unequivocal embrace. But the force of this negativity cannot be denied, and it behooves us to think alongside it, even as it marks the limit of thought.[82]

Palmer's text might suggest that its own contradictory feelings are symptomatic of pursuing critique to the very ends of existence, of what it means to exist. But much of the work of the text is to stake a claim to facing a relentless negativity with a posture of "unequivocal embrace." The rhetorical act of the text distinguishes itself from current clichés of "being otherwise" by unequivocally embracing the End of the World.[83] The theoretical text allows us to rehearse how it feels to face the end of the world, how it feels to imagine a world on the other side of relationality, even as we face many ends of the world, even as we are already after the end of the world.

Our still-unfolding ecological catastrophe has energized a variety of theorizations of relationality, typically organized around assertions of the interconnectedness of all forms of life and matter. Palmer's critique of affect theory builds from Axelle Karera's earlier critique of what she terms "Anthropocene ethics," which maps uneasily onto field formations like object-oriented ontology, posthumanism, and the new materialisms. These discourses and their guiding concepts—among them, relationality—Karera argues, "are unequipped to account for the ongoing and brutal victimization of black people."[84] For Karera, the dominant ethical gestures of the discourses of the Anthropocene are the "constant recognition of our existential interdependency" and the assumption of "the inevitability of our ontological entanglements." In essence, interdependency and entanglement are both abstract renderings of "relationality," different ways of returning relationality to the center of their ethical and political projects. But they cannot account for, nor offer a meaningful challenge to, the forms of violence directed at Black people. More pointedly, Karera then argues, "relationality is inherently not only a position that the black cannot afford or even claim," but the very "structure of relationality is essentially the condition for the possibility of their enslavement."[85]

Within the terms of this argument, there is something inherent and essential to relationality that makes enslavement possible. As an observation, this is perhaps less profound for Orlando Patterson, whose elaboration of slavery as social death is central, perhaps too central, to the interventions called afropessimism. On the first page of *Slavery and Social Death*, Patterson's preliminary definition of slavery is "one of the most extreme forms of the relation of domination."[86] Slavery is a type of relation. Therefore, relationality is a condition of possibility for enslavement. Patterson also says, in the same opening paragraphs, that "all human relationships are structured and defined by the relative power of the interacting persons," and that "power relationships differ from one another not only in *degree*, but in *kind*."[87] There is no relation, no instance of the intersubjective, unmediated by power. But there are also different forms, different kinds of power relations. To try to leave behind power, which is to say the potential for imbalances of power which become abuses of power, is to do away with relationality itself. In short, there is no relationality without the risk of slavery. To risk relationality is to risk enslavement, and enslavement is always the risk of relationality.[88]

Relationality touches something at the unsteady and uneven boundary between being and nonbeing. There is no protection from this. Antiblackness is one name for the desire to be protected from nonbeing. Blackness can be a name for the affirmation of nonbeing. The performance of certainty in some formulations of afropessimism is another type of self-protection, another way of inventing a self that might be protected. The theorization of the nonrelational can be a tactic for inventing a self safe from the risks of relationality. But those risks do not disappear "simply by the use of an analytical apparatus which leaves no place for them."[89] At its best, afropessimism is an affirmation of the risk of nonbeing.

Discourses, like the people who are articulated through them, are not always at their best. In the days and weeks after her surgery, Lorde experienced herself moving around the boundary between being and nonbeing, with all its attendant anxieties. "I was very anxious to go home," she writes, "but I found also, and couldn't admit at the time, that the very bland whiteness of the hospital which I railed against and hated so, was also a kind of protection, a welcome insulation within which I could continue to non-feel."[90] It was a freedom from having to *feel* what she was experiencing, a space of sensation without feeling.[91] "It was," she continues, "an erotically blank environment within whose undifferentiated and undemanding and infantalizing [*sic*] walls I could continue to be emotionally vacant—psychic mush—without being required by myself or anyone to be anything else." As she recovered, the prospect of returning to her home, "to the very people and places that I loved most . . . felt intolerable, like there was an unbearable demand about to be made upon me that I would have to meet."[92] Home meant being made to feel, made responsible to the feelings of others, made responsible to the ways the experiences of the past years had changed her.

Her hospital room was a space where nothing was required of her but to feel miserable, to wish she was somewhere else, to feel the pain in her body and the pain of her loneliness. When she returned home, "it was hard not to feel like a pariah."[93] Her experience had changed her, and was still changing her. Eventually, it gave her a new perspective on her life and her work. In the short term, though, the changes weren't so virtuous. "Pain does not mellow you, nor does it ennoble, in my experience," she says of the early weeks of her recovery, "it was hard not to feel pariah, or sometimes too vulnerable to exist." Further, her experience of cancer, her proximity to a death or dying that awaits so many of us, introduced a distance between herself and others. Nurses turned cold when they learned her status. People moved away from her, consciously or unconsciously. "The status of untouchable is a very unreal and lonely one, although it does keep everyone at arm's length, and protects as it isolates. But you can die of that specialness, of the cold, the isolation. It does not serve living."[94] One can try to make a home of this isolation, can make the nonrelational into a fortress.

Along a similar path to Wilderson, Palmer, and Karera, Rei Terada draws our attention to the tendency to treat relationality as inevitable, or to treat specific forms of relation as inevitable. The racial politics of which modes of relationality become inevitable touch an antiblackness that organizes a set of traditions emerging from, at least, Immanuel Kant.[95] In "The Racial Grammar of Kantian Time," Terada observes the ways that contemporary theorists who insist on "the inevitability of 'relation'" tend to posit "a concept of 'relation' that they bury beneath the political plane." In this way, "relation becomes a natural armature that can be called upon to set a political limit, and to set race outside the political limit. By its criterion, many forms of actual social interaction appear unreal, unpolitical, unmodern, and racialized."[96] In other words, any move to naturalize relationality, to mark it as ontologically prior to power (to the political plane, in Terada's phrase), relies on some exclusion of really existing experiences of the intersubjective that become unreal, unmodern, and racialized. Attempting to expand the field of the relational, the move critiqued by Karera, reproduces the same exclusion in another way.

Elsewhere, Terada explored this thematic within the later project of Jacques Derrida. In a commentary on Derrida's "Faith and Knowledge," Terada follows Derrida in marking "'the experience itself of non-relationship' . . . found in every linguistic social bond."[97] There is an experience of nonrelation internal to every social bond marked by language. In "Faith and Knowledge" itself, Derrida arrives at the nonrelationality internal to every social bond through the figures of testimony, attestation, and bearing witness. What it means to speak, to hear, to be heard. These acts are essential for the existence of any community of faith—and, in a fashion, any community, to the extent that some faith subtends any sociality. Derrida draws our attention to the unsteady border between a community coming together and a community coming apart. "There is no opposition, fundamentally, between 'social bond' and 'social unraveling,'" he writes, "a certain interruptive unravelling is the condition of the 'social bond,' the very respiration of all 'community.'" The breath of community is the interplay between bonding and breaking apart. "This is not even the knot of a reciprocal condition," he adds, "but rather the possibility that every knot can come undone, be cut or interrupted."[98] What is essential to any relation is its capacity to come undone. My argument across this chapter has been that Blackness is one name for the nonrelation internal to every social bond, internal to relation.

The nonrelational is always within relationality. The attempt to imagine something like a "pure" nonrelationality is only a detour toward another relationality. In the elaboration of afropessimism as a theoretical project, the attempt to articulate relationality and the nonrelational at the level of the concept has been marked by a vulnerability presented as invulnerability, as certainty. By attempts to close critical analysis off from the risk of contradiction. The risk of afropessimism is becoming a doxa that closes itself off from its own internal contradictions. One effect of the bad faith attacks on afropessimism is that many in the field—or, if I can speak for myself, as an academic practitioner who has tried to read the relationships between Black feminism and afropessimism, *I* have found myself more than once on my back foot, mounting defenses of an emerging field of inquiry that close off the richness of vulnerability. As Terada writes elsewhere, "the relationships that change us, and thereby change individual and group experience to an extent, are with phenomena that are frail."[99] So often, the phenomena that find us at our most frail are those attached to relation, gender, and sexuality—which is also to say, to Blackness and antiblackness. The anxious admonitions, the whisper campaigns, the hostility generated against afropessimism have made attempts to elaborate afropessimism as a field—and as a debt owed to heterogenous traditions of Black feminist theorizing and feminist Black radicalisms—defensive, closed off, wounded or refusing to be wounded.[100]

Within the texts of afropessimism, the most significant instance of this tendency toward invulnerable theorizing is a general absence of sexuality—in Lorde's terms, the erotic. Or, the absence of sex and sexuality except as forms of violence, where both terms, *sex* and *violence*, exist in an empirical register. In "Uses of the Erotic: The Erotic as Power," delivered in 1978, in the early stages of her missed encounter with Mary Daly, Lorde moves sexuality out of the realm of the empirical. Within this text, the erotic is a short circuit between presence and absence, being and nonbeing, possible and impossible. Lorde writes, "The erotic is a measure between the beginnings of our sense of self and the chaos of our strongest feelings. It is an internal sense of satisfaction to which, once we have experienced it, we know we can aspire."[101] This formulation, of "the beginnings of our sense of self and the chaos of our strongest feelings," returns us to the origins of sexuality, the enigmatic signifiers of our seductions into the world of meaning, and what we will see, in chapter 3, Leo Bersani calls the masochisms of our early existence. The erotic is a form of knowledge and a genre of feeling that connects our sense of ourselves as finite, bound, and boundaried to our experiences of ourselves as expansive, permeable, vulnerable, shattered, and shattering.

For Lorde, our capacity for breaking apart is always also a capacity for connection, for an intersubjectivity of incomplete beings. She calls this the capacity of the erotic to provide "the power which comes from sharing deeply any pursuit with another person." And so, "the sharing of joy, whether physical, emotional, psychic, or intellectual, forms a bridge between the sharers which can be the basis for understanding much of what is not shared between them, and lessens the threat of their difference." And the erotic is also a container for "those physical, emotional, and psychic expressions of what is deepest and strongest and richest within each of us, being shared: the passions of love, in its deepest meanings."[102] Lorde finds the erotic along the uncertain border between being and nonbeing. In the chaos of our strongest feelings there is a generative negativity that brings the intersubjective into action. We might call this the irrelational erotics of a Black feminist negativity.

Ultimately, Lorde seems to insist on the impossible as a source of power. The framing of impossibility can be an alibi for avoiding ontological terror, for domesticating the potential of negativity. Giving oneself over to the risk of nonbeing is a way of touching and being touched by the irrelational. Across the discourses of the old sisterhood feminisms, the texts of Audre Lorde, and the interventions called afropessimism, relationality relies on a negativity, a lack or absence, organized symptomatically around Blackness. In the chapters that follow, that Blackness will be elaborated as a buried subjectivity that makes subjectivity imaginable, as a short circuit between negativity and futurity that enables a Black feminist poiēsis, and the insovereign condition of possibility for sovereignty. None of this is a movement away from theorizing antiblackness and the mechanics of social death, only an engagement with the promiscuous possibility latent in negativity.

"The only answer to death is the heat and confusion of living; the only dependable warmth is the warmth of the blood."[103]

Chapter Two

Buried Subjects, and the Lines from Intersectionality to Abolition

LIMIT

Internal to a tradition of Black women writing in the United States is a practice of critique at, and on, the limits of institutionality.[1] Across a number of major texts, Black feminists have offered pointed critiques of the institutionalization of feminism both as a political movement and as an academic enterprise pursued under the rubric of women's studies. In her preface to *The Black Woman*, Toni Cade Bambara asks and answers, "How relevant are the truths, the experiences, the findings of white women to Black women? Are women after all simply women? I don't know that our priorities are the same, or even similar enough so that we can afford to depend on this new field of experts (white, female)."[2] In her 1971 *New York Times Magazine* commentary on the burgeoning feminist movement, "What the Black Woman Thinks About Women's Lib," Toni Morrison offered more pointedly that "black women have no abiding admiration of white women as competent, complete people. Whether vying with them for the few professional slots available to women in general, or moving their dirt from one place to another, [black women] regarded them as willful children, pretty children, mean children, ugly children, but never as real adults capable of handling the real problems of the world." She added, "There is also a sense among some black women that Women's Lib is nothing more than an attempt on the part of whites to become black without the responsibilities of being black."[3] In Audre Lorde's 1979 commentary on "The Personal Is Political" panel at the conference *The Second Sex*: Thirty Years Later, she asks, "What does it mean in personal and political terms when even the two black women who [presented] here were literally found at the last hour? What does it mean when the tools of a racist patriarchy are used to examine the fruits of that same patriarchy? It means that only the most narrow perimeters of change are possible and allowable."[4] From Lorraine Bethel's "What Chou Mean *We*, White Girl?" to Mikki Kendall's Twitter hashtag #SolidarityIsForWhiteWomen, and beyond, Black feminists have produced a running commentary on the racial politics of institutionality, a body of critique that, in form and content, constitutes an element of Black feminist discourse as such.[5]

At the same time, no body of theorizing has been as widely appropriated during the period of feminism's institutionalization as Black feminism. And no Black feminist concept, save perhaps identity politics itself, has circulated as widely as Kimberlé Crenshaw's formulation of intersectionality. In the decades following the publication of Crenshaw's initial essays, intersectionality has become a central concept in the field of gender and sexuality studies and in feminist and antiracist political organizing. But across these spaces, intersectionality has largely been rendered as a crude topographical instrument, a method for locating oneself at the intersection of multiple discrete identities or modes of oppression. With this handy tool for way-finding, one could account for one's unique experiences as, for instance, a cis white male occupying a particular class position, with specific access to citizenship rights in the place he resides, and an embarrassed et cetera of other possibilities. During the early days of my own undergraduate education in women's studies, the big question seemed to be whether to conceive of the various elements of my identity as lines on a plane or as streets on a map. As time passed, "intersectional" became its own political identity. In a welcome step away from the earlier wave metaphors, the appellation *intersectional feminist* became a de rigueur identity among younger feminists. Under these conditions, it was easy to grow exhausted with the concept's ubiquity, the shallowness of its application, and the moral bent of its prescription. But that exhaustion was, and still is, a commentary on the reception of intersectionality and not a critique of intersectionality itself. Much less is it a reading of Crenshaw's formulation or the genealogies of Black feminist theorizing in which her work is embedded and to which it contributes, such as the traditions of critique with which I opened this chapter.

Crucially, this line of critique internal to Black feminism has not been premised on producing Black women as simply aggrieved, injured, or woundedly attached to white women, white feminism, and white institutions. Instead, what we find is an immanent critique of the institutional life of feminism: a critique not only of feminism's long-standing and continuing normative whiteness but of the very liberal multiculturalism that the incorporation of Black feminism is taken to signify. This tradition within a tradition allows us to interrogate the nature of incorporation and institutionalization. What would it mean for Black feminism, Black feminists, Black feminist concepts, to be incorporated within the institutional life of entities animated—brought to or given life—by antiblackness? Following this line of critique, I would say provisionally that the limits of institutionalization are marked by a remainder, an excess that cannot be incorporated. But this excess does not necessarily resist incorporation in the sense of a heroic and (self-)determined resistance. Rather, it appears, itself, as a resistance of incorporation, as that which institutionality cannot incorporate and so appears only as a monstrous symptom. And Black feminism, as immanent critique, reveals the degree to which each institutionalization of feminism—be it a normatively white feminism or liberal multiculturalism—shares the same limit. Following this line of thought, liberal multiculturalism does not represent an incorporation of Black feminism any more than the normatively white feminism of an earlier moment. Each institutionalization of feminism operates in this way as a resistance to Black feminism, and Black feminist theorizing names the critical practice that operates, that invents, at the impossible limits of institutionality.

Now, any attempt to approach the career of this concept called intersectionality is freighted with an extensive secondary literature. Much of this voluminous literature implicitly or explicitly reads intersectionality within a tradition of Black feminist theorizing on compound subjectivities and interlocking oppressions, or what Vivian May articulates as a "matrix thinking" set in opposition to "single-axis logics."[6] Among others, references are made to Frances Beale, Patricia Hill Collins, and Deborah King as impression points in the development of the intersectionality concept—indeed, all three are mentioned by name by Crenshaw in "Mapping the Margins." This tradition also aligns with certain iterations of feminist standpoint theory (*pace* Collins) and with theorizations of situated knowledges (following Donna Haraway). Much work written in defense of intersectionality focuses solely on these traditions. On these readings, intersectionality is taken to refer to the positioning of particular subjects within structural relations of power. The resulting subject-position is the location upon which standpoint theory stands and within which knowledges are situated. These readings crowd out other Black feminist traditions within which Crenshaw's formulations might be located. This occlusion is endemic to what Jennifer Nash has called the "feminist originalism" animating defenses of intersectionality, the desire to return (again and again) to the text of Crenshaw in search of a true intersectionality.[7] Occluded here are traditions of Black feminist theorizing on placelessness, absence, disappearance, and singularity.

My interest here is to step away from this expansive, even overwhelming, debate in order to read, in Crenshaw, elements of an alternative tradition of Black feminist theorizing. And I would acknowledge that the elements of Crenshaw that interest me are at best marginal in Crenshaw's own text. They are, nonetheless, present and available in Crenshaw, even if they have fallen away in the subsequent rush to incorporate and institutionalize intersectionality. My reading of intersectionality is not meant as a rearguard defense or call for return to some prior plenitude before the purity of intersectionality was besmirched by a hostile academy. Rather, I am interested in the ways a "return" to intersectionality can lead to unexpected new territories and nonterritories. To this end, I turn to the works of Hortense Spillers, particularly her suite of essays from the 1980s on Black female subjectivity, to read intersectionality through the interstitial. It is in the nonspace of the interstice, the empty space of the Black female subject, that I hope to articulate something internal to intersectionality's theorization that exceeds and implodes institutional space.

Hortense Spillers's corpus of criticism offers perhaps the best example in the tradition of Black feminist theorizing of a critical practice "that is and isn't methodologically rigorous and that, as such, cannot be appropriated as a formal reproducible analytic."[8] This practice of reading, which Spillers has developed over half a century of work, is also a practice of writing, specifically, an "idiomatic writing," "the creation of sentences that could *not* be anticipated, that violated the rules within the sights of grammar." Spillers's project is scaffolded by the insistence that "the *materiality of discourse* is as solid an aspect of political economy as the gross domestic product, and its far-flung subtleties and evasions, its coded displacements and well-choreographed insinuations, decidedly more pernicious as the missile that hides its hand."[9] Spillers's critical practice and her formulations of Black female subjectivity are simultaneously pathbreaking in their originality of insight and form, and firmly entrenched in a tradition of Black feminist theorizing. Spillers departs from Crenshaw both formally and theoretically, though in departing from Crenshaw, Spillers's work can expand and deepen the insights of Crenshaw's. Both Spillers's intricate form and her wide-ranging theoretical insights refract the radical obscurity of slavery and recenter slavery and its logic of capture as central to thinking Blackness—as the condition for race, gender, and sexuality—in the modern world.

Across its reception, by friends and by critics, intersectionality is constructed through spatial metaphors operating according to a logic of capture. That is, the spatial politics of the critique of intersectionality (and of Black feminist theorizing, by extension) reveal a desire toward enclosure, a carceral logic that doesn't simply arrest the movement or motion of Black feminist theorizing but produces a world in which *any* movement and *any* motion occur *within* the space of captivity. To anticipate my discussion of Crenshaw below, this logic of capture or desire toward enclosure renders Black women as buried subjectivity, producing the ground upon which all other subjects stand. Put differently, the projects variously called feminist, women's, gender, or sexuality studies are animated by a desire to capture the Black female subject. As I have elaborated above, Black women have written about these desires over at least the past half century. Black women are the object(s) of desire marking the limit that constitutes the field of women's studies. Black feminism and Black feminist concepts are institutionalized to the degree they can be separated from Black women, and they are critiqued to the degree they cannot.

In the following section, I offer a close reading of how the critique of intersectionality operates as a site where broadsides against Black feminist theorizing can be produced under the dispassionate guise of theoretical disagreement. I am particularly interested in the critique of intersectionality produced under the heading of assemblage theory, and especially in the work of Jasbir Puar. Puar's work over the last two decades has interwoven compelling critiques of intersectionality's *reception* in feminist scholarship and activism with a striking and symptomatic anxiety about the status of Black feminism and Black women in the conceptual life of the field. My focus on Puar is not meant to individualize practices of (mis)reading Black feminism, but to read closely symptoms that emerge over a series of texts. While Puar cannot stand in for a field formation, her work is noteworthy for being widely read across multiple fields in and beyond the academy. It is because Puar offers salient and radical political interventions across several fields that I am interested in how the critique of intersectionality operates within her work.[10] Further, Puar's work is important here because it challenges the white supremacy of institutional feminism while simultaneously critiquing the identitarianism associated with women-of-color feminisms. Puar's engagement with a postidentitarian iteration of feminist/queer theory allows an even deeper reading of the limit of institutionality. An analysis of this queer, antiracist, postidentitarian critique of intersectionality, one of the most radical versions of an institutionalized feminism, reveals that a line of argumentation can offer a radical opposition to white supremacy while being subtended by a logic of capture.

THE CRITIQUE OF INTERSECTIONALITY

In her account of the history of feminist theory, Clare Hemmings argues that the narratives feminist theory constructs about itself have had the effect of producing, among several things, a telos of progress. The limited vision of the 1970s gave way to the force of lesbian and woman of color feminist critique in the 1980s, which then gave way to a new theoretical sophistication in the 1990s and beyond. Within this construction, Hemmings argues, "black feminist critique is frequently inscribed in Western feminist progress narratives as *catalyst* to a more general focus on difference" embodied by the poststructural turn of the 1990s.[11] To my mind, Black feminism in the present suffers from a strange double gesture on this score: Intersectionality functions as a synecdoche for Black feminism and is then used to discipline the work of Black feminism. Thus, while "it is no exaggeration to say that intersectionality circulates today as *the* primary figure of political completion in U.S. identity knowledge domains," it has no bearing on the political condition of Black women, in or out of the academy.[12] In this regard, intersectionality appears as a victim of its own success, which is to say that its success is the mechanism of its victimization. As intersectionality takes the place of Black feminism, it prematurely declares the end of Black feminism. To wit, if intersectionality is ubiquitous and Black feminism *is* intersectionality, then Black feminism is ubiquitous and has won the day.

The temporal dimension of this dynamic has been examined in probing detail across the early itinerary of Jennifer Nash, who has elaborated the desires internal to women's studies' encounter with intersectionality across several articles and her 2019 book *Black Feminism Reimagined*.[13] In "On Difficulty: Intersectionality as Feminist Labor," Nash writes that "the fetishization of intersectionality suggests the existence of a kind of feminist theoretical utopia, a promised land where the 'etc.' that marks so much scholarly writing on identity ('race, gender, class, age, ethnicity, etc.') will be replaced by an attention to *all* difference."[14] The apparent embrace of intersectionality in women's studies—its ubiquity on the conference circuit, in department and program descriptions, and in publishing venues—is energized by a desire to displace and move "beyond" Black feminism and Black women. The fetishization of intersectionality and the desire to read *all* forms of difference are, precisely, desires to move beyond the asserted parochialism of Black women, especially if they happen to live in or write about the United States. This desire is akin to the desire described a generation earlier when Ann duCille wrote of an academy eager to "have that 'signifying black difference' without the difference of significant blackness."[15]

In "Institutionalizing the Margins," Nash elaborates what she calls the two "temporal orientations" at work in the institutionalization of intersectionality.[16] On one hand, the project of "feminism-future" operates as a "movement of intersectionality toward the inevitable future" with "calls for more intersectionality, an attention to more intersections, and pleas for more disciplines adopting intersectionality." On the other hand, "feminism-past" locates intersectionality "in an already-transcended past" and issues "a call to move beyond intersectionality—its hegemony, its problematic practice, its shortcomings, and its insistent use of identity-based knowledge and remedies"—because "the valuable insights of intersectionality have already been incorporated into feminism."[17] In both cases, "intersectionality's imagined peril hinges on its attachment to black women's bodies, and its promise comes from its willingness to transcend the (imagined) social location of black women."[18] On Nash's reading, "black women's bodies are not the subjects of the present moment; they are, in fact, constructed as out of time," and the "ongoing preoccupation of women's studies with intersectionality . . . performs a certain kind of violence on black women's bodies and on black feminism: presuming that black women's bodies are always already anachronisms."[19] I am interested in reading Nash's formulations at a slight angle, to say that being excluded from or outside of the present is something different from disappearance or erasure, but rather an enclosure, in the present, *as* the past or *as* the future. Out of time and out of place, Black feminist theorizing can offer a point of access to a no-when and no-where that might disrupt the desire toward captivity that animates feminism's encounter with Black feminism and Black women.

In this section, I turn to one body of writing that understands itself to offer a critique and complication of intersectionality through a turn to assemblage. Across her early work, Jasbir Puar offered a field-defining series of critiques of intersectionality through her explication of assemblage theory. In "Queer Times, Queer Assemblages," *Terrorist Assemblages: Homonationalism in Queer Times*, and "'I Would Rather Be a Cyborg than a Goddess': Becoming-Intersectional in Assemblage Theory," Puar pursued a critique of intersectionality as, first, anachronistically located in and of regimes of discipline; second, collusive with the post-9/11 US national security state; and finally, regressively attached to identity. In the latter piece, Puar wrote self-reflexively on the controversy produced by her early critiques of intersectionality. She characterized responses to her argument that "intersectionality as an intellectual rubric and a tool for political intervention must be supplemented—if not complicated and reconceptualized—by a notion of assemblage" as "anxieties about [her] apparent prescription to leave intersectionality behind (as if one could)."[20] These anxieties produced demands for her to articulate "the political usages of assemblages and assemblage theory," operating from the belief that there is nothing politically useful about nonrepresentational forms of politics. That is, the misreading of Puar as antagonistic to intersectionality was tied to attachments to the subject and to subject-oriented forms of political work. My reading of Puar is not concerned with the political efficacy of assemblages or assemblage theory. Rather, my interest lies in what falls outside of Puar's description of her critique of intersectionality—namely, an anxiety toward the project of a feminist Black radicalism. What critical readers of Puar have caught in her several interventions on intersectionality is a tendency to align Black feminism with state violence, generally, and the post-9/11 US imperial project, specifically, something far different from an anxiety about the political stakes of leaving intersectionality behind, as if one could.

Central to Puar's critique of intersectionality and her advocacy for assemblage is her reading of the relation between disciplinary societies and societies of control; that is, Michel Foucault's elaboration of discipline and punishment as techniques of sovereign power, and Gilles Deleuze's later elaboration of societies in which power is administered through modulations of bodily matter, financial markets, data streams, and affective intensities. For Puar, the shift from discipline to control is also a shift from the self-possessed subject of rights-based and identitarian politics to "bodies as matter," within a "nonrepresentational, non-subject-oriented politics."[21] "To dismiss assemblages in favor of retaining intersectional identitarian frameworks," Puar writes, collapsing "intersectional" and "identitarian" into a single compound adjective, "is to dismiss how societies of control tweak and modulate bodies as matter, not through signification or identity interpellation but rather through affective capacities and tendencies."[22] Put simply, a different society requires a different analytic.

Puar wards against a totalizing account of both the control society and assemblage theory, however, by recognizing that multiple regimes of power can operate at once. "To render intersectionality an archaic relic of identity politics," she offers, while simultaneously producing "identity politics" as a time/place out of sync with the present, "bypasses entirely the possibility that for some bodies—we can call them statistical outliers, or those consigned to premature death . . . —discipline and punish may well still be a primary apparatus of power."[23] Puar's concession to intersectionality is rife with a rhetorical hedging of bets ("possibility," "some," "may well") that renders both intersectionality and those "statistical outliers . . . consigned to premature death" as anachronisms internal to the society of control. Puar's formulation here recalls Ruth Wilson Gilmore's formulation of racism as "the state-sanctioned or extralegal production and exploitation of group-differentiated vulnerability to premature death."[24] The rise of mass incarceration, the militarization of the domestic police force, and the expansion of vigilante violence against Black Americans over the past half century are rendered by Puar as statistical anomaly and historical anachronism.

None of this is to say that the omnipresence of state-sanctioned and extralegal violences against Blacks means that ours remains a disciplinary society. Nor is it to say that resistance to antiblackness requires an identitarian politics, a rights-based politics, or a politics of the (fixed, coherent) subject. Formulations of control societies, assemblages, and postrepresentational politics need not crowd out an analysis of antiblackness. In many ways, when Deleuze imagined the perfection of the control society—capital as finance, education as perpetual training, health care as the management of risk populations, mobility constantly monitored and modulated—he was describing features of the lifeworlds of racial chattel slavery over the past half of a millennium.[25] Such an analysis is disallowed, however, by Puar's alignment of Blackness, the identitarian, and the intersectional on the one hand, with state sovereignty and disciplinary power on the other. Puar's analysis aligns Blackness with state sovereignty through a double movement. First, Blacks, as Puar's unnamed "statistical outliers," are constructed as the paradigmatic subjects of discipline, sovereign power, state violence, and imprisonment. Second, Black resistance is rendered always and already as a plea to the state for rights, and for the redress or repair of an injured status.[26] In this formulation, Black subjection and Black resistance are both buried, anachronisms internal to the present. Indeed, following Puar's analysis, Black resistance (read: "intersectionality," read: "identity politics") colludes with state violence against nonblack people of color.

"As a tool of diversity management, and a mantra of liberal multiculturalism," Puar writes in "Queer Times, Queer Assemblages," "intersectionality *colludes* with the disciplinary apparatus of the state—census, demography, racial profiling, and surveillance—in that 'difference' is encased within a structural container that simply wishes the messiness of identity into a formulaic grid."[27] This is over and against Puar's construction of queerness through assemblage theory, a queerness with "no entity, no identity to queer, [but] rather queerness coming forth at us from all directions, screaming its defiance."[28] At the very moment when Puar is dismissing identity, she anthropomorphizes queerness through tropes of heroic resistance, a sudden shift from the affective to the sentimental. As she seems to abandon politicized identity, Puar produces a figure with which to politically, emotionally, viscerally identify. And it is this figure of heroic queerness that "suggests to me a move from intersectionality to assemblage."[29] Not the plea for rights, but the scream of defiance. Not intersectionality in collusion with the disciplinary apparatus of the state, but assemblages "[working] against narratives of U.S. exceptionalism that secure empire, challenging the fixity of racial and sexual taxonomies that inform practices of state surveillance and control, befuddling the 'us versus them' of the war on terror."[30] To the degree that intersectionality insists on a taxonomically knowable subject, a subject that can be named, that can be known and thereby contained and destroyed, intersectionality "and its underpinnings—an unrelenting epistemological will to truth—presupposes identity and thus disavows futurity."[31] The stakes couldn't be higher. And it is hard to imagine anything like an ethical defense of intersectionality when it is aligned with the murderous program—international and domestic—of US imperialism. Importantly,

Puar's queer assemblage is not only screaming itself hoarse but also "coming forth at us from all directions."[32] That is, assemblage is mobile where intersectionality is stuck in place. In *Terrorist Assemblages*, Puar clarifies the stakes of this binary: "Intersectional identities are the byproducts of attempts to *still* and *quell* the *perpetual motion* of assemblages, to *capture* and *reduce* them, to *harness* their *threatening mobility*."[33] Here Puar inverts the relation, claiming assemblage to be stilled while simultaneously constructing intersectionality as dangerously inert, recalling the logic of capture. Assemblage is constructed as heroic, dynamic, and mobile, in sharp relief to intersectionality's regressive, still, stale attachment to the subject.[34]

And it is specifically the Black female subject to whom intersectionality is so problematically attached. Puar's analysis shifts from the political to the pedagogical, from intersectionality's relation to statecraft to its life in the academy. She notes that, although intersectionality offers a critique of both feminist and antiracist discourses, "it has been more forcefully deployed as a feminist intervention to disrupt whiteness and less so as a critical race intervention to disrupt masculinist frames."[35] Puar never offers an account for this unequal deployment, nor does she do much to substantiate it, except that it plays into a foundational anxiety of feminist institution-building. Puar understands this anxiety as a desire to "[resecure] the centrality of the subject positioning of white women," while I have tried to describe this anxiety as a general desire toward the capture of Black women. Nonetheless, intersectionality's ascendance within feminist studies has reified "the *specific difference* of 'women of color'" as the privileged object of intersectional analysis. This category of women of color, which Puar refers to as WOC (pronounced "wawk"), is "simultaneously emptied of specific meaning in its ubiquitous application and yet overdetermined in its deployment." This is a double motion by which the subject of intersectionality is produced only to be overdetermined. For Puar, WOC is emptied of specific meaning to the degree that it seems to include any nonwhite woman, as long as she can be "shown to be resistant, subversive, and articulating a grievance."[36] At the same time, WOC is overdetermined to the degree that "it is the difference of African American women that *dominates* the genealogy of the term."[37] The category WOC is both emptied of specific meaning and dominated by Black women. To be more precise, WOC is emptied of specific meaning *because* it is dominated by Black women.[38] Puar here is interested in reading WOC as having been hijacked by Black women "driven by anxieties about maintaining the 'integrity' of a discrete black feminist genealogy."[39]

This anxiety runs deep. "This claim to intersectionality as the dominant feminist method can be produced with such insistence," Puar writes, "that an interest in exploring other frames, for example assemblage, is rendered problematic and even produces woc feminists invested in multiple genealogies as 'race-traitors.'"[40] In her critique of a certain deployment of intersectionality, relying on the production of woc (dominated by Black women) as resistant and aggrieved, Puar produces feminist assemblage theorists as the aggrieved victims of identity police. Screaming defiance yet nonetheless bullied by unnamed, nonspecific Black women, Puar's radical critique of the post-9/11 national security state relies on the production of Black citizen-subjects who (re)produce the most profound violences of that state. Puar's critique produces Blackness as the source of the political repression of nonblack people of color.[41]

While not at all limited to Puar, it is this animating desire to displace Black women and Black feminist theorizing that troubles the turn to assemblage theory. Further, and finally, why is it that the conceptual work of Black feminism is so effortlessly aligned with the material work of state violence? Or, why are the works of Deleuze and Félix Guattari not subjected to the same treatment? In *Terrorist Assemblages*, Puar refers parenthetically to the work of Eyal Weizman on the ways Deleuze and Guattari have been operationalized in the course of Israel's military occupation of Palestine. She offers this "on a more cynical note," suggesting that assemblage theory shouldn't be consigned to the trash heap simply because it is useful in some instances to state violence.[42] But Weizman details the teaching of Deleuze and Guattari in Israeli military academies, the direct application of their work to US-backed military operations in occupied Palestine.[43] Puar makes no analogous claim, regarding intersectionality, about the direct use of Crenshaw's work by state or non-state actors. On this point, Puar's argument consists entirely of an asserted *affinity* between the intersectionality concept (shorn of context) and the institutional instruments of state violence. So why this difference between analytics? Why does intersectionality *collude* with state violence while assemblage is *used* by state violence?[44] Certainly, Deleuze and Guattari should not be judged guilty by association because the Israel Defense Forces find their work useful, but this sort of bad faith dismissal is the heart of Puar's critique of intersectionality. As Sumi Cho, Kimberlé Crenshaw, and Leslie McCall observe in their call for an expanded field of intersectionality studies, "It is far from mere coincidence that current debates about intersectionality's capacity to represent anyone other than Black women bear striking resemblance to courts' discomfort with centering Black women in class-action lawsuits."[45] That is, there are resistances to intersectionality that ironically mirror the violences intersectionality means to address.

INTERSECTION

What might we discover if we return to Crenshaw's theorizations of intersectionality? Does Crenshaw's work necessarily rely on the fixity and knowability of the subject, as on Puar's reading? Must it rely on a model of discrete and separable components of subjectivity? In her two foundational essays on intersectionality, Crenshaw's objects of analysis are, primarily, discursive structures. Crenshaw attempts to break the "already established analytical structure" within which "feminist theory and antiracist policy discourse" only function to the extent they engage with "(white) women" or "(male) Blacks."[46] Intersectionality is an attempt to address "the paradigmatic political and theoretical dilemma created by the intersection of race and gender," in which "Black women are caught between ideological and political currents that combine first to create and then to bury Black women's experiences."[47] This double motion, in which the subject position of the Black woman is produced as it is buried, points toward something different from a mere account of subject formation. It is not that Black women are housed at a point on the map where two roads meet, but that Blackness creates a discursive, legal, and political *nonspace*. A being at the intersection of Black and woman is not simply in a difficult place before the law; she is nowhere at all.

To recall my earlier discussion on Nash, antiblackness confines Black beings in the space of subjectivity, but not as subjects. Just as Black women appear in the present as anachronism, as asynchrony, so too do Black women appear in the space of subjectivity as its negative condition of possibility—buried subjectivity. To appear as buried subjectivity is to be out of place, no matter when and where one does (or does not) enter. At the same time, Crenshaw draws our attention to the conditions of possibility for subjectivity as such. That is, the production of Black women as buried subjectivity is the condition of possibility for something like subjectivity in general. Here, I want to call attention to a fundamental slippage between race and Blackness that characterizes not only Crenshaw's work but also writing on race generally. Some have interpreted this slippage, as Puar does, as evidence of the dominance of

Black people in intellectual and political discourse. As Sharon Holland has noted, calls to move "beyond the Black/white binary" operate according to this logic of capture, a desire to "correct" the slippage by subsuming and displacing Blackness within another term: *race*.[48] Another type of corrective moves in the opposite direction. "In the antiblack world," Lewis Gordon writes, "there is but one race, and that race is black. Thus, to be racialized is to be pushed 'down' toward Blackness, and to be deracialized is to be pushed 'up' toward whiteness."[49] Gordon displaces the slippage by identifying race with Blackness under conditions of a global antiblackness. And while Gordon pays careful attention to questions of gender, identifying Blackness solely *as race* can nonetheless have the effect of eclipsing Black women. At an angle to these positions, Black feminist theorizing allows for an articulation of Blackness as neither identical to race (therefore degendered, therefore normatively male) nor a subdivision of race (therefore particular, parochial). Instead, Blackness is *irreducible* to race, to gender, to any mode of categorization. Blackness is the indeterminate scandal to categories that makes categorization possible.

This approach to defining Blackness as a kind of generative negativity is enabled by a long tradition of Black feminist theorizing both in academic discourses and in aconceptual modes of theorizing through political, cultural, and aesthetic practice. While it is not the dominant position in most academic discourses, relying as they do on discrete modes of categorization, Black feminist theorizing resonates with moments in Black critical theory and feminist and queer theory that trouble the desire for coherent categories. We might not only problematize the relation between Blackness and "gender" and "sexuality" but, indeed, reimagine the relation between Blackness and "race." Rather than posit Blackness as a sociological or identity category distinct from gender and sexuality, it might be approached as "a production of bodily (not biological) difference at the nexus of violence and sexuality."[50] In this formulation, Blackness names the relations of force of New World chattel slavery, not a form of social or cultural particularity. Blackness functions as a (non)site within which "gender and sexuality lose their coherence as normative categories."[51] To rest on this point, we might follow Joan Scott's insight that "gender" names "not the assignment of roles to physically different bodies, but the attribution of meaning to something that always eludes definition."[52] Similarly, Tim Dean offers a formulation of "sexuality," when understood in terms of orientation or identity, as "[conforming] to the processes of normalization that regulate desire into social categories for disciplinary purposes."[53] On this reading, both gender and sexuality refer not to pre-existing realities but to social and political tactics for ordering bodies and desires that always and already exceed categorization. It is in this sense that categories "lose their coherence." Blackness disrupts the capacity for these categories to form a body, to be frozen into coherent identities. What is a fraught and incomplete process for all others is structurally prohibited for Blackness. This is all to say that Blackness is ontologically prior to and productive of the paired figure, "gender and sexuality." This is not to reproduce an argument about the *political* priority of "race" over and against gender and sexuality, but to argue that the production and reproduction of Blackness is also the production and reproduction of those categories made possible as the shadows of Blackness.

This is precisely where Crenshaw intervenes, even while she is caught within an analytical structure that presupposes discrete categories. She writes, "Problems of exclusion cannot be solved simply by including Black women within an already established analytical structure. Because the intersectional experience is greater than the sum of racism and sexism, any analysis that does not take intersectionality into account cannot sufficiently address the particular manner in which Black women are subordinated. Thus, for feminist theory and antiracist policy discourse to embrace the experiences and concerns of Black women, the entire framework that has been used as a basis for translating 'women's experience' or 'the Black experience' into concrete policy demands must be rethought and recast."[54] It is the entire "analytical structure" that Crenshaw aims to challenge. Contrary to Puar's claim that intersectionality (re)produces the enabling intellectual frameworks of state violence, Crenshaw offers a formulation of intersectionality that undermines not only the enabling intellectual frameworks of state violence but also frameworks for addressing state violence. And this enabling intellectual framework Crenshaw sets out to undermine is the insistence that race and gender constitute discrete addends combined arithmetically to produce a sum—namely, the Black woman. Instead, the Black woman, as buried subjectivity, appears as something in excess of the sum of any constituent oppressions. This excess constituting "the intersectional experience" is the indeterminate overlap of Blackness and antiblackness. This is not to say, as on some readings, that intersectional analysis can only apply to Black subjects, but that intersectional analysis, on this reading, challenges practitioners to take into account the degree to which antiblackness shapes *all* experiences. Again, this is not antiblackness as a synonym for racism, or even anti-Black racism, but as that force which buries subjectivity, and upon which subjectivity depends for its coherence, however illusory that coherence may be.

Intersectionality is not wedded to the subject so much as it indexes the ways subjectivity relies on Blackness as its negative condition of possibility. This radical critique of the subject seems much more consonant with assemblage theory than Puar's critiques might suggest. The question is less about the degree to which Puar cannot see similarities between intersectionality and assemblage than about why she insists intersectionality is always already a corrupted analytic. To this end, we might note another current across Puar's work: a desire to undermine simple binaries of domination and subordination, complicity and resistance. Puar is interested in the ways power functions to short-circuit this very binary; one is never simply or only resistant or complicit. And here again, Puar is participating in a Black feminist analytic found in Crenshaw's work (though the citational absence of Black feminist scholars in Puar's work might seem to tacitly deny this). Take, for instance, the caveats Crenshaw offers regarding her formulation of intersectionality in "Mapping the Margins": "I should say at the outset that intersectionality is not being offered here as some new, totalizing theory of identity. Nor do I mean to suggest that violence against women of color can be explained only through the specific frameworks of race and gender considered here."[55] And then: "I consider intersectionality a provisional concept linking contemporary politics with postmodern theory. In mapping the intersections of race and gender, the concept does engage dominant assumptions that race and gender are essentially separate categories. By tracing the categories to their intersections, I hope to suggest a methodology that will ultimately disrupt the tendencies to see race and gender as exclusive or separable."[56] Intersectionality itself can be read as a concept becoming. It is a mode of deconstructing rather than solidifying identity, of revealing the subject to be disarticulated and disarticulable rather than either compound or complete. Intersectionality is not an insistence that identity is knowable or nameable. Instead, intersectionality approaches the known and named subject and challenges practitioners to look beyond, underneath, and around it.[57] The Black woman as a discursive figure in either racist and sexist discourse or antiracist and antisexist activism is not a particularity but a buried subjectivity that makes particularity possible.

Crenshaw engages with the production of this buried subjectivity through both discourses of domination and discourses of resistance in order to show the interconnectedness of domination and resistance, not by "[implying] that the disempowerment of women of color is singularly or even primarily caused by feminist and antiracist theorists or activists," but "by capturing, at least in part, the way that prevailing structures of domination shape various discourses of resistance."[58] In other words, because resistance cannot be separated completely from that which it resists (a point with which Puar would readily agree), we must look beyond theories of subjectivity that rely on the whole and discrete subject. Crenshaw is concerned not only with how Black women are constructed in dominant discourse—with its own attendant horrors—but with how they appear within strategies of resistance. When Crenshaw describes the position of the Black woman as a nonplace that resists entering into discourse, she is talking about discourses that are meant to liberate Black women but are animated by the carceral logic producing Black women as buried subjectivity and producing all others as subjects. Thus, "although racism and sexism readily intersect in the lives of real people, they seldom do in feminist and antiracist practices. And so, when the practices expound identity as woman or person of color as an either/or proposition, they relegate the identity of women of color to *a location that resists telling*."[59] This "location that resists telling" is the proper site of emancipatory politics, a nonsite that resists symbolization, and cannot be rendered as or in discourse. Puar might call this quality queerness, but her analysis denies this quality to Blackness by aligning Blackness with an "unrelenting epistemological will to truth" in the service of state power.[60] In this sense, intersectionality has always already been assemblage, for those who care to take either term seriously. Puar's distortions of intersectionality suggest that, rather than a terrorist queerness, Blackness proffers a mode of being too monstrous for both the critique of intersectionality and for many friendly readings of intersectionality to engage. This monstrosity is contained, or domesticated. A monstrous intersectionality or a wild intersectionality, the intersectionality of a tradition of feminist Black radicalism, moves toward another term and another territory, which we might call abolition. This is the intersectionality of an anoriginary Blackness and an anoriginary Black feminist theorizing.

If the theorization of intersectionality, itself, moves to domesticate the radical potential of a Black feminist theorizing, some part of that work is elaborated in the work Crenshaw pursued before she coined intersectionality.

ANORIGINARY BLACKNESS

> The time of slavery is now and the project of freedom remains not only incomplete, but also, in important respects, unbegun.
>
> —JARED SEXTON AND SORA HAN, "THE DEVIL'S CHOICE," 143

Wherever else it might take us, Black feminist theorizing takes us to the relation between meaning and violence. To reimagine the conceptual life of "intersectionality," we might re-frame intersectionality from the vantage of Crenshaw's earliest major statement, "Race, Reform, and Retrenchment: Transformation and Legitimation in Antidiscrimination Law." This is before Crenshaw outlined the vexed status of Black women in antidiscrimination law—the question of how one makes a legal claim of discrimination when the discrimination one faces is based on neither race nor sex but, instead, both—in "Demarginalizing the Intersection of Race and Sex." This is also before she articulated how the same dynamics operated in the contexts of antiracist and feminist political organizing in "Mapping the Margins." Crenshaw's earlier essay hinges on the relationship between Black liberation struggle and the indeterminacy of civil rights law. In the context of Crenshaw's early thought, "intersectionality" names a set of attempts to reckon with the indeterminacy of Black liberation—or, in a word, abolition.

As we have seen, the reception of intersectionality, both critical and laudatory, is largely organized around an anxiety over the subject-position of the Black woman. There are both vocal supporters and vocal critics of the concept who are united by a desire to enclose a disconcerting openness internal to what I, following Crenshaw, call Black women's "buried subjectivity."[61] I want to argue for a critical orientation toward intersectionality, and the larger project of Black feminist theorizing, that holds space for openness. I want to hold on to the promise of openness-as-possibility and risk the perils of openness-as-vulnerability. In the early decades of the twenty-first century, "intersectional feminist" largely supplanted earlier metaphors for naming the center of energy in contemporary feminism. Increasingly, *intersectional* names a feminist mainstream, and *abolition feminism* marks a new cutting edge.

The concept-name *intersectionality* represented Crenshaw's engagement with longer traditions of Black feminist theorizing around multiple and overlapping modes of domination, and Crenshaw has acted as a steward for that concept-name over the past decades. *Abolition* in its contemporary use is less reducible to the work of a single author. One might outline a genealogy including but not limited to the works of prison abolitionists, including Angela Davis, Ruth Wilson Gilmore, Joy James, Mariame Kaba, and Dylan Rodriguez, the work of organizations like Critical Resistance, as well as activist formations calling for the abolition of the US Immigration and Customs Enforcement agency.[62] It also overlaps in significant ways with the movements collated under the heading of Black Lives Matter, and was briefly the watchword of global protests across the summer of 2020, as calls to "abolish the police" were domesticated into calls to "defund the police." *Abolition* has also circulated to the side of (well-funded) nonprofit criminal justice reform organizations, and the growing popularization of resistance to the United States' status as what Loïc Wacquant calls the "the *first genuine prison society*" in world history.[63] *Abolition*, in its present iteration, is a name for calls for the abolition of prisons and jails, for the abolition of the bureaucracy of state violence (especially in the concrete form of law enforcement agencies), and for the abolition of the conditions that produce prisons, police, and criminalized populations.

The Kimberlé Crenshaw of "Race, Reform, and Retrenchment" is not an abolitionist in the sense just outlined. Instead, her project circulates around the status of civil rights law and, to a lesser extent, civil rights activism across three locations: American jurisprudence, conservative legal scholarship, and the field of Critical Legal Studies. Antidiscrimination law, she finds, is founded upon a fundamental ambiguity: "What at first appears an unambiguous commitment to antidiscrimination conceals within it many conflicting and contradictory interests. In antidiscrimination law, the conflicting interests actually reinforce existing social arrangements, moderated to the extent necessary to balance the civil rights challenge with the many interests still privileged over it."[64] Within antidiscrimination law's rhetoric of "equal opportunity," the interests privileged over the civil rights challenge might, depending on the jurist, include the interests of whites in maintaining a political-social-cultural-economic system of racist domination. It is for that reason that the civil rights constituency (that is, African Americans and others committed to racial justice) cannot passively rely on the letter of the law to protect their interests. In Crenshaw's words, "If the civil rights constituency allows its own political consciousness to be completely replaced by the ambiguous discourse of antidiscrimination law, it will be difficult for it to defend its genuine interests against those whose interests are supported by opposing visions that also lie within the same discourse. The struggle, it seems, is to maintain a contextualized, specified world view that reflects the experience of Blacks. The question remains whether engaging in legal reform precludes this possibility."[65]

Crenshaw establishes a distinction here between the "political consciousness" of the civil rights constituency and the "ambiguous discourse" of antidiscrimination law, and she warns against the former being displaced by the latter. Later in the text, Crenshaw also makes a historical argument about the relationship between antidiscrimination law and Black American political formations. The post–Civil Rights American state's formal repudiation of symbolic oppression may have had profound impacts in the lives of Black Americans, but it also displaced structures against which Blacks had forged a collective identity. "Although 'White Only' signs may have been crude and debilitating," she writes, "they at least presented a readily discernible target around which to organize. Now, the targets are obscure and diffuse, and this difference may create doubt among some Blacks whether there is enough similarity between their life experiences and those of other Blacks to warrant collective political action."[66] Crenshaw continues, "As Blacks moved into different spheres, the experience of being Black in America became fragmented and multifaceted, and the different contexts presented different opportunities to experience racism in different ways. The social, economic, and even residential distance between the various classes may complicate efforts to unite behind issues as a racial group."[67] In this historical gloss, Black Americans *did possess* something like an unambiguous set of political desires that were fragmented in the wake of civil rights victories that made inroads against symbolic oppression while leaving material oppression—and the systems, structures, and institutions that reproduce material oppression—intact. Under these conditions, "the task at hand is to devise ways to wage ideological and political struggle while minimizing the costs of engaging in an inherently legitimating discourse."[68]

The challenge, for Crenshaw, is to cultivate the sort of collective vision that had earlier been available to the civil rights constituency, only under the revised circumstances of the late 1980s. But what is the relationship between the ambiguity of civil rights law and the civil rights constituencies that advocated for those laws? Is the ambiguity of antidiscrimination law meant to thwart the desires called civil rights? Are the political desires and demands of the civil rights constituency *unambiguous*? Is the ambiguity of antidiscrimination law an effect of the ambiguity of all law? Is antidiscrimination law *uniquely* ambiguous, in the sense that law is generally literal but antidiscrimination law is not? Or is antidiscrimination law uniquely *ambiguous*, in that law itself is ambiguous but antidiscrimination law is ambiguous in some singular way? Is the ambiguity of antidiscrimination law an effect of the ambiguity of the desires called civil rights? Or are the desires called civil rights and the law of antidiscrimination each ambiguous in different ways? These are questions too large for any one research program to answer. They shape not only Crenshaw's early thought, but the larger project of Black feminist theorizing.

We might ask, have the desires called the Black radical tradition ever been unambiguous? In "Race, Reform, and Retrenchment," Crenshaw treats Blackness primarily as a social-political-legal category: a status one inhabits before the law, within a political order, in the everyday world of the social. As I have shown, there are moments in Crenshaw's analysis that treat Blackness as what we might call, in more contemporary terms, a political-ontological category.[69] Blackness operates at moments of her text as a genre of being that disrupts categorization itself. The two essays that articulate Crenshaw's formative theorizations of intersectionality both reckon with the indeterminacy of a liberation struggle from this anoriginary nonposition. They reveal the degree to which this being at the intersection of Black and woman is not simply in a difficult place before the law, but *nowhere at all.*

At this moment in her work, Crenshaw treats ambiguity as external to the civil rights constituency, as something that infects and fragments that constituency, and thus she proposes a project of unlearning ambiguity. Crenshaw opens, and closes, the door to the indeterminacy of a feminist Black radicalism that might avow an anoriginary, an-archic Blackness. The demands and desires of a feminist Black radicalism are indeterminate, and the remedies available through the law are inadequate to their demands, and can only be. Crenshaw's work over the ensuing decades has largely operated from within a certain left-liberal position within Black politics that makes a virtue of the (putative) necessity of making concrete demands in the name of indeterminate desires.

The challenge remains to pursue the promise of an anoriginary Blackness, to seek out the impossible inventiveness of abolition against the violence of the word. Intersectionality might approach this inventiveness through and alongside the interstitial as another figure of Black feminist theorizing.

In her "Interstices: A Small Drama of Words," Hortense Spillers offers a metacommentary on Black women's sexuality as "discursive static," an object of study existing only in a distorted and obscured state within feminist discourse. In her twin orientation toward the discursive and semiotic registers of Black female sexuality, on the one hand, and the structures of relation inaugurated by chattel slavery, on the other, Spillers offers an account of Black female sexuality as a discursive field that resists location (or, a telling that resists location alongside a location that resists telling). "Before one could venture conceptualization on the sexual performative," Spillers writes, "she had to confront the entire landscape of prohibitions that literally mire its subjects in the nostalgic reiterative gestures of a frozen temporality."[70] For Spillers, there is no object of study called Black women's sexuality absent the "landscape of prohibitions" anticipating and locating Black women within the symbolic universe of New World slavery. Thus, while "the black female is, if anything, a creature of sex . . . *sexuality* touches her nowhere." In Spillers's formulation, "She became instead the principal point of passage between the human and the non-human world. Her issue became the focus of a cunning difference—visually, psychologically, ontologically—as the route by which the dominant modes decided the distinction between human and 'other.' At this level of radical discontinuity in the 'great chain of being,' black is vestibular to culture. In other words, the black person mirrored for society around her what a human being was *not*."[71] This constitutes, for Spillers, "the paradox of non-being" the Black woman inhabits: to exist in a place prior ("vestibular") to culture, to only appear within "lexical gaps" in dominant discourse.[72] To this end, "[the] black woman subject demarcated a sexual limit, at which point 'sexuality' did not have a name anymore. Sheer phenomena, *this* sexuality refused category, as a staging ground for the abnormal. . . . Focus on this supercharged investment became the obsessive property of this essay, which wanted to say, at last, that 'superwoman' had a sister with a very peculiar name, . . . 'we-don't-do-sex-here.' Actually, this sister is a twin, a study of a double text that says two things the same way except that one would not necessarily detect it."[73] Spillers locates the source waters of this bifurcated model of Black female sexuality in the original absence of Black women from the field of the sexual. To this end, Spillers writes that for Black women, "the absence of sexuality as a structure of distinguishing terms is solidly grounded in the negative aspects of symbol-making," in which "the missing word" is "the interstice," the nonsite of Black women's sexuality.[74] This is all to say that Black female subjectivity occupies a nonplace within the field of Western discourse. The violence that occasions the appearance of the Black woman as a historical actor is so great that this subject can only enter our field of view as a distortion, a gap, a black hole.

The work of "Interstices" was continued in "Mama's Baby, Papa's Maybe: An American Grammar Book," which returned to American chattel slavery "to try to generate a discourse" that might create space in the discourses of the academy for Black women, a position from which to theorize.[75] To this end, Spillers's project extends beyond the ensemble of questions and the constellation of concerns presented in her essay, and extends also beyond a demand for the mere inclusion of Black (gendered) subjects in the intellectual projects of modernity. Rather, Spillers's project endeavors to understand Blackness not as "a figure of supplement to the dominant intellectual technologies" but "as their 'blindness' in the field of vision that enabled their 'insight' as a tool of speech performance."[76]

We can trace an outline of this project through Spillers's engagements with psychoanalytic theory throughout "Mama's Baby, Papa's Maybe." The essay opens with a suggestive analogy between the figure of the "color line" as articulated by W. E. B. Du Bois and "the split subject that psychoanalytic theory posits."[77] We might intuit here that both Jacques Lacan's split subject and Du Bois's subject of the color line are split by the Lacanian symbolic order, but Spillers offers that "the symbolic order that I wish to trace in this writing, calling it an 'American grammar,' begins at the 'beginning,' which is really a rupture and a radically different kind of cultural continuation."[78] For Spillers, the psychoanalytic subject's entrance into language is anticipated by the Du Boisian subject's entrance into the "American grammar." Indeed, the entrance of the Black subject into the Lacanian symbolic order of modernity is "withheld," for Spillers, "by the requirements of the engines of domination."[79] The presence of a buried subjectivity called "Black" is conditioned by a violence *anticipating* the Black subject. The "American grammar," what I have called antiblackness, is that which positions the Black subject before any emergence into the Lacanian symbolic order. To this end, Spillers offers a suggestive account of the power of returning to the site of Middle Passage—a practice seemingly unaccountable to the law of diminishing returns—when she writes that "in a very real sense, every writing as revision makes the discovery [of slavery] all over again."[80] Spillers describes an originary site that is both placeless and timeless, returning us to the space and time of the Freudian unconscious and the Lacanian Real. For Spillers, the Middle Passage is a utopian site within which African persons were transformed into Black flesh: "Those African persons in 'Middle Passage' were literally suspended in the oceanic, if we think of the latter in its Freudian orientation as an analogy on undifferentiated identity: removed from indigenous land and culture, and not-yet 'American' either, these captives, without names their captors would recognize, were in movement across the Atlantic, but they were also *nowhere* at all."[81]

Blackness is utopian, is anoriginary, in that it emerges from "nowhere" and functions in something like the time of the unconscious explored by Freud, a nonlinear temporality in which the past lives continually in the present. Indeed, likening slavery to the Freudian symptom, Spillers elsewhere observes that "slavery . . . offers an analogous spectacle of successive displacements" in which "nothing is what it appears to be" and "little or nothing is called by its name." Under these conditions, critical or interpretive work must "try to stand up this anarchically inverted arrangement of the social in order to hear its stutter more clearly."[82] For Spillers, the figure of the interstice is a method for occupying a field of discursive static, to experience what is meaningful in the chaos of a world formed from antiblackness. In a world that does everything to evade the indeterminacy internal to being, that calls this indeterminacy Blackness and organizes the world to contain Blackness as an encircling exclusion, the work of critique can show us how that indeterminacy inflects and infects every dream of coherence, and all of the violences necessary to make coherence possible. There is a theorization, between Crenshaw and Spillers, of the ways those violences produce a subject of law and a subject of discourse. Rather, the Subject, as a residuum of the world formed from antiblackness, coalesces—imperfectly, incompletely—from the violence of the law *as* the violence of the word.

THE VIOLENCE OF THE WORD

> Words set things in motion. I've seen them doing it.
>
> —TONI CADE BAMBARA, "WHAT IT IS I THINK I'M DOING ANYHOW," 163

In "Violence and the Word," Robert Cover begins from a simple claim: "Legal interpretation takes place in a field of pain and death."[83] Within that field, "the judges deal pain and death. That is not all that they do. Perhaps that is not what they usually do. But they *do* deal death, and pain. From John Winthrop through Warren Burger they have sat atop a pyramid of violence, dealing. . . ."[84] In his attention to this defining feature of the law and the act of legal interpretation, Cover recalls a moment in Walter Benjamin's "Critique of Violence," when Benjamin reaches capital punishment as the founding gesture of the law. "For if violence, violence crowned by fate, is the origin of law," Benjamin wrote, "then it may be readily supposed that where the highest violence, that over life and death, occurs in the legal system, the origins of law jut manifestly and fearsomely into existence."[85] The essence of law is its capacity to organize and deploy violence. In Benjamin's formulation, there are forms of violence that found the law and there are forms of violence that preserve the law, that continually reproduce the founding of the law. In a precise sense, the capacity of law to deal in pain and death is the foundation of any political order founded on the "rule of law."

Cover was responding, in part, to what was then a new interest within legal scholarship in the act of interpretation.[86] In different ways, Cover and Crenshaw both noted the influence upon legal scholarship of what was then called "postmodernism," what now would be called "poststructuralism," that manifested in an acute concern for how (legal) meaning was *produced*. As Cover notes, earlier scholarship focused more exclusively on "the traditional set of questions about how a particular word, phrase, or instrument should be given effect in some particular context."[87] Crenshaw's work engaged with these new discourses, with their expansive sense of the connections between legal and other forms of interpretation.[88] Cover, on the other hand, was careful to hold on to a distinction between the interpretation of laws and all other forms of interpretation, which do not, he argues, take place in the field of pain and death. Cover allows a space for constitutional interpretation, which may "carry the seeds of violence," but, he argued, "it is precisely this embedding of an understanding of political text in institutional modes of action that distinguishes *legal* interpretation from the interpretation of literature, from political philosophy, and from constitutional criticism. Legal interpretation is either played out on the field of pain and death or it is something less (or more) than law."[89] Against the tide of a new movement of literary theory that paid special attention to the relationship between violence and the production of literary meaning, Cover insists that "such views do not in any way claim for literary interpretations what

I am claiming about legal interpretation—that it is part of the *practice* of political violence."[90]

Indeed, it is around the question of *political violence* that the liberalism of Crenshaw's formulations take shape. At the moment Crenshaw wrote "Race, Reform, and Retrenchment," and into the present, liberal politics formed around and operated through the mystification of political violence and the violences that produce and reproduce law. Among the left legal theorists Crenshaw identifies with Critical Legal Studies, Crenshaw diagnosed an inability to conceive of the state—as that which possessed a monopoly on the legitimate uses of violence—as a mechanism for pursuing radical social change. For Crenshaw, state power was a tool that might be put to multiple uses. With reference to histories of state intervention on behalf of Black Americans, from Reconstruction to the height of the Civil Rights Movement, Crenshaw argues for the *potential* of state intervention, though she is clear that the results had been decidedly mixed.

> Some critics of legal reform movements seem to overlook the fact that state power has made a significant difference—sometimes between life and death—in the efforts of Black people to transform their world. Attempts to harness the power of the state through the appropriate rhetorical/legal incantations should be appreciated as intensely powerful and calculated political acts. In the context of white supremacy, engaging in rights discourse should be seen as an act of self-defense. This was particularly true because the state could not assume a position of neutrality regarding Black people once the movement had mobilized people to challenge the system of oppression: either *the coercive mechanism of the state* had to be used to support white supremacy, or it had to be used to dismantle it. We know now, with hindsight, that it did both.[91]

"The coercive mechanism of the state" is another name for a field of pain and death. When Crenshaw extracts the moral credibility of Black freedom struggle in the name of reformism, she also collapses Black self-defense and state violence. State violence is un-made as violence and re-made as Black self-defense. Of course, power always understands its own violence as defensive, as self-protection, as life-preserving. Claiming state power means claiming the (legal, rhetorical) power to transform violence into defense. Claiming violence *as violence* would augur a different politics altogether.

With the benefit of even more hindsight, we now know the retrenchment of white supremacy that was at such an intense pitch during the

1980s would metastasize into a delirious and headlong rush into nothingness. In the present, decades of what Ruth Wilson Gilmore calls "organized abandonment" has produced a state formation in the United States that operates primarily as the enforcement wing of a new era of extractive racial capitalism.[92] As public services have been privatized and dismantled, notions of (political) legitimacy have been nullified. What is left of the liberal state in the United States is an apparatus for producing and collecting debts while also dispensing gratuitous violence.[93] These dynamics were, and remain, open to challenge through collective action. At the moment of Crenshaw's writing, the possibility that "the coercive mechanism of the state" might be put to progressive ends was not unthinkable. But it was only thinkable as a parody of state power.

A state founded on something other than violence would be something other than a state. A world founded on something other than antiblackness would be something other than a world. The subject of such a world, a Black subject, would be a stateless, worldless subject.

The historical moment that has seen the popularization of "intersectionality" is the same moment that has seen the emergence of the interventions called afropessimism. It is the same moment that has seen a new energy around scholarly projects animated by Black feminism, Black queerness, and Black transness. It is also the same moment that has seen the speculative tradition within Black studies, afrofuturism, move from an exterior interiority to an interior exteriority. And all of these projects in different moments speak to each other, speak past one another, speak with each other's voices. It is at their confluence that Blackness might today be theorized as anoriginary in two senses. First, in the sense that it can dispense with the need to locate some concrete historical origin of Blackness. Second, this Blackness, that breaks history from within, signals the emergence of a genre of being called the Human. It is in this context that Blackness might be theorized as an-archic, as having "no beginning and no foundation."[94] The world we inhabit is a reaction-formation; it invented, and continually reinvents, itself against the Blackness it brought into existence. Antiblackness is a desire against negative being. Antiblackness is violence that gives the world meaning. There are otherwise worlds that endeavor only to inhabit the desire to exist in an antiblack world differently. The desire for a Black world is another violence—the violence of a feminist Black radicalism, a violence against the origins of the world—and another word.

That word, in this moment, might be *abolition*. Abolition is something like the lacuna internal to intersectionality. Abolition radicalizes the desires collected under the name of intersectionality. *Abolition* and *intersectionality* are both place-names for desires. *Abolition*, as a place-name for a set of desires, is not immune from the same forms of conservatism that can crystallize within and around *intersectionality*.[95] Crenshaw's formulations of intersectionality, and their predecessors in her earliest work, contain both the desires of a feminist Black radicalism, a radicalism emerging from an anoriginary Blackness, and the desires for coherence that manifest as a parody of state power. *If we act as if the state can protect us, if we act as if we* are *the state, then perhaps the state will protect us*. This is a politics that cannot imagine a world founded on something other than antiblackness. Perhaps no politics can hope to hold that image, not for more than moments. The challenge is to pursue a politics of the unimaginable, and so abolition remains not unfinished but unbegun.

Finally, the Black female subject in a space-time ontologically prior to and productive of the symbolic order has two distinct features with respect to the symbolic. First, she is its condition of possibility; her exclusion is the traumatic kernel that inaugurates the symbolic. Second, we can only glimpse the Black female subject looking backward; we see her through (beneath) the symbolic order that her "*being* for the captor" founds.[96] To this end, Spillers opens "Mama's Baby, Papa's Maybe" with those names that "isolate overdetermined nominative properties," in which the Black female subject is "embedded" and "buried beneath."[97] Spillers offers us a Black female subject placed "out of the traditional symbolics of female gender" that must be *thought*—to say nothing of liberated—in a different way.[98] Just as Spillers's intellectual project conceives of Blackness as a foundational scotoma in the Western field of view rather than a potential additive to that tradition, "Mama's Baby" asks us to think about the Black female subject through an analytic lens completely different from that with which we understand nonblack subjects. Not to be "free" as nonblacks are free, but to pursue a *Black* emancipatory politics that operates by "*claiming* the monstrosity" of a Black subjectivity. This is a politics that "might rewrite after all a radically different text" of emancipation, a freedom struggle reconfiguring freedom by way of struggle.[99]

We might now return to Black women writing at the limits of institutionality. If institutionality is the site for the production and reproduction of subjects, is there an unsite of the unsubject? A nonspace of the buried subjectivity of the Black woman? Toni Morrison offers something like a negative formulation of intersectionality that points the way. The Black woman, Morrison writes, "had nothing to fall back on: not maleness, not whiteness, not ladyhood, not anything. And out of the profound desolation of her reality she may very well have invented herself."[100] This practice of invention under conditions of "profound desolation" recalls an even older Black feminist formulation, the motto of Nannie Helen Burroughs's National Training School for Women and Girls, since widely repurposed: "We specialize in the wholly impossible." A political, cultural, intellectual practice of invention under impossible conditions—a Black feminist poiēsis. Indeed, this practice, honed to the point of specialization, is something like an intersectional project invested in claiming monstrosity. If "the only possible invention would be the invention of the impossible," "the invention of that which did not appear to be possible," then it could be that *only* a feminist Black radicalism offers the possibility of a monstrous politics, rather than a politics of those "normal monstrosities" cataloged by an assemblage theory anxious about Blackness and Black feminism.[101] If we take Black feminist theorizing seriously, not only as "a discipline with a history and a body of rigorous scholarship and distinguished scholars underpinning it," but as the practice of an impossible inventiveness, then we allow for ourselves the possibility of opening up those nonspaces feared by both state power and its most radical critics.[102] Taking intersectionality seriously, understanding it as one line of Black feminist theorizing that frays and tangles toward abolition, opens a door to those parts of the map that don't yet exist, the proper domain of monsters.

Part II
Fields of Static

Chapter Three

Hope Against Hope, and the Queer Negativity of a Black Feminist Poiēsis

The polemical edges of the interventions called queer negativity and queer futurity opened a debate on hope and hopelessness that left little room for middle ground, much less an altogether different terrain. This chapter tries to find different spaces from which to theorize queer negativity and, or as, Black feminist theorizing. That is, to find in the interventions called queer negativity—with its prehistory in theories of the shattered subject of sexuality and the indeterminacy of sexuality and violence, and with its critiques of reproductive futurity, the family, and the politics of hope—prefigurations and alter-articulations within Black feminism. This is not to say that queer negativity simply reproduces Black feminism in whiteface, but that Black feminist theorizing anticipates and haunts the conceptual and political imaginaries articulated as queer negativity. Returning to Black feminist theorizing opens onto yet another imaginary, one different from both queer pessimists and their queer futurist critics. Black feminist theorizing offers a way of short-circuiting the dialectic of hope and hopelessness and allows for different theorizations of sexuality, violence, invention, and the ways they coalesce in the figure of a reproduction without futurity—a Black future or a Black feminist poiēsis.

The discourse of queer negativity opened a new space in feminist and queer cultural studies for theorizing the relationship between sexuality and violence. Where a tradition of dominance feminism had theorized sex under patriarchy as laden with violence, or as an extension of patriarchal violence, queer negativity began from an alternative theorization of sexuality as the disruptive force of indeterminacy extimate to subjectivity—that is, at once internal and external to the subject. Sexuality shatters subjectivity and, with it, sociality. Violence, too, shatters the subject and the social bond, even as it constitutes subjects and social orders. In this chapter, I hold on to the theoretical utility and conceptual clarity of queer negativity's accounts of sexuality and violence and, at the same time, draw connections to moments in the archive of Black feminist theorizing that articulate the vexing nexus of violence and sexuality, and ask what other forms of living might emerge from it.

For a time, the debate over what Robert Caserio called "the antisocial thesis in queer theory" represented perhaps *the* key nodal point in queer scholarship.[1] Practitioners of queer theory were obligated, it seemed, to locate their work in some relation to this debate as a partisan of one side or the other. The two camps staked their territory primarily around questions of how relationality, a posture toward sexuality and intersubjectivity, and temporality, a posture toward the past, present, and future, should inform queer theorizing. In one camp, so-called antirelational queer theorists like Leo Bersani and Lee Edelman held that because queerness represented for the dominant culture a foundational negativity, its radical potential emerged from its capacity to throw *all* forms of relationality into irresolvable crisis, which might also undermine the iron grip the future holds on the present. Liberating the present from the future, in their view, created the conditions for queers to live differently, to "rethink what we mean and what we expect from communication, and from community."[2] For Bersani, sexuality shatters the self in ways that reveal other ways of inhabiting our common being.

For another camp, sexuality forms the basis of a kind of community. A shared experience of sexual desire, sexuality inhabited as an identity, is the basis of queer community and queer theory. So-called utopian queer theorists, theorists of a queer futurity, such as José Esteban Muñoz and Jack Halberstam, pursued a different path toward radical queer politics. For these queer theorists, the future was itself a queer site and the work of collectively imagining and producing alternative futures was the work of queer theory. "This mode of queer critique," Muñoz wrote, "depends on critical practices that stave off the failures of imagination that I understand as antirelationality and antiutopianism in queer critique."[3] In Muñoz's formulation, a certain negativity was always present, lurking in queer theory's political or conceptual imagination, threatening to undermine the project of queer critique. Both positions were freighted with the anxiety that something more was at stake in their debate than the practice of critique in one narrow sector of the academic humanities. While the debate centered on these questions of relationality and futurity, the disagreement between utopian and antirelational queer theorists was also a signpost for related disagreements regarding the proper status of other forms of difference (i.e., race, gender, class) in queer theory. The queer debate over negativity and futurity was also presented as a debate between the theorizing of white gay men and the theorizing of queer feminists and queers of color.[4] These lines calcified as the debates themselves receded from view. Eventually, to say "queer negativity" or "queer futurity" was also to invoke a racial politics.

But this easy outline eclipses both the heterogeneity within these critical positions and the symptoms they share. The queer negativity of Lee Edelman pursued a theorization of queer positionality that aligned it conceptually, if not politically, with the project of afropessimism (as one expression of a Black feminist negativity). Meanwhile, the queer futurity articulated by Muñoz expressed itself through an antiracist politics that, nevertheless, seemed to aim for the radical promise of a relationality prior to antiblackness. Rather than dwelling in the moment of that debate, such as it was, this chapter also excavates prehistories of these queer theories through a pair of contemporaneous discourses: the critical itinerary of Leo Bersani, whose theorizations of sexuality read psychoanalysis alongside Michel Foucault's work on power and subjectivity in a way that laid the groundwork for what became queer theory, and works by Toni Morrison, Beverly Smith, and Barbara Smith, as figures of a burgeoning Black feminist literary renaissance, whose accounts of the relationship between power and sexuality anticipate queer theory from another angle. This chapter reads queer negativity and queer futurity through these discourses for the ways the archive of Black feminist theorizing allows for new understandings of the work Blackness performs for both discourses, and for finding within (queer) negativity a Black feminist practice of invention, or poiēsis, that gestures toward what Kara Keeling has called Black futures.

The next section examines Toni Morrison's 1976 essay, "A Slow Walk of Trees (as Grandmother Would Say), Hopeless (as Grandfather Would Say)," to consider the dialectics of hope and hopelessness within the Black radical tradition. While Morrison reads these dialectics across the generations of her own family, the essay troubles any easy formulation of reproductive futurism. And, even as it dramatizes the tension between pessimism and optimism in a familiarly gendered way, it opens a space for rereading queer negativity in relation to Black feminist theorizing.

HOPELESS (REPRODUCTION WITHOUT FUTURITY)

Toni Morrison's essay, "A Slow Walk of Trees (as Grandmother Would Say), Hopeless (as Grandfather Would Say)," was originally published in the 4 July 1976 issue of the *New York Times Magazine*, as a featured commentary on "The Black Experience" at America's bicentennial. It appeared alongside a plea for "democratic capitalism" from the economist Arthur Okun (creator of the "misery index"), a celebration of the sexual revolution from the pioneering sex therapist Helen Singer Kaplan, and a sardonic commentary from the Native activist and academic Vine Deloria Jr. on the situation of "the first Americans." Morrison's essay outlined the situation of Black America as the Civil Rights Movement faded and the era of racist retrenchment settled into place. "Ten years ago," she reflected, "young, bright, energetic blacks were sought out, pursued and hired into major corporations, major networks, and onto the staffs of newspapers and national magazines." And, while "many survived that courtship, some even with their souls intact, . . . many more spend a lot of time on the telephone these days, or at the typewriter preparing résumés, which they send out (mostly to friends now) with little notes attached: 'Is there anything you know of?' Or they think there is a good book in the story of what happened to them, the great hoax that was played on them."[5] The enthusiasm of their countrymen for racial justice proved to be short-lived, and what felt like profound and irreversible institutional changes turned out to be anything but: "Now when we describe what has happened we cannot do it without using the verbs of upheaval and destruction: Open admission *closes*; minority-student quotas *fall* or *discontinue*; salary gaps between blacks and whites *widen*; black studies departments *merge*. And the only growth black people can count on is in the prison population and the unemployment line."[6]

Morrison places the whiplash of the previous decade into historical context through a series of portraits, beginning with her maternal grandparents, John Solomon Willis and Ardelia Willis, and moving on to her mother and father. The generations of Morrison's family represent dyads of optimism and pessimism, hope and hopelessness, that Morrison generalizes toward the situation of Black Americans at the beginning of America's third century, two hundred years after the signing of the Declaration of Independence. The essay opens on her grandfather: "His name was John Solomon Willis, and when at age 5 he heard from the old folks that 'the Emancipation Proclamation was coming,' he crawled under the bed. It was his earliest recollection of what was to be his habitual response to the promises of white people: horror and an instinctive yearning for safety."[7] On the other hand, Morrison's grandmother "was of a quite different frame of mind and believed that all things could be improved by faith in Jesus and an effort of the will."[8] Within the essay, Morrison's grandparents represent two possible political and affective orientations for Black subjects, left negotiating the historical border between slavery and what was to come after slavery. Her grandfather caught in a pessimism of the intellect, a totalizing sense of the world that could be misrepresented as "an unflinching paradigmatic analysis." Her grandmother, with her optimism of the will, holding an evangelical belief in the counterhegemonic force of individual or collective agency.

Morrison's parents repeat this dynamic, with a difference. Where her grandparents wondered and worried over what futures were possible for Black people, her parents "assumed that black people were the humans of the globe; but had serious doubts about the quality and existence of white humanity." While Morrison's father "[distrusted] every word and every gesture of every white man on earth," her mother "*believed* in them—their possibilities."[9] Morrison describes her early encounters with whiteness, framed between her father's rage and her mother's attempts at comity. Within this formulation, Morrison productively troubles one version of the critique of the Human. In the present text, I have argued that antiblackness names the tactics, methods, strategies, and impulses that push away the indeterminacy, incoherence, incompleteness, negativity, deathliness, and excess internal to living, life, or aliveness, and, following Patrice Douglass, that the Human is "the modern philosophical and scientific social construction of a being that is actionable and willful because it is not a slave or an animal."[10] These formulations might be reformulated through the lens of Morrison's text, to say that antiblackness is a stripping away of various essential parts of the experience of the human animal and that whiteness, the first quality of the Human, creates a compromised and denuded form of life.[11] In this way, Morrison's rendering of her parents is less an expression of ethnic chauvinism or the ego-shielding pride of the subaltern. Instead, it recognizes the cruel optimism of whiteness, the dominant culture of a "nation [that] has spent a large part of its time and energy looking away from . . . the principal facts of its life."[12]

The generations of Morrison's family represent the evolving dialectics of Black life inhabiting the aftermath of the slave estate. In her own life, Morrison synthesizes the different possibilities represented by her grandfather and grandmother, her father and mother, to navigate what she calls the "racial vertigo" of her present. Morrison's vertigo "can be cured only by taking what one needs from one's ancestors. John Solomon's cynicism and his deployment of his art as both weapon and solace; Ardelia's faith in the magic that can be wrought by sheer effort of the will; my mother's open-mindedness in each new encounter and her habit of trying reasonableness first; my father's temper, his impatience, and his efforts to keep 'them' (throw them) out of his life." These are all different tools for inhabiting a world organized around reproducing her presence as an absence, her speech as sound, her reason as unreason. For Morrison, these conflicting approaches to the problem of navigating antiblackness were "held not only by me, but by most black people." She continues, "Some I know are clearer in their positions, have not sullied their anger with optimism or dirtied their hope with despair. But most of us are plagued by a sense of being worn shell-thin by constant repression and hostility as well as the impression of being buoyed by visible testimony of tremendous strides."[13]

When Morrison imagines how her grandparents, decades after their deaths, would make sense of her present, she is sure that "each would have selected and collected enough evidence to support the accuracy of the other's original point of view. And it would be difficult to convince either one that the other was right."[14] Morrison pictures her grandparents grappling with the raw matter of the Black present:

> Hopeless, he'd said. Hopeless. For he was certain that white people of every political, religious, geographical and economic background would band together against black people everywhere when they felt the threat of our progress. And a hundred years after he sought safety from the white man's "promise," somebody put a bullet in Martin Luther King's brain. And not long before that some excellent samples of the master race demonstrated their courage and virility by dynamiting some little black girls to death. If he were here now, my grandfather, he would shake his head, close his eyes and pull out his violin—too polite to say, "I told you so." And his wife would pay attention to the music but not to the sadness in her husband's

> eyes, for she would see what she expected to see—not the occasional historical repetition, but, like the slow walk of certain species of trees from the flat-lands up into the mountains, she would see the signs of irrevocable and permanent change.[15]

In Morrison's construction, the figure of John Solomon's violin, as both weapon and solace, disrupts the dialectic of pessimism and optimism. For Morrison, the truth of her grandfather lay less in his bleak pronouncements on the nature of things and more in his musical performance. In his performance, her grandmother experiences his desire to believe something better of the world. In this common construction, performance, invention, and poiēsis become optimistic attachments to the world.

In his own account of the affective structures of Black radicalism, Cornel West offered a formulation consonant with Morrison's reading of her grandfather's performance. For West, "black radicalism hopes against hope if only to hold out the dream of freedom in a never-never land . . . in order to survive in the deplorable present."[16] This is Black radicalism as "survival and sustenance," set in anticipatory opposition to his later, famous formulation of "nihilism in Black America."[17] But this mode of optimism crowds out another possibility, of there being something beautiful or generative or sustaining in negativity and pessimism. We might challenge a logic that holds an "unreconstructed Black pessimist" and the violin as contradictions; we might close the gap between pessimism and possibility.

From another vantage, the project of queer negativity inhabits just this gap between pessimism and possibility. In the work of literary theorist Lee Edelman, the antirelational position that developed across the oeuvre of Leo Bersani shifted from a critique of the sanitization of sexuality into a position against the reproduction of society—futurity—itself. Edelman's *No Future: Queer Theory and the Death Drive* offered an iconoclastic revision and reenvisioning of the antirelational project. Edelman's text positioned itself against "reproductive futurity," or "the dominant ideology of the social" that "represents futurity in the image of the innocent child."[18] This image of the Child is central to Edelman's work, insofar as the force of the Child's presence polices queerness and queer politics. For Edelman, the Child "remains the perpetual horizon of every acknowledged politics," and "the fantasmatic beneficiary of every political intervention."[19] Thus, Edelman offers a vision of a queer ethics that is against the future and against the Child that symbolizes the future.

Indeed, the force of Edelman's polemic obtained in his insistence that queers embrace the very disorder imputed to them by the dominant society. In a much-cited passage, Edelman argues that resistance must *affirm* "what the Law and the Pope and the whole of the Symbolic order for which they stand hear anyway in each and every expression or manifestation of queer sexuality: fuck the social order and the Child in whose name we're collectively terrorized; fuck Annie; fuck the waif from *Les Mis*; fuck the poor, innocent kid on the Net; fuck Laws both with capital *l*'s and with small; fuck the whole network of Symbolic relations and the future that serves as its prop."[20] For Edelman, this is precisely to argue that "what is queerest about us . . . is this willingness . . . to insist that the future stop here."[21] The queer, in other words, "is the figure currently capable of unraveling the libidinal economy of signification through which a particular dominant socius reproduces itself."[22] It is in the rejection of the future—indeed, an embrace of this rejection—that Edelman discovers the possibility of fundamentally undoing the dominant social order.

Critiques of Edelman have included accusations that his arguments amount to little more than a dissembled optimism, that he ignores the polymorphous perversity of really existing children, that he misapprehends Lacan entirely, and that his polemic is overwritten by an intransigent, smirking whiteness that limits the applicability of his conclusions.[23] For my own part, I am interested in how the latter critique has been marshaled by some utopian (or, to borrow from José Muñoz, anti-antiutopian) queer theorists whose critiques rely on the figure of the "other" child.[24] In a 2007 *GLQ* roundtable, Jack Halberstam described Edelman's project as "utterly compelling . . . for certain subjects in certain social locations. For others, that place of pure critique might constitute epistemological self-destruction."[25] In response, Edelman challenged, especially for Halberstam's unidentified "others," "Why not endorse, to the contrary, 'epistemological self-destruction' for all? Why not accept that queerness, taken seriously, demands nothing less?"[26] In their endorsement of Muñoz's *Cruising Utopia*, Halberstam restates this position, that "for some queers, particularly for queers of color, hope is not something one can afford to lose and for them giving up on futurity is not an option." Indeed, Muñoz himself offers that "the future is only the stuff of some kids. Racialized kids, queer kids, are not the sovereign princes of futurity."[27] For Halberstam and Muñoz, Edelman's stubborn refusal of futurity is structured by the privilege of having a guaranteed future, foreclosing the possibility that his project can speak to the concerns of queer subjects who are not also bourgeois white men.

More interesting, perhaps, is to consider how Edelman's avoidance of race in *No Future* actually weakened his analysis of the Child and futurity. Neither Edelman nor his utopian critics were willing or able to imagine a mode of reproduction that is not reproductive futurism; that is, a Black reproduction. On this score, we might consider, again, Hortense Spillers's "Mama's Baby, Papa's Maybe: An American Grammar Book." In her gloss of the Moynihan Report, Spillers seems to anticipate Edelman's well-known passage, quoted above: "According to Daniel Patrick Moynihan's celebrated 'Report' of the late sixties, the 'Negro Family' has no father to speak of—his name, his law, his symbolic function mark the impressive missing agencies in the essential life of the black community."[28] On Spillers's reading, the father, the L/law, and the "whole network of symbolic relations" that Edelman rejects in the name of the queer are foreclosed a priori for the Black. Spillers marks how "the Black family" is refused entry into the symbolic order, except negatively as a site of pure dysfunction. The incoherence that accrues around Black filiation is also what Orlando Patterson called "natal alienation."

One of the "constituent elements" of slavery described in his *Slavery and Social Death*, Patterson offers natal alienation as "what is critical in the slave's forced alienation, the loss of ties of birth in both ascending and descending generations."[29] I want to rest on this point for a moment, because it is a point that queer negativity was unwilling to theorize and that queer futurity theorized only to the extent that it could still enable an orientation toward the future. What does reproductive futurity mean for the natally alienated? What is the status of the Child or of the family for those "alienated from all 'rights' or claims of birth"?[30] What does reproductive futurity mean for a "genealogical isolate"? Indeed, Patterson offers a formulation much like those of Edelman and Spillers in describing the natally alienated: For the enslaved, seeking out, creating, or maintaining synchronic and diachronic bonds "meant struggling with and penetrating the iron curtain of the master, his community, his laws, his policemen or patrollers, and his heritage."[31]

Rather than argue, following the anti-antiutopians, that "others" cannot "afford" to give up on hope for the future, we might argue instead that Edelman doesn't account for those modes of reproduction that are not future-oriented, those figures of the Child who do not register as such, and those "families" denied the security of nuclear bonds. And we might find with this reproduction without futurity not a crisis scenario demanding redoubled attention to either the family (Moynihan et al.) or the future (the anti-antiutopians), but an opportunity to develop a politics of position that inhabits the incoherence of a Black reproduction. Reproduction without futurity, then, names nothing more (and nothing less) than the queer capacity of Blackness to reproduce without being productive and to orient lives extimate—simultaneously internal and external—to sociality as Edelman might theorize it.

Toward this end, what is most useful in Edelman's account is his reading of queerness as a structural position. No matter what sorts of liberal or conservative politics individual queer persons might affirm, for Edelman, "the structural position of queerness . . . and the need to fill it remain."[32] But this structural position that Edelman attempts to theorize from is not the unraced (read: white) queerness he offered in *No Future*. While the experience, the archive, and the politics of Edelman's queer are white, the position of Edelman's *sinthomosexual* is Black. This dissonance is not so much the fatal flaw of Edelman's thesis, as queer futurity might have it, but its enabling condition. The conceptual architecture of *No Future* opens onto the possibility of reckoning with Blackness as a (queer) structural position—something Edelman began in later work—and reckoning with the sort of epistemological violence that might undo a social order.

In "A Slow Walk of Trees," Morrison articulates another, related, problematic: "There *is* repetition of the grotesque in our history. And there *is* the miraculous walk of trees. The question is whether our walk is progress or merely movement."[33] Rereading the prehistory of queer negativity in canonical queer theory alongside archives of Black feminist theorizing opens space to consider this question. The archives of canonical queer theory and Black feminist theorizing each reckon with the indeterminate space between progress and mere movement. Around the same time Morrison posed this question, new activist formations, organized under the headings of gay liberation and Black feminism, pursued a range of political, aesthetic, and conceptual interventions around desire, sexuality, and the experience of being un-made; negativity and the politics of violence; and futurity and the practice of invention. The two sections that follow engage with different aspects of the prehistory of queer negativity in canonical queer theory in conversation with writings by Beverly Smith and Barbara Smith. After those sections, I consider queer futurity's critique of queer negativity in conversation with the work of Alexis Pauline

Gumbs, as a theorist and culture worker in the same tradition of Black feminist theorizing as the Smith sisters. For Morrison, these activist and aesthetic formations were one source of hope. "In the shambles of closing admissions, falling quotas, widening salary gaps, and merging black-studies departments, builders and healers are working quietly among us," she wrote.[34]

SHATTERING (SEXUALITY)

> A deep underlying fear I have is that I can't have anyone to whom I'm really attracted. I mean I can't decide "I'm interested in that woman" and end up getting involved with her. I have a real lousy record in this department. In fact I've never been successful, ever. So the new rule is that I can have sexual relationships but not with women whom I choose. Besides the negative pattern I'm frightened that maybe I get interested in women who are wrong for me. Oh shit. I'm tired of all this.
>
> —BEVERLY SMITH, "DIANE," 61

Leo Bersani's theorization of the shattered subject of sexuality is, perhaps, the signal theoretical contribution of his "Is the Rectum a Grave?," an essay credited as a foundational moment in the emergence of queer theory (as a radicalization of the emerging project of gay and lesbian studies). Although Bersani grounds his theorization in a range of earlier works—his own, as well as the psychoanalysis of Sigmund Freud and a cast of French thinkers—it has been tempting to credit Bersani with discovering something new about sexuality. His famous opening gambit, about "a big secret about sex: most people don't like it," invites the reader to experience the subsequent text as a series of revelations, as the report of a great discovery or as an initiation into an esoteric underground of forbidden knowledge. But the worst-kept secret about desire is that we are undone by it.

Seven years before Bersani's essay, in 1980, at the height of a flourishing lesbian/feminist underground print culture, the inaugural issue of an unassuming lesbian feminist quarterly out of Iowa City, Iowa, called *Common Lives/Lesbian Lives* presented another view of the shattering force of sexuality. In "Diane," Beverly Smith collected a series of journal entries from late 1978 and early 1979 around her relationship with a white woman active in Boston's lesbian feminist community. *Relationship* is perhaps a fraught word for her experiences with Diane; it's more like an attraction or an attachment. Though it doesn't appear in the text, *crush* is a suggestive alternative because it captures some of the affective experience of unreciprocated longing—*am I crushing them? because I'm being crushed.* Offered "as affirmation and documentation of our lives as lesbians," Smith's writing conveys the depth of feeling and the contradictory affects at work in the dramas we stage for ourselves when we're lonely.[35] In one of several drafts of an author bio Smith includes among the journal entries, she writes, "Beverly Smith is in love with a woman who says it's best for Beverly that they not get involved in a sexual relationship. This woman has a poet's spirit, a lovely voice, muscles, thick, brown, curly hair, lips with more curves than Beverly has ever seen, rough, ancient gentle hands, a mind like a steel trap and a great heart."[36]

Over the previous decade, Beverly Smith had been one of the builders and healers working quietly toward a Black feminist movement. After completing her degree at the University of Chicago, Smith married and lived for several years in New York City with her husband. There, she took a job at *Ms.* magazine that connected her with feminists across the Northeast, including Margaret Sloan, an editor at *Ms.* who was organizing the Eastern Regional Conference of the National Black Feminist Organization (NBFO), which took place at the end of November 1973. Smith passed news of the conference to her twin sister, Barbara, who was living in Boston at the time. By the next year, Beverly Smith had separated from her husband, begun a graduate program in public health at Yale, and moved to Boston. Around the beginning of 1975, the Smith sisters and Demita Frazier, recently relocated from Chicago, reconstituted the Boston chapter of the NBFO, which would be reorganized into the Combahee River Collective.

Alongside her work in the Collective and her training in public health, Beverly Smith worked on a creative writing practice that built out from her journals. Smith had journaled since college, but she burned her journals and stopped writing during the years she was married. "Partly," she wrote elsewhere, "because I felt I had no safe place for them away from my husband and partly because one of my duties in that marriage was to forget who I had been before it."[37] She returned to journaling shortly before she left her husband, and journaling became an important practice for making sense of her identity as a Black lesbian and feminist.

In this context, "Diane" offers a raw, unvarnished account of experiencing desire as a destabilizing self-shattering. Over the course of a single week in October of 1978, Smith documents the arc of her initial attraction.

On Monday, "I'm feeling very attracted to Diane. I'm going a bit nuts over it." On Wednesday, "I feel like I'm losing it." On Thursday, "Maybe what I like more than anything is falling in love. Those early exciting times. The problem is I don't know a whole lot else." By Friday, "Oh shit. I'm tired of all this." On Sunday, "Rampant insomnia."[38]

A month later, on her thirty-second birthday, Smith is exhausted again: "I got about four hours of sleep and have cried a lot. It's Diane. What to say. I'm going to cry again, am crying."[39] Smith's writing is bracing for all the ways it eschews the romance, and also the softness, of an idealized or pastoral lesbian desire that so easily circulated in lesbian feminist writing of the time. Smith's desire is, instead, often terrifying. "I am very scared," she writes. "To name the fear. I am scared of how much I want her in my life. . . . I think I'm also crying because I'm not sure we will have a sexual relationship." Smith tries to use her journal "to sort out how I feel about her sexually," with all of the conceptual and practical messiness of sorting through sexuality and the sexual: "I know I'm attracted to her but it interests me that I don't fantasize a lot about making love with her. Actually I do, but in very fleeting instances, my mind veers away. Of course I know some of the fears. Of my physical imperfections and of my inhibitions. I know that I want to touch her and do. Yesterday at the meeting I imagined putting my hand on her throat, on the 'V' of her throat outlined by her plaid shirt."[40] The fleeting flashes, the way desire breaks its object into pieces, the way it attaches itself to a smile, or the shape of a curl, and the longing to feel a specific softness beneath the fingers. The fantasy of the body in pieces as the subject of desire finds herself broken apart.

The shattering Bersani articulates in "Is the Rectum a Grave?" is something different than the madness of love and the ambivalence of sexual desire, but to see this we have to go deeper into his project. The antirelational is only one moment in Leo Bersani's theoretical and conceptual itinerary. It sits on a continuum between his explorations of the psychoanalytic subject and his later exposition of an aesthetic subjectivity. This transition marked the major terrain of Bersani's late work. (It is worth remembering that Bersani was approaching the fourth decade of his published work when "Is the Rectum a Grave?" appeared in 1987.) Tim Dean has called this shift in Bersani's work a move "beyond the largely negative ethics and aesthetics of antirelationality toward a greater emphasis on new kinds of relationality," or what he elsewhere calls "new relational ontologies."[41] For Dean, readers who identify Bersani singularly with the antirelational moment in his work have missed the "foundational . . . place of aesthetics" in his thought.[42] Situating antirelationality as a moment in Bersani's work allows us to unpack, in a more holistic way, what exactly Bersani means by "self-shattering," the theory of subjectivity that emerges from the antirelational, and the racial politics of that moment in his project.

What becomes the antirelational in works like *The Freudian Body*, "Is the Rectum a Grave?," and, later, *Homos*, appears in an inchoate form in his earliest work, and especially as he began to engage with structuralist and what became poststructuralist thought.[43] In *A Future for Astyanax*, Bersani's theorizations around "desire" anticipate his later work on the shattering of the subject. Bersani introduces "desire" with a sense of its conceptual contingency—"desire" occupies a space in the text that might just as well be expressed by terms like *enthusiasm*, *vision*, *freedom*, or *frontier*, he claims. Each term "[suggests] an area of human projection going beyond the limits of a centered, socially defined, time-bound self, and also beyond the recognized resources of language and confines of the literary form."[44] The term of art that organizes the text touches on the space where subjectivity and aesthetic form cohabitate. This rich and contested space, the space opened up by "desire," though not only by "desire," offers "an alternative to both the socially defined self and the free or universal or transcendent self."[45] In this alternative space, "there are marginal or partial selves or, perhaps most interestingly, *a scattered or disseminated self*."[46] And, anticipating his work with Ulysse Dutoit on the Marquis de Sade and Pier Paolo Pasolini, Bersani notes that the "delights of self-scattering may include putting 'persons in pieces,' an enterprise which, in certain pornographic writing, becomes an appropriate image for the process of violently deconstructing the self."[47] For Bersani, there are certain acts of writing, certain instances of the literary, that make it possible to imagine a violent deconstruction of subjectivity.[48] Or, more than possible, it opens space for this violence to be pleasurable.

In his engagements with Michel Foucault's *Discipline and Punish* and the first volume of his *History of Sexuality*, Bersani theorizes the relation between violence and sexuality, between power and subjectivity. Bersani's "The Subject of Power" opens with a characteristic Bersani flourish, as he follows Foucault's hypothesis in *Discipline and Punish* that imprisonment was being superseded by more subtle modulations of the subject—the shifts Deleuze would characterize as the emergence of societies of control. Bersani writes, "The era of prisons may be nearly over."[49] Unknown to itself, Bersani's summary of Foucault was witnessing the opening moments of a world-historic expansion of incarceration in the United States, as new regimes of state violence were cultivated and deployed to eviscerate Black freedom struggle and to curtail the incipient radicalism internal to Black collectivity itself. Certainly, Bersani and Foucault were not the only thinkers to predict a collapse of incarceration that never arrived.[50] But this blindness in Bersani's text allowed for a different set of insights. The concrete forms of violence that coalesced at the site of the prison could inure us to what Bersani calls "the violence intrinsic to our perception of the universe as multitudinous mobile forms." What he calls "the narrative violence of human history" monopolizes our attention—in art and criticism as in everyday life—and prevents us from engaging with what he calls, alternatively, "formal violence" and "the body's inescapable implication in violence."[51] Turning to the Foucault of *The History of Sexuality*, this formal violence becomes the center of Bersani's account of power relations. There is "something fundamentally incomprehensible in power." For Bersani, "all intentional uses of power" are subject to "the infinitely perverse movements of desire." To that end, "the desiring subject is indispensable to a treatment of the subject of power."[52] A micropolitics of power demands a theorization of desire, of desire as one name for the body's inescapable implication in violence. Bersani's variation on Foucault insists on an engagement with the psychoanalytic problematic that Foucault famously resists.

Within the wider ambit of Bersani's practice, psychoanalysis represented "an unprecedented attempt to give a theoretical account of precisely those forces which obstruct, undermine, [and] play havoc with theoretical accounts themselves."[53] Psychoanalysis offered a way of thinking, with theory, about the ways theory got in its own way. This theme cuts across the theorization of the antirelational. There is something within the subject that undermines or obstructs subjectivity. There is something internal to the intersubjective that breaks relationality. In Slavoj Žižek's suggestive phrase, "Desire itself is a defense against desire."[54] Desire is a way of keeping what we want opaque to ourselves so we can keep desiring. Fantasy is a name for the infrastructures we build to keep desiring everything *but* what we want, because what we "really" want is an absence—or an enigma. Bersani would come to argue that we needn't disavow these failures. They may make possible other forms of politics, other ways of organizing collectivity, other forms of sociality.

As the months passed, Beverly Smith's attraction to Diane only got more complicated. Diane sent some passionate postcards while she was out of town, but passionate friendship doesn't necessarily keep one up journaling all night. In the meantime, being alone took on its own inertial force: "I feel very lonely. Very alone. Because I am."[55] In January, one of Smith's great aunts, Rosa, died. The Smith sisters grew up in Cleveland, Ohio, in a home with their mother, grandmother, and many aunts and great aunts who came to stay at different times. Her Aunt Rosa taught in the segregated schools of the South. She took courses at Spelman but never earned a degree. She never married and she taught her nieces all the arts and crafts she had taught her students back in the South.

After Aunt Rosa dies, Smith describes being caught between mourning and desire. She writes, "I feel very alone. I want someone to hold me and to comfort me. Yet I'm afraid when it happens. I'm so unused to physical contact." The old problem—of obtaining your object of desire only to lose desire, the pleasure or delicious agony of desiring—might not be the issue. Something more like the ambivalence of wanting only a safe amount of the other, of wanting to be undone but only but so much. Or the unbearable proximity of mourning and desire: "Diane came over on Friday afternoon. She held me but I told her I was uncomfortable. What I meant was that I was afraid of the feelings of tenderness and the sexual feelings her touching me evoked. Ever since I've been wanting to see her again, wanting more hugs and being afraid. Christ. I'm trying to get up the nerve to call her."[56] The next entry is dated two weeks later: "I realize that I'm furious at Diane."[57]

Whether Smith is describing her desire for Diane, or for physical intimacy with Diane, or for physical intimacy itself, and whether she is mourning the loss of her Aunt Rosa, or the in-process losing of Diane (a loss without having possessed), Smith is caught up in processes that confound any attempt at a complete account. And this experience of mourning in its relation to desire opens onto the nature of subjectivity itself.[58] We might ask, as Freud asked, why the loss of an object of desire does not simply cause us to replace it with another object. If Diane, with her curls and her good politics and her lips and her eyes, won't return your affections, why can't your unconscious, notoriously open to the contingent and indifferent to propriety, simply conjure another object?

Smith herself is troubled by this as she spends a marathon evening at her typewriter unloading her feelings: "A thought which has been going around in my head as I've typed and typed is WHY I'm still attracted to her. I cannot figure it out quite. Is it an obsession? I feel like I must be acting on some atavistic longing, that she reminds me of someone or something before conscious memory or even in another life. I cannot figure it out."[59] The desire that destabilizes Smith, that fixes itself around the figure of Diane, grabs ahold of something so central to Smith that she can only name it as prior to memory, or even prior to her living itself.

In *The Freudian Body*, Bersani's rereading of Freud's *Three Essays on the Theory of Sexuality* turns toward the antisocial within sexuality. Bersani is interested in the tension within Freud's articulation of sexuality. Bersani finds in Freud a view of sexuality that, on one hand, is in line with a normative, developmentalist framework, where sexuality is a mature expression of a specific type of relationality. But on the other hand, sexuality for Freud seems to name those moments of human experience "when the organization of the self is momentarily disturbed by sensations or affective processes somehow 'beyond those compatible with psychic organization.'" In this way, sexuality in Freud is "that which is intolerable to the structured self." Sexuality is both the province of the developmentally mature subject and that which unmakes the subject. The "mature" subject might be that subject who can (generally) withstand sexuality as an experience of being unmade. But it is through infancy and childhood that we most experience the pleasurable unpleasures of our "vulnerability to being shattered into sexuality."[60] In order to survive the many unmakings of our childhoods, we develop an expertise in masochism. Bersani's occasional coauthor, the British analyst Adam Phillips, has written on the ways that we, as children whose desires cannot, by definition, be met, "had to make a virtue of necessity, turn privation into a thrill, and develop a talent for masochism."[61] The masochism of childhood, our initiations into sexuality, bring us toward our essential *openness* as subjects—our essential incompleteness, incoherence, vulnerability, and indeterminacy. If we characterize this experience as a masochism, it is because it is bound in a necessary way to questions of power. Our power to control the world around us, or our powerlessness against the world around us. Our power to get what we want, or our powerlessness in the face of our desires. Our power to express what we want, or our inarticulate impotence. Our power to control our own bodies, or the failures of self-control.[62] Sexuality is that realm of human experience where we can engage with power and powerlessness in pleasurable ways, in ways that unmake us, where we can experiment with self-annihilation, where we can touch something essential about the impossibility of subjectivity.

This theorization of sexuality as a shattering of the subject builds from the work of the French psychoanalyst Jean Laplanche. For Bersani, Laplanche's work offers two key annotations to Freud's theorizations of sexuality: self-shattering and a return to the theory of general seduction.

Self-shattering emerges as an intervention of "Is the Rectum a Grave?," though it takes up precious little space in the text itself (to which I return in the next section). In a later essay, Bersani would offer more of a theorization of this moment in Laplanche's work, reflecting on Laplanche's "theory of sexual excitement as an effect of *ébranlement*—perturbation or shattering—on the organism, an effect that momentarily undoes psychic organization."[63] This unmaking of the subject opens a space for new relationships to power. This theorization of sexuality can be thought of "as a defeat of power, a giving up, on the part of an otherwise hyperbolically self-affirming and phallocentricly constituted ego, of its projects of mastery."[64] If we cultivate a relationship to ourselves as unmade subjects, we open up a new space for an intersubjectivity "in which the individuating boundaries that separate subjects, and that subjects for the most part fiercely defend, are erased."[65] If there is a political project within Bersani's theorization of the antisocial, this is it. Sexuality is a way of reaching beyond the limits of selfhood, but it is also a reaching toward the enigmatic signifier that sets desire in motion.

From Laplanche's recuperation of seduction in the theorization of general seduction, Bersani aims at the foundations of relationality. Freud abandoned the idea that many or most neurotic symptoms were produced by actual experiences of sexual or sexualized abuse.[66] In his revisions on Freud, or his effort to rescue Freud from himself, Laplanche recuperated seduction theory as a theory of *general seduction*. Not the idea that all neurotic symptoms are caused by actual experiences of abuse, but the idea that there is an originary trauma in the relationship between prelinguistic children and their caregivers. By necessity, infants inhabit a world of adults (at least, children much older than themselves), a world they are not yet capable of making sense of. As caregivers communicate with prelinguistic children, they communicate messages that cannot be understood—in some combination, both because they exceed the child's developmental capacity for comprehension, and because the messages are, themselves, unconscious; they are messages caregivers do not realize they are communicating. The enigma of these messages is an originary trauma that occurs alongside the child's entrance into language, an entrance that constitutes the formation of the unconscious mind.

These enigmatic signifiers are the medium of what Laplanche calls seduction; they are invitations into a world of meaning that is also the world of sexuality. For Bersani, "the implication here is that we are originally seduced into a relation by messages we can't read, enigmatic messages that are perhaps inevitably interpreted as secrets. The result of this original seduction would be a tendency to structure all relations on the basis of an eroticizing mystification."[67] Tim Dean takes the argument a step further: "It is because the other has an unconscious that I have a sexuality." Because the other communicates messages that they cannot realize they are communicating, because the other seduces me into the world of meaning, "my sexuality is thus ineluctably relational."[68] The origins of sexuality are somewhere in the relation between a being who is not yet closed off from the world (the child) and a split subject (the caregiver). Sexuality shatters the subject across these fault lines—our "internal" divisions and the extimate openness of our existence.

This theorization of sexuality anticipates a type of aesthetic subjectivity, a subjectivity organized around "a certain appetite for formal representations."[69] That is, the aesthetic is a site where the excessiveness of desire is shaped into something at once self-contained (the aesthetic object) and constitutively open-ended (its possible meanings). The aesthetic, for Bersani, is not simply oppositional, but is "one of those resistances to power created by all moves of power."[70] This aesthetic subjectivity creates a space for new theorizations of sociality. When we experience ourselves as aesthetic subjects, contained and uncontainable, we can find a type of universal solidarity among ourselves as sentient objects. For Bersani, "we relate to difference by recognizing and longing for sameness." When we love others as "inaccurate replications of ourselves," we express "the security humans can feel when they embrace difference as the supplemental benefit of a universal replication and solidarity of being."[71] In short, "each subject reoccurs differently everywhere."[72]

In this way, the antisocial thesis ultimately elaborated in *Homos* might be reread through Bersani's later theorization of an aesthetic subjectivity and sociality. So much of the antisocial or antirelational is about moving away from a form of subjectivity intent on mastering the world it finds itself caught in, where other subjects are also part of the world to be mastered. The antirelational is a project against specific forms of mastery: "While a certain degree of anxiety about an unmastered world is inevitable, it is also true . . . that we correspond to the world in ways that don't necessitate or imply the world's suppression. The world will always resist embodying our anxieties, or our desires, but we are also in it independently of our need to master it."[73] The aesthetic for Bersani is a space where our anxious grasping at mastery might be redirected, where the world can be unknown to us and we can be unknown to ourselves. In this lapse of knowing, we are *held* by the world. This is a subjectivity in abeyance of mastery, of the anxious desire to *know*. A subject that is shattered such that it is open to a world that cares for us. But "it is part of the complexity of a human destiny that we may fail to find that care sufficiently satisfying, and so we will undoubtedly never stop insisting—if only intermittently—that the jouissance of an illusion of suppressing otherness can surpass the pleasure of finding ourselves harbored within it."[74] The subject of the antirelational is open to the world, it touches at the radical openness of our earliest lives, before we become closed off from others, before we become whatever our selves might be.

"The self is a practical convenience," Bersani writes, before warning, "promoted to the status of an ethical ideal, it is a sanction for violence."[75] The fantasy of the self, as the vessel of the subject of modernity, as a Human "that is actionable and willful because it is not a slave or an animal," justifies a violence without limit against those beings that bear "the burden of embodying . . . the abyss that the world would negate."[76] At the level of the social, the characteristics of those beings are culturally and historically contingent, though they are always formed through the indeterminate nexus of violence and sexuality. Here, Bersani finds space for sexuality to undermine the self in a way that makes other forms of collectivity possible: "If sexuality is socially dysfunctional in that it brings people together only to plunge them into a self-shattering and solipsistic *jouissance* that drives them apart, it could also be thought of as our primary hygienic practice of nonviolence."[77]

The self sanctions violence at the level of the social, violence that becomes properly *structural* or *structuring*, but the fantasy of the self can also sanction other violences that operate outside or underneath the allowances of the state or community. The self that is shattered by sexuality has a repertoire for bearing the unbearable that can vacillate between cliché and pure invention. Almost four months after she first articulates her attraction toward Diane, Smith sets herself down at her typewriter to process what her desire has done to her. "I realize that I'm furious with Diane. I am furious at her for rejecting me. I am furious at her because she has precisely what she wants, I assume, in our relationship and I don't. . . . I'm tired of it. It's not working. I'm mad that I feel that I've got to bury, *annihilate* my sexual feelings for her. How the hell am I supposed to do that and how can I not?"[78] Rage, resentment, exhaustion, madness. Smith is destroyed, annihilated, by the desire she feels she has to destroy within herself. At the end of four pages, Smith finds herself, literally, a tragic figure, quoting from *Hamlet*: "I feel like I've gotten to something with all this mad incessant typing, 4 pages. Where I've got to feels close to despair, full of fear. I'm cold. 'It is bitter cold and I am sick at heart.'"[79] When Smith offers her journal entries "as affirmation and documentation of our lives as lesbians," she offers the gift of melancholy and melodrama, and the shattering madness of desire. If we want to reach through the page and stop her from sharing so much about herself, so much more than propriety permits or our embarrassment allows, it is because we see and feel our own anguish reflected back at us—all of the ink spilt, all of the messages sent or left unsent, our own pages of recriminations, bargaining, and despair.

Near the end of "Diane," after a dream leaves her among "flowers surrounded by inky blackness," Smith aches for some form of connection with the real. She writes, "I feel very alone, in silence. I've often felt recently that there are few ways that my tenderness and passion get expressed. Certainly not in my paid work—that's out. Only in writing and in my political work. But these two outlets are for passion and not for physical tenderness. Little gestures. Touching friends. Arranging flowers."[80]

NEGATIVITY (VIOLENCE)

Around the time "Diane" ends, in the spring of 1979, death intrudes upon the lives of Black women in Boston. Over the winter and spring of 1979, Smith's sister, Barbara, wrote in her own journals of the murders of nearly a dozen Black women over the course of four months, and the organizing of the Combahee River Collective to put forward an analysis of the racial and sexual politics that produced Black women's vulnerability to lethal violence. After a long discussion of the problems of organizing a multiracial feminist coalition, Smith pauses and adds, "Then there is the emotional level of this, the level so much harder to write about. We are dying. Again the truth I've always talked about that at bottom Black feminism is about keeping Black women from dying, is made frighteningly real."[81] "Keeping Black women from dying" is a challenging foundation for Black feminism, and one might reduce "keeping Black women from dying" to preventing murder, preventing individual instances of lethal violence. But keeping Black women from dying is a challenge to the structure of both a global political economy emerging from racial slavery and a libidinal economy in which Black women dying is the basis of sexual subjectivity.[82] Smith poses Black feminism as a challenge to the distribution of resources and energies from the global to the intrasubjective: "I thought about what I was doing yesterday as our sister was dying. Waiting in front of the Harvard Coop for Beth. Eating quiche, but talking about the murders too. Lord help."[83] Smith's everyday life, her inner life, is structured by the same regimes of violence, of antiblackness, that rendered vulnerable the victims of the Boston murders.

What might we make of this proximity of fear and pleasure, violence and sexuality? The drama of a failed romance and the fearful vulnerability to violence, eating quiche while yet another murder is occurring. Violence and sexuality both reveal the essential incompleteness and incoherence of the subject. In the experience of violence or sexuality, a subject can experience the loss of their coherence, can experience themselves as limitlessly open or affectable. Black feminist theorizing points toward the ways that sexuality and violence both represent indeterminate disruptions of the self, or how sexuality and violence both reveal the incompleteness internal to subjectivity, the indeterminacy and incoherence of being.

Black life cannot be reduced to the violences that produce lives as Black. Likewise, Black life cannot be reduced to the pleasures that produce lives as Black. No life is lived outside of a relation to the forces that produce lives as Black. We cannot escape the question of death by insisting on the power of life, and we cannot escape the question of social death by engaging erotic life. Each term descends into the other. As I argued in my discussion of Audre Lorde and afropessimism, one doesn't escape the ugly discomforts of erotic life by insisting that social death is ontologically prior. If, in an antiblack world, Black death is a condition of possibility for the erotic, at scales large and small, we are no less *responsible* to the erotic as "a measure between the beginnings of our sense of self and the chaos of our strongest feelings."[84]

This responsibility to the erotic cuts across Black feminist theorizing and the antecedents of queer negativity. Here, we might pause to elaborate the negativity of queer negativity, and begin to see how Bersani attempts to think the relation between sexuality and violence, and between homosexuality and Blackness. Queer negativity has been read in a range of ways that reflect the conceptual openness of "negativity": as an affective disposition, a pessimism, a refusal, et cetera. . . . The "negativity" of queer negativity is not a disposition, it is not oppositional (it is not the "no" to some "yes"), and it is not dialectical (it is not the antithesis to some thesis).[85] Instead, negativity refers to a fundamental or foundational lack or absence. Within a Lacanian conceptual framework, lack is what sets desire into motion (akin to the case of the enigmatic signifier in the previous section). At the level of the social, the symbolic order is organized around a foundational absence—a gap between the world of the Real and the signifiers available for making sense of that world. Queer negativity is interested in the ways that the figure of "the queer" functions as a stand-in for this primal negativity. For Bersani, the "self-shattering and solipsistic *jouissance*" of sexuality is an experience of negativity that makes sexuality, at once, so endlessly compelling and so fundamentally unbearable, an ambivalence that is mirrored in our relations to violence.

Counterintuitively, "Is the Rectum a Grave?" spends precious little time on subjectivity and self-shattering. Instead, the essay features some of Bersani's most direct engagements with questions of politics, with questions of how we experience matrices of power and violence. The politics that occupy Bersani in 1987 are not the politics of his earlier "Subject of Power." Instead of imagining the end of prisons, Bersani imagines the beginning of quarantine camps. Echoing many gay men during the early years of the epidemic, Bersani anticipates concentration camps, extermination factories awaiting populations of gay men who had been reconfigured through the AIDS crisis as living threats to public safety. Questions of power and violence come front and center in a way they only do in the face of an indeterminate apocalypse. In this context, Bersani reaches for other forms of bare life, for Blackness and Jewishness, as points of comparison. Bersani's references to Nazism are striking, and befitting the polemical project of the essay, but his treatment of antisemitism comes and goes. Within "Is the Rectum a Grave?," it is the ascendant political power of Black Americans that throws the political status of gay men into sharpest relief. On this score, the long paragraph that begins Bersani's elaboration of the vexed political status of gay men merits a full reproduction:

> The peculiar exclusion of the principal sufferers in the AIDS crisis from the discourse about it has perhaps been felt most acutely by those gay men who, until recently, were able to feel that they could both be relatively open about their sexuality and still be thought of as belonging to the "general public," to the mainstream of American life. Until the late '60s and '70s, it was of course difficult to manage both these things at the same time. There is, I believe, something salutary in our having to discover the illusory nature of that harmonious adjustment. We now know, or should know, that "gay men," as Watney writes, "are officially regarded, in our entirety, as a disposable constituency." "In our entirety" is crucial. While it

> would of course be obscene to claim that the comfortable life of a successful gay white businessman or doctor is as oppressed as that of a poverty-stricken black mother in one of our ghettoes, it is also true that the power of blacks as a group in the United States is much greater than that of homosexuals. Paradoxically, as we have recently seen in the vote of conservative Democratic senators from the South against the Bork nomination to the Supreme Court, blacks, by their sheer number and their increasing participation in the vote, are no longer a disposable constituency in those very states that have the most illustrious record of racial discrimination. This obviously doesn't mean that blacks have made it in white America. In fact, some political attention to black interests has a certain tactical utility: it softens the blow and obscures the perception of a persistent indifference to the always flourishing economic oppression of blacks. Nowhere is that oppression more visible, less disguised, than in such great American cities as New York, Philadelphia, Boston, and Chicago, although it is typical of the American genius for politically displaced thought that when white liberal New Yorkers (and white liberal columnists such as Anthony Lewis) think of racial oppression, they probably always have images of South Africa in mind. Yet, some blacks are needed in positions of prominence or power, which is not at all true for gay people. Straights can very easily portray gays on TV, while whites generally can't get away with passing for black and are much less effective than blacks as models in TV ads for fast-food chains targeted at the millions of blacks who don't have the money to eat anywhere else. The more greasy the product, the more likely some black models will be allowed to make money promoting it. Also, the country obviously needs a Civil Rights Commission, and it just as obviously has to have blacks on that commission, while there is clearly no immediate prospect for a federal commission to protect and promote gay ways of life. There is no longer a rationale for the oppression of blacks in America, while AIDS has made the oppression of gay men seem like a moral imperative.[86]

Bersani's sense of the evolving political status of gay men is linked to fantasies about the political status of Black Americans. Bersani argues that there was no longer a rationale for the oppression of Black people in America—as if the oppression of Black people had ever *required* a rationale. "By their sheer numbers," some Blacks were needed in positions of prominence or power, he argues, which was not at all true for gay people. On this analysis, positions of prominence or power operate through a hydraulics by which gay people lost as Black people won, a zero-sum game. Faced with the (possible) loss of a relatively recent political status, the loss of the capacity to be both openly gay and a member of the general American public, Bersani grasped vertiginously at the fantasy of an oppressive Black power. The debasement of (white) gay men, real and potential, actual and anticipated, was made worse by the specter of Black political power, even a Black political power that Bersani recognized as illusory. Bersani seems to envy there being a handful of mainstream Black public figures, even as he possessed a working analysis of Black poor and working-class people's experiences of massive structural violence. In fact, Black Americans were, at that very moment, experiencing forms of concentration, social quarantine, and disappearance into a massively expanding apparatus of punitive warehousing that he saw as the horizon of possibility for gay men. The polemical energy of Bersani's essay, and all the qualities that made the project of the antirelational so provocative, so seductive, so energizing, emerged from this inchoate fear of being *made Black*.

The moment of antirelationality in queer thought occurred when the subjective shattering internal to sexuality collided with the politics of HIV/AIDS. Or, when the Blackness internal to the sexual was forced to the surface in the form of a sexualized deathliness.[87] The emergence of HIV/AIDS collapsed the social and psychic distance between homosexuality and Blackness. Gay men were marked proximate to a viral deathliness, to an ominous potential for self-annihilation. Bersani marked his unfolding present as a moment when academic analysis might "be an indefensible luxury," a moment when "morally, the only *necessary* response to all this is rage."[88] Bersani's rage felt like moral clarity. But that gay male rage held both the rage of being left to die, of being *killed*, en masse, *and the rage of being made proximate to Blackness*. Of being contaminated, collectively, by the odium of "social equality." This was the rage Bersani could not name. And so Bersani's rage coalesced around the apparatuses of state power and all the moral and social authorities that consigned gay men to death, but also to phantasms of Black political power. Newly proximate to Blackness, Bersani obsessed over measuring their relative political potency. Bersani wrote of "those very cities where white gay men could, at least for a few years, think of themselves *as decidedly more white than black* when it came to the distribution of privileges in America," before losing the racial marker to say that "gay men . . . must now accept the fact that, unlike the underprivileged blacks all around them whom, like most other whites, they have developed a technique for not seeing, they—the gays—*have no claims to power at all.*"[89] It is not enough to be without power, though this "power" is no longer the "power" he theorized elsewhere, but to be without power *relative to Blacks.* "Frequently on the side of power, but powerless," Bersani continues, "frequently affluent, but politically destitute; frequently articulate, but with *nothing but a moral argument*—not even recognized as a moral argument—to keep themselves in the protected white enclaves and out of the quarantine camps."[90] This is Bersani's remarkable fantasy: that white gay men were something other than white, and that whiteness was something other than nothing. That is, nothing but the power that produced both "protected white enclaves" and "quarantine camps." In a fundamental way, Bersani lacked an analysis of what would later be called racial formation. Rather, Bersani relied on a phantasmatic distinction between race and sexuality. In an unwelcome way, HIV/AIDS revealed the proximity between Blackness and the sexual. While Bersani was compelled by the potential for an intimacy with death at the site of the rectum, Blackness called forth with another, unbearable, deathliness.

Race appears in the essay at just the moment Bersani delineates the specifically *sexual* dimensions of political identity. Gay men must contend, he argued, with the reality that "the logic of homosexual desire includes the potential for a loving identification with the gay man's enemies."[91] This is a political identity that cannot avoid the proximity between what one loves and what one is hated by, between being subject and object. There is an intimacy here between oppression that is constituted externally, as a function of power, and the inner workings of subject formation. Bersani distinguishes this form of political identity from those identities that might be called race: "What I'm saying is that a gay man doesn't run the risk of loving his oppressor *only* in the ways in which blacks or Jews might more or less secretly collaborate with their oppressors—that is, as a consequence of the oppression, of that subtle corruption by which a slave can come to idolize power, to agree that he should be enslaved because he is enslaved, that he should be denied power because he doesn't have any." Now Bersani has introduced Blackness, Jewishness, and slaveness. For Bersani, these are forms of political identity that are *primarily* or *essentially* produced externally. "Blacks and Jews don't *become* blacks and Jews as a result of that internalization of an oppressive mentality," he writes, "whereas that internalization is in part constitutive of male homosexual desire, which, like all sexual desire, combines and confuses impulses to appropriate and to identify with the object of desire."[92] But Bersani does not have an account of how Blacks and Jews *do* become Blacks and Jews.

In short, this theorization of sexual subjectivity is effectively *pre-racial*: On Bersani's reading, sexuality and desire are separate and ontologically distinct from race. Rather, for Bersani, race is pre-theoretical. Pure sociology. But even with his folk-sociological understanding of Blackness, Bersani's theorization of sexuality touches at a Blackness internal to sexuality as the knot of fantasy, desire, violence, and subjectivity; the intersubjective as the space where we become unmade together; and the intrasubjective as the space where we inhabit fantasies of ourselves as bounded and discrete. To the extent that there is a self to shatter, that self is formed in the shadow of Blackness. The antirelational as it is elaborated across Bersani's later career touches something internal to sexuality that is also a peculiar quality of Blackness: Blackness is a hard kernel of negativity, of the nonrelational that sutures relationality and makes relation meaningful. Bersani's analysis short-circuits around the figure of Blackness, as an incoherence that makes politics possible. Despite its critiques of queer negativity, and the traditions of canonical queer theory from which queer negativity derives, Blackness functions in much the same ways across the elaboration of queer futurity.

Here, we may say that queer negativity and queer futurity, as they emerged around the turn of the century, were two responses to what it meant to live on after an apocalypse. The advent of HIV/AIDS ruptured something in queer life. The epidemic marked gay men through a matrix of violence and sexuality that had produced and reproduced Blackness across the long duration of modernity. But the quarantine camps never came, not for white gay men, and, as the epidemic evolved, gay liberation lurched rightward and assimilation displaced revolution. Negativity and futurity became two competing responses to having survived this end of the world. Queerness was touched by a regime of violence that characterized Black life and living before and after the AIDS crisis disrupted queer sociality. To recall Bersani's other, earlier prediction about imprisonment, the "era of prisons" was not nearly over. Although the quarantine camps were never erected, the carceral regime meant to undermine Black liberation struggle and community autonomy, meant to warehouse and kill Black people, saw an unprecedented expansion. The incarcerated population only began to decrease as incarceration was replaced, partially, by new technologies of permanent surveillance, capture, and indebtedness.[93] And the Black experience of state and state-sanctioned violence, of which Bersani adroitly demonstrated his awareness, never subsided. After Eleanor Bumpers, the police only became more violent. After Rodney King, the police only became more violent and more militarized. After Amadou Diallo, Oscar Grant, Aiyana Stanley Jones, Tamir Rice, Sandra Bland, Michael Brown, George Floyd, and Breonna Taylor, the police have only become more violent. After oversight committees, civilian review boards, community policing, body cameras, mandatory trainings, and consent decrees, the police have only become more violent.[94] In the psychic life of queer theory, HIV/AIDS was an apocalyptic experience of being made to inhabit Blackness, and queer negativity and queer futurity became approaches to what it meant to continue living after that Blackness, to return to social life on the other side of the violence of having borne Blackness.

FUTURITY (INVENTION)

> Yet when I was a child
> whatever my mother thought would mean survival
> made her try to beat me whiter every day
> and even now the color of her bleached ambition
> still forks throughout my words
> but I survived
>
> —AUDRE LORDE, "PROLOGUE," IN *CHOSEN POEMS, OLD AND NEW*, 59

In her reading of Audre Lorde's poem "Prologue," in its connection to later Black women's vampire novels, Alexis Pauline Gumbs argues that Lorde's poem, as well as the project of a number of other Black women writers of speculative fiction and fantasy, "draws on both horror and utopia" in a way that "hinges on the stakes of reproduction and the possibilities of productive relationality on different terms."[95] That is, these Black women writers attempt to imagine different modes of kinship across generations in the face of a world that does not recognize the filial claims of Black people, generally, and the maternal claims of Black women, particularly. On Gumbs's reading, the vision of a different future of Black queer kinship across generations is the utopian, and the threat posed to the status quo in a world that is antiblack, anti-woman, and anti-queer is the horror. For Gumbs, this simultaneity of horror and utopia is distinctive of a "queer Black feminist futurity" insofar as, and here she follows José Muñoz, "for queer young people of color to even survive, to even imagine that they would exist within the future is quite a queer proposition in the face of state and hate violence used to erase them from the planet as themselves."[96]

While Gumbs certainly distances herself from the project of Edelman's *No Future*, described as his "hell and Hitchcock polemic," her embrace of the horror of Black female subjectivity is of a piece with Edelman's articulation of the death drive and queer negativity. Just as Edelman insists that queers "should listen to, and even perhaps be instructed by, the readings of queer sexualities produced by the forces of reaction," Gumbs offers that, perhaps, "conservatives have been telling us the truth all along. Black women are queers raising up an underworld that threatens the light of a capitalist day. Black lesbians will destroy the American family. Our kind are dangerous because we show that there is something better beyond the tick of capital where life breaks down into differentially billable hours."[97] Gumbs's affinity for the project of queer futurity alongside her Black feminist revision of Edelman's embrace of horror offers an instructive disjuncture that strikes at the heart of the debate over negativity and futurity. It captures the ambivalence of realizing that nothing is better than the present—that is, *nothing* is preferable to *this* present. It also brings to light the dissonance that arises when an analysis attempts to reconcile position with politics, the structural with the performative, and the historical force of slavery with futurity.

To my mind, the ways queer negativity is dismissed in Gumbs's text indicates some of the difficulties intrinsic to merging utopia and horror, of imagining the utopian from the position of social death. This dismissal of pessimism in the realm of political thought has been well documented in Joshua Dienstag's study of pessimism as a mode of political theorizing. He writes that while pessimists "are often admired for their style, or respected for the critiques they offer, their apparent lack of a 'positive project' is made to appear as a badge of second-rank philosophical status. They interest us; but, it is believed, they cannot possibly orient us."[98] Gumbs describes her project in the essay as "looking at the two rhetorically impossible claims 'Black maternity' and 'queer intergenerationality' together" in Black feminist speculative fiction.[99] But the latter claim is not *rhetorically* impossible in a political and critical context that offers a queer futurist position that projects the liberal gay notion that "it gets better" onto an unseen and unseeable future in the name of "queer of color youth" who "cannot afford" despair. Rather, we arrive at the *structural* limit that precludes Black maternity and Black intergenerationality from cohering, what I have in this study called antiblackness, and the limit that interests but does not orient both queer negativity and queer futurity.

I want to suggest that what is characterized as hopeless, pessimistic, nihilistic, negative, or cynical offers instead a hope *against hope*, the possibility of politics not simply as hope for a different or better world, but as the nonagential affirmation of the Blackness internal to living. And, further, embracing horror, embracing pessimism, might also create space for thinking beyond the nuclear family, for thinking a Black feminism that follows neither the father nor the mother, but that embraces the sorts of queer kinship networks that have always shaped Black life in the New World.[100] Returning to Gumbs, "Blackness is already external to patriarchy, a haunting presence that the (white) patriarchal structures characterize as antithetical and destructive of the norms they were built to perpetuate." Instead of the reproductive futurity Edelman finds at the site of the Child, we have "a Black, and therefore deviant, future."[101] Here we might have something different than the optimists' injunction to think something better of the world in the name of young people who, we are told, "can't afford" pessimism.

For José Muñoz, the project of what would come to be called queer futurity emerged, in part, from its distance from the antisocial or antirelational turn in queer theory. He would describe his own interests as a "project of thinking beyond the moment and against static historicisms," and a "project [that] depends on critical practices that stave off the failures of imagination in queer critique that I understand as antirelationality and antiutopianism."[102] In *Cruising Utopia: The Then and There of Queer Futurity*, Muñoz re-frames his anti-antiutopianism as a "queer futurity," the position that "queerness is essentially about the rejection of a here and now and an insistence on potentiality or concrete possibility for another world."[103]

But what work does Blackness perform in *Cruising Utopia* and Muñoz's critique of *No Future*? His most sustained rebuke of queer negativity appears in "Cruising the Toilet: LeRoi Jones/Amiri Baraka, Radical Black Traditions, and Queer Futurity," his chapter on Amiri Baraka's 1964 one-act play *The Toilet*. The play, written while Baraka went by LeRoi Jones, details the story of two teenage boys, one Black and one white, who are compelled to fight each other in a high school boys' bathroom. The Black boy, Ray (nicknamed Foots), is forced into the encounter by the gang of boys he leads. The primary instigator of the encounter is an especially sadistic member of the gang, Ora, who is poised to take over Ray's position of leadership. The white boy, Karolis, is forced into the encounter after Ora intercepts a letter meant for Ray. The letter circulates among the boys in the gang to become "the letter Karolis sent Foots telling him he thought he was 'beautiful' . . . and that he wanted to blow him."[104] What seems to be an open secret, hidden in view, is the pre-existing romance between Ray and Karolis. The action of the play revolves around the gang gathered in the bathroom, Karolis being beaten and dragged into the bathroom, and Ray appearing in the bathroom and being compelled to fight Karolis, who is already badly injured. When Karolis takes the upper hand in the fight, Ora leads the gang in an assault on Karolis that is also a coup d'état removing Ray from power and leaving him disgraced. The play ends with Ray alone in the bathroom, cradling Karolis's head and weeping.[105]

However, the action of the play is largely secondary for Muñoz's analysis, which focuses more on moments in the life of Baraka. Time is spent on the Baraka who may or may not have explored a romance with fellow Greenwich Village artist Frank O'Hara. Muñoz pores over details from secondary accounts before telling us they are not relevant. Muñoz is also interested in the Baraka who later rejected the work of LeRoi Jones and adopted a particularly homophobic stream of Black nationalist thought and politics. Muñoz's reading of *The Toilet* constructs an allegory to the life of Baraka (at least, to Muñoz's gloss of his life). The final moment of the play, which Baraka later disavowed as an empty gesture toward racial integration and harmony, is for Muñoz freighted with the possibility of queer futurity. As a rejoinder to Edelman, Muñoz suggests that the end of the play "shows us that relationality is not pretty, but the option of simply opting out of it, or describing it as something that has never been available to us, is imaginable only if one can frame queerness as a singular abstraction that can be subtracted and isolated from a larger social matrix."[106] That is, relationality is only something to be rejected for those who can "afford" it—white gay men, those for whom queerness is "subtracted and isolated from a larger social matrix."

Muñoz argues that Edelman's critical enterprise, however attractive it may be, excludes queer people who aren't white or male. Further, the critique of reproductive futurism in Edelman is "enacted by the active disavowal of a crisis in afrofuturism." But what is this "crisis in afrofuturism" for Muñoz? Muñoz turns to the details of Baraka's real life to make his point. He refers to the 2003 murder of Baraka's thirty-one-year-old daughter, Shani, and her partner by the estranged husband of another of Baraka's daughters. Her killing led to an expansion of Baraka's activist work, along with his wife, Amina, to include raising awareness around homophobic violence. Muñoz writes that "real violence has *ironically* brought Baraka back to a queer world that he had renounced so many years ago." Muñoz also refers to the murder of Sakia Gunn, a fifteen-year-old Black queer girl, to refute Edelman's provocation that "the future is kid's stuff." The murders are described not "to serve as proof" for his argument regarding Baraka's play, but "because it makes one simple point. The future is only the stuff of some kids. Racialized kids, queer kids, are not the sovereign princes of futurity."[107] In articulating queer futurity in opposition to queer negativity, Muñoz recruits Amiri Baraka's daughter and reproduces the violence that ended her life.

Does this make her, or Sakia Gunn, images of the Child? Across these discourses, can there be a Black Child? That is, not a racialized child, but a figure of futurity that is also a figure of negativity? If really-existing instances of antiblack violence don't make the analysis of *No Future*, they seem to appear gratuitously in *Cruising Utopia*. Along those lines, there is something unseemly about Muñoz's construction of Shani Baraka's death as ironic. Her death brought Baraka "back to a queer world he had renounced so many years ago." But are they the same queer worlds? Is the Greenwich Village of LeRoi Jones's youth that Muñoz details, in which he was a simultaneous site of sexual desire and racist disgust, a "stud" among his white male counterparts, really the same queer world occupied by his daughter or by Sakia Gunn? Is queer futurity nothing other than the reproduction or return of an imagined queer past? And is the path to that futurity found in cultural critique that plays with the pain of a Black artist or the deaths of Black women? The queer futurity pursued in *Cruising Utopia* constructs Blackness symptomatically, mobilizing Blackness to guarantee a relationality sutured by antiblackness.

In later work, Edelman rearticulated the distance between the Child, as a privileged figure of futurity, and "any actual or historical child, whose sociopolitical value rests on its ability to embody that position."[108] As he clarifies, "While the figure of meaning and cultural promise in a racist and antiblack order will disproportionately find representation in images of the dominant racial class, the Child itself does not have any intrinsic relation to whiteness and can, where useful, be embodied, even by that dominant order, in (the image of) children of color as well."[109] Edelman separates the *figure* of the Child from really existing children, and adds that the Child *as a figure* has no *intrinsic* relation to race or to any other form of socially constructed difference. "The Child," as a figure that anticipates difference, "has no qualities in itself, but will assume those qualities as needed in the context of a dominant social order. At the same time, racial and ethnic communities within that social order may hold out their own hopes for the future in the form of a Child of their own."[110] Edelman emphasizes the racial contingency of the Child, writing that "the image of the Child has no transcommunitarian racial specificity," and offers as one example, of many possible examples, "antigay legislation recently proposed by members of Ghana's parliament."[111] For Edelman, the *image* of the Child is not racially specific and is deployed by all sorts of communities. Indeed, the figure of the Child is an important way communities consolidate themselves *as communities*. In this way, Edelman's Child could encompass the "queer kids of color" mobilized by critiques of *No Future* and the project of queer negativity.

This formulation shares with Muñoz's queer futurity an understanding of Blackness as an identity, as a particular racial identity, as a socially and culturally constructed basis of community. Over time, Edelman began to incorporate engagements with afropessimist critiques of queer negativity into his own critical practice, without moving away from the engagements with Lacanian psychoanalysis that form the center of that practice. In his *Bad Education*, Edelman orients his new engagements with Blackness (as a primary figure of Black critical theory) around a Lacanian concept that Edelman renders as "ab-sens." On Edelman's reading, *ab-sens* names a constitutive outside or excess of meaning, a "primal negativity" the exclusion of which makes the entire world of meaning possible.[112] In different ways, different figures come to embody this ab-sens for different cultural and historical contexts—to paraphrase the French linguist and philosopher, Jean-Claude Milner, its appearance is infinitely contingent.[113] In our present, Edelman understands "those read as Black, queer, woman, trans*, or any other category of social (non)'being'" as embodiments of ab-sens, and "the stigma attached" to those identities "corresponds to their inflection . . . as embodiments of a negativity inassimilable to being, reflecting their figural status as personifications of ab-sens."[114] Where an afropessimist might insist on the singularity of Blackness or of "the Black" as an embodiment of ab-sens, Edelman "insists on the myriad names" that "share . . . the burden of embodying, however differently, the abyss that the world would negate."[115]

If antiblackness is one expression of a resistance to indeterminacy, and if there are, as Edelman argues, many resistances to indeterminacy, then antiblackness may be singular for its centrality to several centuries of

Western social formations (with their properly *global* reach), and the ways it touches so much of lived experience (from the intrapsychic to global geopolitics). The project of queer negativity has tended to set those questions aside as matters of politics rather than structural analysis. But there was also something convenient in the ways queer negativity bracketed Blackness. Queer futurity, on the other hand, offered a different sort of missed encounter with Blackness and Black feminism. Understanding itself as an extension of the political and theoretical project of Black feminism, its political imagination nonetheless appears to be bound by antiblackness.

The argument that "young queer people of color," with that figure's imprecise relationship to Blackness, cannot "afford" to give in to queer negativity, or to (afro)pessimism, is subtended by "a politics of scarcity at the level of subjectivity" that mischaracterizes the entire question of futurity.[116] The argument that young Black queers cannot "afford" pessimism "understand[s] current forms of being as inadequate, rather than over abundant."[117] This is to say that something like queer negativity, rather than queer futurity, makes it possible to recognize the overwhelming *overpresence* of futures for those racialized and queer kids that Muñoz argues "are not the sovereign princes of futurity." What does it mean that the argument that futurity is a scarce resource relies so heavily on figures of Black queer people who have been murdered? Muñoz's argument summons three murdered Black lesbians to demonstrate that young queers of color (we note, again, the slippage from "Black" to "of color" in the argument) cannot abandon futurity-as-hope and hope-as-futurity. That is, focusing on the spectacle of state and state-sanctioned Black queer death obscures the structuring violences that accrue around Black queer survival.

On this front, Gumbs's long engagement with the figure of Audre Lorde is instructive, demonstrating the multiple ways that premature death is something other than the foreclosure of futurity as such. In her reading of "Preface," Gumbs refers to the ways Lorde's words continually appear and re-appear in feminist writings, at protests, and in other venues, constituting "a sacred repetition," one way that Lorde "survives into the present."[118] Elsewhere, Gumbs has written of Lorde's multiple denied requests for medical leave while teaching at Hunter College, noting that "Black feminists are a trouble more useful as dead invocation than as live troublemakers, raising concerns in faculty meetings. And those institutions continue to make money and garner prestige off of their once affiliated now dead faculty members."[119] Access to the future as "sacred repetition" exists alongside access to the future as "dead invocation," complicating the implicit collapse of optimism onto futurity at work in this politics of scarcity. Disentangling optimism from futurity is essential here. There are many ways of accessing and inhabiting the future, and the problem is not that young Black queers have *no* access to the future but that the future is, itself, structured by an antiblackness that shapes access to future(s) for *all* subjects. In her own reading of Edelman alongside Frantz Fanon, Kara Keeling has observed that "from within the logics of reproductive futurity and colonial reality, a black future looks like no future at all."[120] By reading antiblackness solely through spectacular acts of violence, rather than as a structural and structuring violence, the project of queer futurity ironically precludes the recognition or embrace of a "black future," or the invention or inventiveness of Black feminist theorizing.

A SLOW WALK OF TREES (THE QUEER NEGATIVITY OF A BLACK FEMINIST POIĒSIS)

Although "A Slow Walk of Trees" is framed around descending generations of married couples in Toni Morrison's family, the essay arrives at something other than a coupling convention or reproductive futurity. For Morrison, the "builders and healers [who] are working quietly among us," like Beverly and Barbara Smith, navigating the antimonies of Black lesbian life in Boston, or, two generations later, Alexis Pauline Gumbs reimagining the living legacies of Audre Lorde, were also time-workers: "They clarify our past, make livable our present and are certain to shape our future." She continued, "And since the future is where our immortality as a race lies, no overview of the state of black people at this time can ignore some speculation on the only ones certain to live it—the children." The Black children born after 1960 were "both exhilarating and frightening" to Morrison. "They are the baby sisters of the sit-in generation, the sons of the neighborhood blockbusters, the nephews of jailed revolutionaries, and a huge number who have had college graduates in their families for three and four generations." These children were born into the Civil Rights era, came of age into Black Power, and approached adulthood during an era of retrenchment when the mass media portrayed their very existence as a social crisis. Against the propaganda of teenage crime and the pressing need for Law and Order, Morrison experienced them as "either magnificent hybrids or throwbacks to the time when our ancestors were called 'royal.'" In the wake of midcentury Black freedom struggle, Black children were figures outside of time. Those children represented at once the successes of Black freedom struggle and an unfinished revolution, as those successes were clawed back jealously by revanchists and liberals who had met their limit for imagining a new world or a new way of being in the world.

What did those children make of the failures of Civil Rights and Black Power? "I thought we had left them nothing to love and nothing to want to know," Morrison wrote. "I thought that those who exhibited some excitement about their future had long ago looked into the eyes of their teachers and were either saddened or outraged by the death of possibility they found there. I thought that those who were interested in the past had looked into the faces of their parents and seen betrayal. I thought the state had deprived them of a land and the landlords and banks had deprived them of a turf."[121] Those children had come into a lifeworld where all of the scripts for living had been interrupted, a world where their erstwhile countrymen had "woke up one morning to find the sun shining and all the stars aflame," and they saw everywhere around them contests over what the new scripts for living might be.[122] For some, it was a moment of a new Black feminist inventiveness, a Black feminist poiēsis, the invention of new ways of inhabiting life and living. But that moment was also radically open-ended, and the inertial force of antiblackness asserted itself in fantasies of reclaiming a bygone past, a lost greatness, and banishing incoherence and indeterminacy. "So," Morrison asks, "how is it that, with nothing to love, nothing they need to know, landless, turfless, minus a future and a past, these black children look us dead in the eye?"[123]

The figure of the Black child in Morrison's essay is not queer negativity's sovereign prince of futurity, nor is it queer futurity's queer kid of color who cannot afford pessimism and negativity. The Black child Morrison describes is "certain" to inhabit the future, even as they live in the radical indeterminacy of a broken temporality, minus a future *and* a past. The Black child of Morrison's essay lives in a queer time and builds a Black future. In her *Queer Times, Black Futures*, Kara Keeling asks, "If we were never meant to survive *as such*, what do we do with 'the time that remains,' while we suffer, while we rejoice, while we exist within conditions not entirely of our own making, yet still open, currently defined by, but not confined by, flesh that dies and lives in its time?"[124] Here, Keeling invites us, as readers, scholars, and practitioners, to experience the openness and endure the open-endedness of a Black future. The emergence of this future is tied to our capacity to engage with our desires, our deepest desires, as Keeling establishes her conceptual coordinates between surrealism and the Black feminist theorizing of Audre Lorde. Keeling's conceptual architecture enables a mode of writing that takes ambivalence seriously without claiming to have mastered ambivalence, moving toward what Leo Bersani called an aesthetic subjectivity, or a mode of living that lets go of mastery altogether.

Futures can take many forms, and Keeling holds those many forms in generative tension, as when she writes, "Our deepest internal desires can be violent and cruel, as well as expansive, generous, and delightful."[125] Already, this pushes against a tendency in both minoritized critical discourses and radical political discourses (to say nothing of their overlap) to *omit the possibility* that our deepest desires—our personal desires or our political desires (to say nothing of their overlap)—might be desires to do violence, enact cruelty, obliterate the agency of others, and delight in naked abuse and violation.[126] *But there is no one truth to our desires.* Our desires cannot, finally, tell us the truth about ourselves. We must live with, or live in denial of, the multiplicity of our desires, the potential ugliness of their promiscuity, and the certainty that we will be guilty of giving ground relative to them.[127] But we must also live with everything in our desires that is expansive, generous, and delightful—which is no less unbearable. We circumvent the unbearable delights of a Black future by omitting the unbearable horrors of our deepest desires.

How might we pursue a radical politics without bracketing away the indeterminacy and incoherence of our lives as subjects of desire? Keeling introduces recurring interruptions from Herman Melville's story, "Bartleby, the Scrivener," as attempts "to meditate on the (im)possibility of a politics of radical refusal."[128] Keeling makes use of a common rhetorical gesture, marking the simultaneity of the possible and the impossible through the use of parentheses, but to uncommon ends. She is not saying that, though we believe this or that thing is possible, it is, "in fact," impossible. Nor that, though some of us claim this or that thing is impossible, it is, "in fact," possible. Instead, Keeling marks a politics of radical refusal with the essential indeterminacy that the concept requires. Within this open formulation of Black futures, Keeling draws us to a conceptualization of Blackness, Black existence, and Black invention as radically open-ended and in relationship to a multiplicity of futures. These temporalities are the queer times that ground Keeling's analysis—like the dead letters Bartleby sorts in Melville's story, with "good tidings for those who died stifled by unrelieved calamities."[129] In any present, we can look back to futures that were imagined but never pursued, foreclosed freedom dreams that molder in archives and fade in memories.

Still, Keeling is attentive to the historical force of antiblackness and the ways it "continues to delimit otherwise visionary movements and possibilities, shaping existing geopolitics and other present realities."[130] Put differently, antiblackness shapes the political imaginaries of both the largest and most regressive international forces (state and capital) *and* the most insurgent and radical forces. This is not a source of despair, but the condition of the labors of an emancipatory politics. The fact of antiblackness is, indeed, a valuable source of knowledge, and drawing our attention to its mechanics can offer an outline of a knowledge of freedom, to borrow Fred Moten's formulation. For Keeling, "Black existence has called modernity-as-progress narratives into question since the dawn of modernity during the transatlantic slave trade and as European colonization of African, Asian, Aboriginal, and other Indigenous peoples' lands. [Black existence] carries within it alternative organizations of time in which the future, if there is such a thing, has not been promised; it has had to be created by reaching through and beyond what exists."[131] Keeling's formulation takes Black existence as the source of both a global knowledge of freedom and a knowledge of global freedom. Black freedom dreams do not eclipse any other Indigenous dreams, though the academic marketplace and the dynamics of antiblackness surely encourage formulations of Indigeneity mutually exclusive from Blackness (a question I take up in the next chapter).

To this end, Keeling operates within a tradition attentive to the distinction "between 'Blackness' and 'Black people,'" and the "ways 'Blackness' itself is a historical becoming, tied to the human and therefore available to all."[132] Blackness, in Keeling's formulation, "both exceeds and supplements those who are called 'Black people,' but cannot be divorced from Black people without epistemological and ontological violence to both the concept and the material realities it currently participates in organizing."[133] Keeling takes seriously the liberatory potential, and the potential for violence, within the non-identity of Blackness and Black people. What Keeling calls "the longue durée of modernity" are those "historical conjunctures" within which "Blackness" has operated across an array of systems, structures, and institutions. "In the neoliberal multicultural phases of racial capitalism," Keeling says of the present, "'Blackness' is *available* in various ways to those who are not immediately recognizable as 'Black' according to existing common perceptual cues."[134] Blackness is *available* to persons who are not positioned as Black across a range of sensory indicators. What is done with Blackness remains an open question, the answer to which cannot always be anticipated in advance. At the same time, Blackness "might wander, errantly, becoming perceptible, as of now, in a variety of places, terrestrial, extraterrestrial, and, through the work of the imagination, intergalactic and beyond."[135] Keeling finds in the fungibility of Blackness an opportunity to be authorized by Blackness.[136]

And so we might return to the figure of the Black woman as a figure of a Black invention, as a figure linked historically to the bind of a reproduction without futurity, as a being that (re)produces non-futures. "What we recognize today as Black femininity, regardless of the official sex of the body that expresses it, has been a site of the oftentimes violent suturing of individuals to racial collectives over time."[137] We all inhabit a world in which being, belonging, and becoming perpetually return to the figure of the Black woman. The non-belonging she reproduces sutures collectivity. Too often, "the Black woman" becomes a metaphor for resistance without passing through the radical openness of her futurity—that is, the end of the world. But, as Keeling reminds us, it's already after the end of the world: "Although the historical continuity of the identity category 'Black women' has been unevenly associated with femininity, the nexus at which Black race meets feminine genders has been significant to the calculus involved in the distribution of property, profit, and power. It is a store of value. The resulting figure, whom we might recognize today as 'the Black woman,' stitches processes of racialization to those of political economy, and thereby carries a potential to disrupt both."[138] It is not because this figure is a store for opacity, or something unknown or unknowable, that she carries a potential for disruption, for a new politics, but because this figure joins libidinal economy to political economy. This may be the impossible politics of a feminist Black radicalism, the point of departure of a mode of critique authorized by a queer Black feminism, and the anoriginary or anarchic form of a Black invention or inventiveness—a Black feminist poiēsis.

For Morrison, those Black children who "look us dead in the eye" embody a generative negativity, they possess a discomfiting ingenuity. She asks, "What species of black is this that not only does not choose to grovel, but doesn't know how? How will they keep jobs? How will they live? Won't they be killed before they reproduce? But they are unafraid. Is it because they refuse to see the world as we did? Is it because they have rejected both land and turf to seek instead a world?" In Morrison's view, those Black children are inventors and artists of new forms of living in collectivity, "they watch us with the eyes of poets and carpenters and musicians and scholars and other people who know who they are because they have invented themselves and know where they are going because they have envisioned it."[139]

To this end, we might consider Joy James's formulation of Afrarealism as an orientation to the side of pessimism or optimism, negativity or futurity, that avows the generative negativity of Blackness as the basis for a form of realism. For James, Afrarealism names a resistant mode of Black feminist theorizing attuned to "the beauty of resistance to denigration," and a practice of politics that is "terrifyingly beautiful because it is violently transcendent."[140] There must, in James's formulation, be room to think about the "beauty and pleasure in confronting the real."[141] And here we might also read "the real" of Afrarealism in a Lacanian idiom as that which both resists symbolization and is the condition of possibility for symbolization itself.[142] This real is also Hortense Spillers's "interstice," the Black woman fallen "into the great black hole of meaning," which is also the hard kernel of what Spillers calls an "American grammar."[143] In this account, beauty is not the sole property of futurity; possibility is not the sole property of optimism. This reading of beauty and possibility in Black feminist theorizing is related but not identical to the project of queer negativity. It's related insofar as both articulate a possible politics from the position of Black subjectivity, but queer negativity does so symptomatically while James does so in an open avowal. Just as we move beyond the apparent contradiction of the pessimist with a violin, we might square the circle of a reproduction without futurity—a Black future. If we extricate ourselves, our politics, our theorizing, from a dialectic of optimism as the slow walk of trees and pessimism as hopelessness, we might find that the horror of the Real is the beauty of a Black feminist poiēsis. This politics, which begins from no-place, may be the abolition glimpsed from the vantage of a buried subjectivity. Against the common sense of some traditions of radical thought and practice, it is a politics that begins *nowhere.*

Chapter Four

Nowhere, and Notes to Not Belonging

> My uncle was not a scholar of African art of any kind. He did not know of the personal masks of the Bassa people, he did not know of the men's society masks of the Manding people or Guinea, nor the dance mask of the Igbo or the Bawa or Bamana people. He had no recall of the Baule, the Oan, the Mossi, the Ogoni, the Sennefo, the Ngbaka, or the Akwaya. My uncle only had the gaping Door of No Return, a memory resembling a memory of a thing that he remembered. And not so much remembered as felt. And not so much felt as a memory which held him.
>
> **Dionne Brand, *A Map to the Door of No Return*, 121**

> It is the stray detail that does not stay in place that stands against the monumentalism of state terror.
>
> **Gayatri Gopinath, *Unruly Visions*, 144**

BELONGING, DERACINATION

This chapter builds from the conceptual interventions of the previous chapters—from theorizations of relationality, subjectivity, and negativity that emerge across traditions of Black feminist theorizing and their missed encounters with and in the discourses of feminist and queer theory—toward a concept that appears at the confluence of relationality, subjectivity, and negativity: belonging. The first chapter examined histories of lesbian and sisterhood feminisms and the foundational conflicts that continue to shape how feminist thought imagines relationality and the question of coalition. From Audre Lorde's missed encounters with

Mary Daly, the chapter argued for a relationality that breaks the distance between the relational and the nonrelational, that emerges from a Black feminist negativity toward the irrelational as a relationality touched by impossibility. The second chapter read Kimberlé Crenshaw's theorizations of intersectionality as an attempt to theorize Blackness as a buried subjectivity. Reading Crenshaw alongside Hortense Spillers, the chapter charted the ways intersectionality moves between the interstitial incoherence of a buried subjectivity and a domesticated, disciplined intersectional subject, moving with and against the desires now called abolition. Then, the third chapter traced queer negativity's ambivalent relationship to the Blackness internal to queerness, and the ways it was anticipated by the canonical queer critique of Leo Bersani and the Black feminist theorizing of Beverly Smith and Barbara Smith. It argued that queer futurity, as a counterpoint to queer negativity, is organized around anxious attachments to the antiblackness of the present as a way of mitigating a reproduction without futurity, a Black future, that finds expression across the works of Alexis Pauline Gumbs, Toni Morrison, Kara Keeling, and Joy James. All of those discourses were organized in some way by a negativity, a lack or an absence, that reveals the incompleteness and incoherence internal to being, an indeterminacy the world calls Blackness. A Black feminist poiēsis imagines new forms of living from the indeterminacies called Blackness.

Here, I extend these theorizations of relationality, subjectivity, and negativity toward the question of belonging. Across the academic, activist, and aesthetic discourses of Black feminism, *belonging* names something more and less than sociality, the social life of social death, and the matter or material of what, in the context of an antiblack world, is called the political.[1] Belonging is also something more and less than what is called the intramural, an undercommon and underground Black sociality that sustains itself despite or to spite an antiblack world.[2]

The recent career of Black studies seems to offer two approaches to the problem of belonging and the politics of deracination. For one approach, deracination makes belonging "impossible." For the other, deracination makes belonging essential. The preceding chapters have tried to show that, besides nihilism or an otherwise futurity, another orientation is possible, something like the indeterminate anarchy of Black feminist theorizing. The relation between deracination and belonging revises each of the terms that organized the previous chapters, turning them toward broader organizations of power and the dynamics of hegemony and counterhegemony; to questions of governmentality, citizenship, rights, and the matter of collective being; and to the nature of sovereignty at the level of the state as well as the subject. In short, the interventions of the previous chapters arrive here at the matter of deracination and the politics of the deracinated.

In the years after the end of the Cold War and into the era of the war on terror, the most salient expressions of feminist and queer cultural studies' concern for the politics of belonging were organized through the figures of the transnational and the diasporic. In the following sections, I read Inderpal Grewal and Caren Kaplan's early work to articulate and define a transnational feminist cultural studies, Grewal's later study of consumer citizenship in the United States after 11 September 2001, and Gayatri Gopinath's work on queer diasporic visual art. What interests me in these authors' texts is an ensemble of relations to Blackness, Black women, and Black feminism that shapes their discourses. How do Black figures enter these texts and what work are they tasked with? I will say, first, that there is something pathological about how Black women appear in the texts of transnational and diasporic feminisms—that is, pathological in the sense that they appear along the edges and in excess of the arguments at hand, or, when they are the object of study, they prompt magical thinking and motivated misreadings that distort and invert relations of power. They appear seductively, as abjected objects of desire, rendering the powerful weak and structures of power inconsequential.

When Grewal and Kaplan offer an extended critique of Pratibha Parmar's 1993 documentary film, *Warrior Marks*, and the companion book coauthored with one of the film's executive producers, Alice Walker, their reading is organized around a critique of a hegemonic "global womanism," Grewal and Kaplan's pejorative take on Walker's neologism. The titular chapter of Grewal's 2005 monograph, *Transnational America: Feminisms, Diasporas, Neoliberalisms*, structures itself as a series of observations on the beleaguered citizenship status of Muslims and people interpreted as Muslim in the United States during the early years of the war on terror, juxtaposed with the (putatively) newly untroubled citizenship of Black Americans. Finally, in her *Unruly Visions: The Aesthetic Practices of Queer Diaspora*, Gopinath offers a reading of diasporic queer visual art through an engagement with Saidiya Hartman's *Lose Your Mother: A Journey Along the Atlantic Slave Route*. In Hartman, Gopinath finds a text mirroring the sovereign aspirations of the postcolonial African nation-state. This chapter is organized around these three figures—hegemony, citizenship, and sovereignty—as figures that anchor the transnational turn's encounters with Blackness, where transnational feminism and diasporic queer theory oppose hegemony to the degree that Blackness is hegemonic, trouble citizenship to the degree that Black people have access to citizenship, and destabilize sovereignty to the degree that sovereignty is touched by Blackness.

Transnational feminism and diasporic queer theory reckoned with the problematic of belonging in an American context at once triumphalist and beleaguered, the last remaining superpower and an empire in decline. At a moment when free trade agreements and American cultural production had opened borders around the world, opened them to exploitation by Western business interests and the products of US cultural imperialism, feminist and queer cultural studies turned toward the subjectivities produced through the matrices of American global hegemony—its mix of cosmopolitanism, nativism, and militarism, and its discourses of human rights, neoliberalism, and neoconservatism. In this chapter, I argue that the transnational turn, in its initial formulations around the turn of the millennium and in its reformulations through the figure of the diasporic, was shaped by its missed encounters with Black feminist theorizing.

As transnational feminism began to circulate in the academy, a number of feminist theorists argued that it reflected a desire to move "beyond" Black women in the United States.[3] It allowed the academic community to have antiracism without addressing antiblackness. At a time when the cultural productions of Black Americans had reached new levels of popularity both in the cultural mainstream and in the academy, the hypervisibility of Black art and Black thought seemed to prompt a reflexive call to move "beyond the black/white binary." At a 1997 symposium at Yale, the legal scholar Mari Matsuda offered an unvarnished assessment of this tendency: "When we say we need to move beyond Black and white, this is what a whole lot of people say or feel or think: 'Thank goodness we can get off that paradigm, because those Black people made me so uncomfortable. I know all about Blacks, but I really don't know anything about Asians, and while we're deconstructing that Black-white paradigm, we also need to reconsider the category of race all together, since race, as you know, is a constructed category, and thank God I don't have to take those angry Black people seriously anymore.'"[4] Fifteen years later, Sharon Holland connected the desire to move "beyond" Black and white to the project of a transnational American studies: "Having thought of all things American as purblind, scholars began focusing on the 'larger' picture—a picture in which they themselves play little part."[5] For Holland, the desire to widen the geographic aperture of cultural studies in the United States was an extension of the move beyond a "black/white binary that many theorists were happy to leave behind," and that, as a matter of critical self-reflection, "that glee alone should tell us there is unfinished business."[6] I am less interested here in the matter of avoidance or moving beyond than in the ways Black women and Blackness enter the texts of transnational feminism, the work they perform, and the anxieties they index.

In a 2015 dialogue with Jennifer Falcón on *intersectionality* and *transnational* as key terms in contemporary feminist studies, Jennifer Nash articulated some of the ways the transnational turn seemed to construct and solidify a distinction between Black women in the United States and non-Black women of color in the United States and abroad. While, nominally, both Black feminism and transnational feminism advance radical critiques of the Enlightenment tradition, Western colonialism and imperialism, patriarchal and white supremacist orderings of power, and the limitations of feminist, antiracist, and decolonial social movements, another motivating force seemed to emerge through the cracks and margins of the transnational. "I was surprised to see," she writes, "how transnationalism was deployed . . . to exculpate women's studies from talking about U.S. processes of race-making, and to shift scholarly conversation away from the fleshy materiality of black women's bodies."[7] Building from Nash's observation, this chapter aims to lay out the theoretical foundations of transnational feminism, how and why the field formed at the moment it did, and the centrality of the encounter with Black feminism to the psychic life and political aspirations of transnational feminism.

In its early formulations, transnational feminism was marked by shifts away from the twentieth century's nationalisms, internationalisms, and Third Worldism, as figures that represented the messy materialities of hegemony, citizenship, and sovereignty. Transnational feminism offered a postmodern rebuke to post–Civil Rights cultural nationalisms and the universalism of second-wave feminism; to the operative assumptions and institutional forms of a new international community; and to essentialisms of race, nation, gender, sexuality, and culture. Essentialism, especially, is a form of belonging, a way of taking collectivity for granted and for avoiding the question of who gets left out of collectivity. These questions of belonging and the limits of belonging were central to transnational feminism's relationship with Black feminist theorizing, particularly in an intellectual and political context in which hegemony, citizenship, and sovereignty were dominant terms.

As a counterpoint or counterpart to these theorizations of hegemony, citizenship, and sovereignty, this chapter also moves through the itinerary of Saidiya Hartman as an exemplary figure of the Black feminist cultural studies that developed after the signal works of the 1980s (those of, among others, Barbara Christian, Audre Lorde, Hortense Spillers, Patricia Williams, bell hooks, Nellie McKay, Valerie Smith, Sylvia Wynter, and Hartman's former teacher, Hazel Carby), as well as contemporary writers and theorists whose works explore the transnational hydraulics of Blackness and antiblackness (in particular, Dionne Brand and M. NourbeSe Philip). Hartman's practice has anticipated, inspired, challenged, and interrupted the most significant tendencies within contemporary cultural studies in its feminist, queer, and Black iterations. At different moments, Hartman's projects speak to tendencies as varied as the new empiricisms of thick description and postcritique, the speculative or sentimental inventions of a critical fabulation, and the feminist Black anarchism incipient in the discourses of Black insurgency. Across the chapter, I ask what Hartman's interventions make possible for a feminist critique of belonging in the contexts of global capitalism and global antiblackness, and how we might differently understand hegemony, citizenship, and sovereignty as aspects of belonging.

Before turning to each of those concepts, their articulations within transnational feminist and queer discourses, and how they are productively interrupted by traditions of Black feminist theorizing, I am interested in the ways Black feminism has theorized the relation between belonging and deracination. This book has explored the different ways that Black feminist theorizing is animated, in part, by the problem of enslavement and the question of abolition. The racial slavery that created a status called Blackness, and that produced the Human as a universalizable category, is characterized by deracination. Deracination refers both to loss—the loss of culture or land or bodily autonomy or subjectivity—and to the uneven production of the capacity for loss. Both the endless repetition of losses, of being deracinated again and again, of being reminded of one's deracination, and that which produces the capacity for loss in the context of a global racial modernity. Deracination is the irrelational force of enslavement and the problem for relationality posed by enslavement.

In Orlando Patterson's formulation of slavery as social death, slavery is a relation of domination that cannot be reduced to a labor relation—slaves could be made to labor, or not, in many different ways in different slave societies. But slavery is also something more or other than a property relation.[8] For Patterson, the intersubjective experience of enslavement was characterized by natal alienation, and this "loss of ties of birth in both ascending and descending generations" was "the heart of what is critical in the slave's forced alienation." The slave was alienated from their near and distant ancestors and their progeny, but also their natal community. Crucially, enslavement entailed an ongoing and permanent experience "of a loss of native status, of deracination."[9] For Patterson, "it was this alienation of the slave from all formal, legally enforceable ties of 'blood,' and from any attachment to groups or localities other than those chosen for him by the master, that gave the relation of slavery its peculiar value to the master. The slave was the ultimate human tool, as imprintable and as disposable as the master wished. And this is true, at least in theory, of all slaves, no matter how elevated."[10] Later in the text, Patterson would describe the peculiar value of the slave relation for the master as a kind of parasitism. "To all members of the community," he writes, "the slave existed only through the parasite holder, who was called the master." It was "on this intersubjective level" that "the slaveholder fed on the slave to gain the very direct satisfactions of power over another, honor enhancement, and authority."[11] In this formulation, which Hartman builds from in her *Scenes of Subjection*, the relation of slavery is not, at its core, a relation of labor or of property, but a relation of satisfaction, of *enjoyment*.

Across *Scenes*, Hartman revises Patterson by way of Hortense Spillers. In "Mama's Baby, Papa's Maybe," Spillers attends to the ways enslaved Africans were renditioned and rendered through the various documents of the slave trade (ledgers, insurance documents, bills of sale, ship manifests, diaries, travelogues, contracts, etc.): "Everywhere in the descriptive document, we are stunned by the simultaneity of disparate items in a grammatical series: 'slave' appears in the same context with beasts of burden, *all* and *any* animal(s), various livestock, and a virtually endless profusion of domestic content from the culinary item to the book."[12] But there is something that separates the enslaved from other commodities. While the slave exists along a chain of equivalents with other commodities in terms of political economy, the slave occupies a distinct space in the libidinal economy of the slave trade, as well as the world that emerged from the racialization of slavery. The slave is distinct even from "all the magic and necromancy that surrounds the products of labor" that Marx called the fetishism of the commodity.[13] The form of life animating the enslaved sets that life, that living, apart from the world of commodities she brings into being in her wake.

In "Seduction and the Ruses of Power," Saidiya Hartman explores the strange and terrible magic that makes the slave at once subject and object. Hartman's reading of slave law examines how and why property acquired personality before the law. The demand for the perfect submission of the enslaved required that the will-lessness of the object cohabitate with the conquered will of the subject. This submission, Hartman argues, "not only encompassed the acquisition of power but also explicitly addressed the power of affection in influencing the relations between master and slave."[14] That is, the injunction to recognize a limited humanity for the enslaved was at once legal and sentimental. But, "contrary to pronouncements that sentiment would abate brutality, feelings intensified the violence of law and posed dire consequences for the calculation of black humanity, for the dual existence of the slave as object of property and person required that feelings endowed to the enslaved be greatly circumscribed."[15] Through her reading of the legal foundations of slavery, Hartman shows that it is precisely the truncated and malformed *humanization* of the enslaved that is the mechanism of slavery's perfection.[16] Sentimentality, affection, and enjoyment bridged the slave's dual status as object and subject.

At this enjoinment of person and property, the enslaved are defined not only by a capacity to be property, but by a capacity for enjoyment and a capacity to be enjoyed. To be deracinated is to carry this capacity to be enjoyed as a sentient object, an irrelational encounter between those who can claim humanity and those who can be enjoyed by humanity. In this way, deracination anticipates enslavement, which anticipates relationality, belonging. Deracination is the irrelational moment that sets relationality into motion and gives meaning to belonging. In Jared Sexton's formulation, "Racial blackness, as the necessary condition for enslavement in the modern era, entailed manifold processes of deracination and homogenization, such that previous fictions of descent and destiny, distribution and direction were thrown into permanent crisis. To become New World African or African-derived, whether enslaved or nominally free, would involve a tradition of ceaseless invention without foundation, a tradition wherein all sorts of internal dissent, distinction, and diversification would require efforts best described as unlawful or lawless."[17] In this context, abolition could be understood as an insovereign politics of dissolution, the anarchic invention of a Black feminist poiēsis. The subjects (and sentient objects) of deracination may be incommensurate, asymmetrical, antagonistic, while also being co-constitutive and interrelated—irrelational rather than nonrelational. Deracination is at once monumental and non-monumental. The terrors that produce the subjects of deracination are non-state and extra-state terrors, mundane terrors, quotidian terrors, non-monumental state terrors. Deracination is a species of the violence that produces stateness and it also exceeds the state form. Deracination is both the condition of possibility and the condition of impossibility for something called resistance, what Gayatri Gopinath calls "standing against." The terror of deracination operates at a larger scale than that of the State and it contains the state form but it is also more intimate than state terror.

For Dionne Brand, deracination is not remembered, but resembles memory. Deracination might resemble a memory of a memory, rather than being itself a memory or even being one's *own* memory. Deracination possesses the deracinated. Regardless of what one might stand for or stand against, one is always standing within deracination. What is called resistance, or standing against, operates at a different scale than deracination and is also within deracination. State terror, even at the most radical outposts of cultural studies, is an insufficient rubric for understanding deracination. The question remains, however, how transnational feminism arrives somewhere between state power and the deracinated, and how another orientation toward deracination can help articulate the insovereign anarchism of a feminist Black radicalism.

HEGEMONY, AGENCY

> The chronicle of black pain doesn't mobilize a response, it doesn't arrest the reader, and it doesn't incite a crisis.
>
> —SAIDIYA HARTMAN, IN SAUNDERS, "FUGITIVE DREAMS OF DIASPORA," 10

In this section, I trace how hegemony emerges in the discourse of transnational feminism, with what effects, and the politics of its deployment. Across a publishing itinerary that included nearly a dozen jointly authored articles and book chapters, an edited volume, an introductory women's studies textbook, and a book series at Duke University Press, Inderpal Grewal and Caren Kaplan spearheaded a project that inaugurated, consolidated, and set an agenda for a field of inquiry called transnational feminism. This section traces the racial logics of transnational feminism across Grewal and Kaplan's formulation of "scattered hegemonies" and their only published collaborative work of cultural criticism, "*Warrior Marks*: Global Womanism's Neo-Colonial Discourse in a Multicultural Context." Along with M. Jacqui Alexander and Chandra Talpade Mohanty's *Feminist Genealogies, Colonial Legacies, Democratic Futures*, Grewal and Kaplan's 1994 collection, *Scattered Hegemonies: Postmodernity and Transnational Feminist Practices*, has been called "canonical in defining and conceptualizing transnational feminisms."[18]

Grewal and Kaplan's approach to transnational feminism was unique for the degree to which their shared writing was concerned with the politics of language in the creation and consolidation of the field. Between the early 1990s and late 2000s, the bulk of their collectively authored work delineated the proper boundaries of a project alternatively called "transnational feminist cultural studies," "transnational feminist practices," "transnational studies of sexuality," "transnational practices and interdisciplinary feminist scholarship," and "feminist transnational studies." Reflecting these several names and this persistent return to naming, much of their shared work concerned itself with the politics of how to articulate a feminist transnational cultural analysis. In "Transnational Practices and Interdisciplinary Feminist Scholarship," Grewal and Kaplan remark at some length on their choice of *transnational* over and against terms like *international, global, multicultural,* or *cosmopolitan*. For Grewal and Kaplan, "all of these terms and critical practices reinforce governmentality over and against cultural effects or reinforce cultural effects over and against governmentality and economic considerations. In this regard, the term 'transnational' can mark critical practices that bring the economic and governmental into cultural criticism."[19] On the specific distinction between *transnational* and *international*, they argue that the former allows them "to trace circuits that are produced by problematic political, economic, and social phenomena," and that "if we speak of transnational circuits of information, capital, and labor, we refuse to valorize a system founded on inequality and exploitation."[20] Finally, "both internationalism and critical internationalism display a stubborn reliance on state and nation that ignores the scattered hegemonic effects that evade governmentality."[21] In this way, Grewal and Kaplan are representative of a wider tendency in literary and cultural studies to posit a certain *performative autonomy of language*. That is, words are imbued with a remarkable capacity to act on the worlds in which they are used, autonomous from wider structures of power and meaning. Some words reinforce governmentality, or reinforce cultural effects, or ignore scattered hegemonic effects that evade governmentality. And, though a reader may arrive at their text with their own understanding of what is meant by "governmentality," or what exactly a "cultural effect" might be, or what it means for hegemonies to scatter, they are unlikely to discern what, precisely, Grewal and Kaplan mean by them. On one hand, Grewal and Kaplan are careful to the point of obsession about which words to use and when. On the other hand, much of the specialized vocabulary built into their various constructions of transnational feminism is untheorized, undefined, or presented without context or comment.

The terms *hegemony* and *scattered hegemonies* arrive in their discourse in just this way. The titular concept-metaphor of Grewal and Kaplan's 1994 edited volume, *Scattered Hegemonies*, was meant to intervene in the dominant neo-Gramscian approaches of contemporaneous scholarship in cultural studies. Interestingly, the authors introduce their concept of "scattered hegemonies" as an aside within a defense of the term *postmodern*. Rejecting a line of argumentation that *postmodernism* only named a style of abstract, ironic detachment, or "the apolitical celebration of Western popular culture," Grewal and Kaplan instead claimed to pursue an alloyed practice combining theoretical rigor with radical political practice. Postmodernism could, within their framework, "be read as part of the operations of transnational culture; as the cultural expression of what Inderpal Grewal describes as 'scattered hegemonies,' which are the effects of mobile capital as well as the multiple subjectivities that replace the European unitary subject."[22] The reference to Grewal's previous articulation of "scattered hegemonies" leads to a conference paper delivered at Berkeley in 1992 and not apparently published elsewhere. Other references to scattered hegemonies in the text are fragmentary, as though adding nuance to a fully elaborated concept.[23]

For Grewal and Kaplan, "scattered hegemonies" intervened in the dominant practices of cultural studies and revised the figure of hegemony as it had arrived from the English-language reception of the Italian Marxist, Antonio Gramsci. In his *Posthegemony: Political Theory and Latin America*, Jon Beasley-Murray offers a substantial intellectual history of cultural studies and the routes by which "hegemony" came to prominence, especially as it was taken up in the ideology critique popularized by Stuart Hall beginning in the 1980s—a practice that would later be bowdlerized and function as a stand-in for cultural studies itself.[24] By the early 1980s, "the idea of hegemony was, as it were, in the air; it had been invoked by Althusser and, separately, already been introduced to cultural studies by [Raymond] Williams" around 1973.[25] But, Beasley-Murray argues, Stuart Hall's theorization of hegemony was not so much indebted to Althusser, Williams, or Gramsci—nor even to Hall's colleague at the *New Left Review*, Perry Anderson, who offered seventy pages on Gramsci's thought in 1976.[26] Rather, Hall's theory of hegemony built from the Argentine political theorist Ernesto Laclau's 1977 book, *Politics and Ideology in Marxist Theory*. Beasley-Murray draws a convincing line of influence from Gramsci through Laclau, to Laclau's work with Chantal Mouffe, and then to major essays like Hall's "Gramsci's Relevance for the Study of Race and Ethnicity" and "The Toad in the Garden: Thatcherism Among the Theorists."

In *Politics and Ideology in Marxist Theory*, Laclau introduced Gramsci's theorization of hegemony as a corrective for the twin perils of class reductionism and economism among Marxist and ultra-left intellectuals and national and international Communist parties. For these orthodox Marxists, Laclau argues, all democratic political struggles were irreducibly linked to the bourgeoisie and, therefore, "were now obsolete and . . . it was necessary to confine the struggle to a pure revolutionary class perspective." On this reading, "democratic ideology can be nothing but bourgeois ideology."[27] Laclau challenged these foundational assumptions. He argued that popular democratic ideologies could be appropriated by the working class and that "the basic ideological struggle of the working class consists in linking popular-democratic ideology to its discourse, avoiding both class sectarianism and social-democratic opportunism."[28] An analysis that succumbs to neither bourgeois liberalism nor class reductionism, Laclau contends, "lies in the struggle of the working class for its ideological *hegemony* over the remaining popular sectors."[29]

It is in this context that Laclau introduces and elaborates hegemony as a Gramscian concept, as a corrective to the class reductionism of orthodox Marxism. That is, the tendency to reduce all social phenomena to effects of the antagonism between workers and capitalists. In the proceeding footnote, Laclau bases his analysis "on the interpretation developed by Chantal Mouffe in an unpublished paper on the Gramscian notion of hegemony." This paper was likely published two years later in the collection, *Gramsci and Marxist Theory*, edited by Mouffe. According to Laclau, Mouffe's analysis argues that "the notion of the specific autonomy of democratic interpellations is implicit in the concept of 'hegemony,' of democratic ideology as the domain of class struggle and, consequently, it permits Marxist theory to overcome class reductionism," adding that,

"Gramsci's great originality did not lie so much in his insistence on the importance of superstructures in the determination of historical processes . . . but in his effort to overcome *at the same time* economism and class reductionism."[30] For Laclau, "the development of all the *theoretical* implications of the Gramscian concept in terms of the non-class character of democratic ideology constitutes to a great extent a task to be accomplished."[31]

The promise of hegemony, in the historical and political context of the 1970s, was a shift away from a politics that reduced all social conflicts to expressions of economic conflict. In her contributions to *Gramsci and Marxist Theory*, Mouffe traced the development of hegemony across Gramsci's works. His *Notes on the Southern Question* emphasized coalition politics and the necessity of alliances by which the working class might lead other social classes in a struggle against capital. This was a gentle revision of hegemony as theorized by Vladimir Lenin, placing new emphasis on the specifically political character of working-class struggle.[32] Mouffe argues that later, in his *Prison Notebooks*, Gramsci developed the ideological dimensions of hegemony, where it "becomes the indissoluble union of political leadership and intellectual and moral leadership, which clearly goes beyond the idea of a simple class alliance."[33] Quoting the *Notebooks*, Mouffe explores how hegemony becomes "a complete fusion of economic, political, intellectual and moral objectives which will be brought about by one fundamental group and groups allied to it *through the intermediary of ideology* when an ideology manages to 'spread throughout the whole of society determining not only united economic and political objectives but also intellectual and moral unity.'"[34] Put differently, the theorization of hegemony Mouffe offers, by way of her reading of Gramsci, challenges a long-prevailing class essentialism in Left theory and practice, while also opening space for the analysis of the political and ideological as linked with, but ultimately autonomous from, the economic. Hegemony allows for theorizations of power that are less concerned with outright economic domination than with the production of subjects spontaneously consenting to prevailing social structures.

None of this is to say, however, that hegemony is a singular, global, or universal phenomenon. As Laclau and Mouffe note in *Hegemony and Socialist Strategy*, "Hegemony is, quite simply, a political *type of relation*, a *form*, if one so wishes, of politics; but not a determinable location within a topography of the social." They add, "In a given social formation, there can be a variety of hegemonic nodal points. Evidently some of them may be highly overdetermined: they may constitute points of condensation of a number of social relations and, thus, become the focal point of a multiplicity of totalizing effects. But insofar as the social is an infinitude not reducible to any underlying unitary principle, the mere idea of a centre of the social has no meaning at all."[35] Within the Gramscian tradition Grewal and Kaplan would claim, hegemony is always already scattered, it is always already multiple, plural, incomplete, fragmented, and fragmentary.

How, then, are Grewal and Kaplan modifying the conceptual itinerary of "hegemony" through their formulation of "scattered hegemonies"? They suggest that "feminists can begin to map these scattered hegemonies and link diverse local practices to formulate a transnational set of solidarities."[36] Grewal and Kaplan arrive here at a politics of microrelations of power across the social matrices of a globalized postmodernity, what they elsewhere call the "current phase of globalization."[37] Under these conditions, hegemony is not only autonomous from the economic, but uncoupled from *structures* of domination, and any subject might be the site of a hegemonic agency. Around this formulation of hegemony, Grewal and Kaplan offer a transnational feminism that is most passionately concerned with the political choices of Black women in the Global North, elevated to the status of hegemonic operations. Hegemony might be diffuse, but it crystallizes around the power wielded by Black women. In other words, this diffuse, plural concept reveals a singular anxiety. This anxiety about the subject position of Black women in the Global North is central to the psychic life of transnational feminism.

In their only jointly authored work of cultural criticism, "*Warrior Marks*: Global Womanism's Neo-Colonial Discourse in a Multicultural Context," published in *Camera Obscura* in 1996, Grewal and Kaplan offer an extended critique of Pratibha Parmar's 1993 documentary film *Warrior Marks*, as well as the accompanying book Parmar coauthored with Alice Walker. Much of the critique put forward by Grewal and Kaplan, regarding what they call the neocolonialism of the film and book's representational strategies, is directed at Walker, who appears in *Warrior Marks* and served as an executive producer on the film. The film and accompanying book blend performance and literary art with reportage and interviews on practices across sub-Saharan Africa that Parmar and Walker call "Female Genital Mutilation." Contemporary work in gender and sexuality studies, global public health, and human rights advocacy have shifted toward the less judgmental language of female genital surgeries. These practices, which vary considerably across local and national contexts, have been the object of contentious debates over the status of women's sexual, personal, and political autonomy as well as the contradictions of cultural relativism and universal human rights. While there are many opponents of nonvoluntary genital surgeries in the countries and cultures of sub-Saharan Africa, as well as diasporic communities in the Global North, feminists in the Global North have been (appropriately) criticized for patronizing, sensationalist, and racist advocacy campaigns that have reproduced forms of seeing and knowing the Global South that characterized the imperial projects of previous centuries.

For Grewal and Kaplan, Alice Walker's contributions to the international campaigns against nonvoluntary genital surgeries performed on young girls and women are analytically interesting because she is a Black woman from the United States who is also a literary celebrity. "The cultural producers of this work are two women of color," they observe, which "raises important issues about new forms of racialization and power relations between women from First and Third World locations."[38] The novelty of *Warrior Marks*, as a cultural object, is that women of color, and particularly a Black feminist woman, become the agents of colonial epistemic violence. Grewal and Kaplan then direct their critique toward Walker's own personal investments in pursuing feminist activism and advocacy outside of the Global North.

In the companion book to *Warrior Marks*, Walker describes one Christmas when she was a young girl. Her brothers all received toy guns that shot copper pellets, meant for killing birds. Because she was a girl, she did not receive a gun. One day, an elder brother, who often frightened young Alice with his size and capacity for violence, shot his gun into Alice's face, striking her in the right eye and blinding her. Her family called the event an accident—"Alice's accident." It belonged to her rather than having been done to her. Her eye covered over with scar tissue. Her disability and its visible manifestations led to her being bullied at school. She was sent away to live with her grandparents. She describes years at the edge of suicide. She describes several surgeries that eventually removed the scar tissue from her eye. She describes learning to walk and to experience the world without the use of her right eye. Walker describes her contingent experience of forms of violence that are intrinsic to the particular patriarchal context into which she was born, and connects those experiences to the forms of patriarchal violence she sees on the African continent.[39]

For Grewal and Kaplan, Walker's representation of a personal investment in connecting different forms of patriarchal violence, different obliterations of the agency of women and girls, relies on a "logic of identification" that "depends upon a notion of interpretation whereby one subject comes to 'know' another or others based on a perceived similarity that precludes any self-consciousness of the contingent and power-laden nature of relations between women."[40] According to this line of argument, by drawing connections between her experience of patriarchal violence as a young girl and the experiences of young girls in other times and places, by seeing her experiences refracted through the lives of others, Walker is forgetting both her own subject position as a woman in the West and the specific lives of the women and girls that the film documents. But the authors raise the stakes from mere obliviousness, precluding "any self-consciousness," toward something far more sinister:

> *Warrior Marks* utilizes visual colonial tropes not only to identify the "natives" but also to enable Walker herself, as narrator, to identify with this native. Doris Sommer has argued that a romanticized identification with cultural Others can be "the ultimate violence" as appropriation and can foreclose the possibility of any political alliance or solidarity across identities. Thus, Walker legitimates her view of African genital surgeries by projecting her own tragedy—her brother's assault and her injured eye—onto the bodies of women whom she perceives to be in peril from patriarchal violence. . . . Like so many acts of identification, it enacts its own epistemic violence and erasures.[41]

In this formulation, Walker is not merely a rich, oblivious, Western feminist, but a hegemonic agency colonizing the experiences of African women and girls. Her romanticized identification with these "cultural Others" can be, could be, might be, "the ultimate violence." Rhetorically, Grewal and Kaplan distance themselves from their claim that Walker has committed "the *ultimate* violence" against girls who, we recall, have also experienced nonvoluntary genital surgeries. Her desire to connect with these cultural Others leads her to epistemic violence and erasure.

But Grewal and Kaplan do leave space for other forms of identification, ones that do not enact epistemic violence. They posit authentic solidarities, untouched by sentimentality and essentialism. These scattered solidarities would be premised upon recognizing the absolute alterity of any particular historical and social context. This form of solidarity would evade the violence of identification and the violence of essentialism. I wonder, though, whether the desire for identification without violence, for a purely *nonviolent* practice of politics and culture, simply obscures the violence internal to all identification, the force internal to all politics.

By positing transnational feminism as a nonviolent alternative to "the ultimate violence" of a "global womanism," Grewal and Kaplan claim the fictional terrain of a pure radical politics. Or, if *pure* is insufficiently nuanced, a radical politics inflected with just the right amount of contingency, complicity, and contradiction.

What if we shift the aperture of Walker's identification with the women and girls represented in *Warrior Marks*? While not a Buddhist by faith, Walker had been practicing in Buddhist traditions for over a decade by the time she began work on *Warrior Marks*, and her engagement with Buddhist thought has been a recurring topic in Walker scholarship.[42] From the perspective of the Plum Village Tradition of the late Thích Nhất Hạnh, when we see another, we see the interconnected being or the nothing that is common to all things.[43] This is not an obliteration of the other, but the recognition that the contingencies of context are secondary to the obliteration that all being things share. It might be in the overlap of such a Buddhist tradition and a Black feminist negativity that we could say that the condition of living is the sharing of an irreducible alterity. *Blackness* is one name for the irreducible alterity internal to living, what is shared prior to any agency to give or to receive. Antiblackness, then, is one strategy for containing that alterity, for curtailing that sharing, for imagining or willing living into the confines of the sovereign subject.[44]

Grewal and Kaplan work from a tradition of pure separability, a tradition wherein subjects are embedded within social contexts that overdetermine the common negativity of being. This would also be to say that their form of analysis belongs to a tradition of political-theological thinking that is essentially Euro-American and Christian.[45] In this precise way, their scattered hegemonies are no less an epistemological imperialism than Walker's internationalist Black feminism.

None of this is to argue for the purity of one type of theorizing or one type of politics against another. If Grewal and Kaplan produce their own epistemic violences, it is at least in part because this violence is irreducible. In one elaboration of "strategic essentialism," Gayatri Spivak makes just this point: "Since the moment of essentializing, universalizing . . . is irreducible, let us at least situate it at the moment; let us become vigilant about our own practice and use it as much as we can rather than make the totally counter-productive gesture of repudiating it."[46] Every politics contains the potential for imperialism, just as there is no relationality without the risk of slavery. Every desire to reach out risks harming the other, just as it risks our imagined self-sovereignty.

Not for nothing, Spivak's suggestion of a strategic essentialism is one of the only points where Grewal and Kaplan distance their project from (what they take to be) Spivak's. Spivak is a key figure and reference in the early formulations of transnational feminism, and Grewal and Kaplan chart the ways her "methodologies . . . enable us to question any emphasis on similarities, universalisms, or essentialisms in favor of articulating *links* between the diverse, unequal, and uneven relations of historically constituted subjects."[47] In a footnote, Grewal and Kaplan refer their reader to a "critique of strategic essentialism" by Vivek Dhareshwar, published in the short-lived journal of the Group for the Critical Study of Colonial Discourse at the University of California, Santa Cruz.[48] For Dhareshwar, "the problem with that concept [strategic essentialism] is, of course, that it is unable to specify the difference between the strategic and nonstrategic use of essentialism. Whatever argument is going to justify strategic essentialism should be available to the nonstrategic version as well, unless one constructs a version of essentialism to which no one is likely to subscribe."[49] In short, Dhareshwar returns again to the problem of risk. Every strategy entails a risk, and there is no critical or political practice that eliminates the risk that something internal to that practice will produce its failure. Inevitably, something internal to the act of criticism fails.

Grewal and Kaplan's critical procedure becomes a practice of intellectual risk management—an attempt to contain the risks of contingency and contamination, the risks of Blackness. The symptomatic appearance of Alice Walker in Grewal and Kaplan's shared cultural criticism is an index of the absolute contingency of the figure of the Black woman as an absolute stimulus to anxiety.

Another relation to hegemony is possible, beyond the intellectual genealogies of cultural studies and the hope that some formulation over another formulation will protect us from our own inadequacies. Hegemony is belonging imbued with agency. Hegemony operates through the collaboration, the consent, the agential will of the subordinated classes in the reproduction of their subordination. Domination subordinates through force, but hegemony subordinates in the interplay of the agencies of the dominating and dominated classes. One of the ideological lures of liberal capitalism is to conflate agency and freedom. To reckon with the political and social force of hegemony would mean to take seriously the contradictory coexistence of a desire for freedom and a desire for unfreedom. It would mean reckoning with the promiscuity of agency.[50] Ultimately, the micropolitics of power articulated by transnational feminism, through the figure of scattered hegemonies, concerned itself with the putatively ironic status of a postmodern Black feminist colonialism. But the insovereign politics of a Black feminist negativity gestures toward another possible relation to agency, hegemony, and the analysis of racial capitalism and the nation-state.

In the same span of years that Grewal and Kaplan were formulating and reformulating a project called transnational feminism, Saidiya Hartman was constructing another critique of hegemony. One of the "hidden polemics" in her *Scenes of Subjection* "was an argument against the notion of hegemony, and how that notion has been taken up in the context of looking at the status of the slave."[51] Hartman was responding to the radical cultural historiography of the previous twenty years—the recoveries and revisions of Antonio Gramsci, the projects of the *New Left Review* and the Centre for Contemporary Cultural Studies at Birmingham, and the revisionist historiographies emerging from the "new social movements." Across that terrain, Hartman saw a "desire to look at the ravages and the brutality of the last few centuries, but to still find a way to feel good about ourselves," and to "locate the agency of dominated groups," which "resulted in celebratory narratives of the oppressed."[52] "Ultimately," she argues, "it bled into this celebration, as if there was a space you could carve out of the terrorizing state apparatus in order to exist outside its clutches and forge some autonomy."[53] Those projects sought to recover a radical agency from the debris of history, from an archive of defeat, conquest, and loss. From that recovered agency, they sought to redeem the defeated, conquered, and lost, and to lay the foundations for the creation of a counterhegemonic bloc in the present. For Hartman, that notion of hegemony, as the medium of social struggle and the terrain of a war of position, was inadequate for understanding the status of the enslaved.

Around the time she was writing *Scenes of Subjection*, Hartman would offer another name for the slave system's social, cultural, political, economic, and legal technologies of discipline and control: "The history of the black body in the Americas is *a chronicle of terror*: enslavement, domination, subjection, and confinement."[54] Across *Scenes*, "terror" recurs as a strategy of domination that confronts the modern reader with both its incomprehensible materiality—its brutality, violence, and depravity—and its "sheer unrepresentability"—the ways it fades into the fabric of daily living or, following Christina Sharpe's later work, the ways it becomes an atmosphere or climate.[55] Too often, terror is monumentalized as spectacle, but Hartman's project sought to stress the terror in the mundane, in the everyday experiences of Black life on either side of emancipation. By placing the accent in this way, Hartman aimed, in part, to avoid simply re-presenting and re-producing the violence and degradations experienced by the enslaved.[56] But she was also reckoning with a problem she would later describe to Patricia Saunders: "The chronicle of black pain doesn't mobilize a response, it doesn't arrest the reader, and it doesn't incite a crisis."[57] What Hartman calls a chronicle of terror and the chronicle of Black pain are the foundational violences of the American project. Antiblackness is the terror that sets the drama of civil society into motion; it is unthought and unseen when it is invisible and when it is hypervisible.

In this formulation of terror, Hartman was also articulating a theory of what her student, Frank Wilderson, in his own critique of the Gramscian tradition, would call "civil society's foundation of despotic terror and white pleasure by way of the accumulation of black bodies."[58] On this reading, terror, rather than hegemony, is the foundation of the civil society that emerged in the wake of racial slavery. The discourse of hegemony could only mystify the relations of domination and structures of terror that characterize American society. Reading those relations and structures through the language of hegemony was the dominant strategy of a generation of post–Civil Rights radical historians and critics, who sought to recover a heroic agency from the archive of slavery. But those "representations of slave agency . . . intensified the effects of subjugation and dispossession in the guise of will and denied the abject and ambivalent personhood of the captive in the facile and spurious attempt to incorporate the slave into the ethereal realms of the normative subject through demonstrations of his consent and/or autonomy."[59] The discourse of hegemony relied on notions of autonomy, selfhood, and subjectivity that Hartman found "inadequate and, more important, inappropriate to thinking through the issue of slave agency."[60] With its emphases on a particular form of agency and on "complementarity, reciprocity, and shared values, this hegemonic or consensual model of slave relations neutralizes the dilemma of the object status and pained subject constitution of the enslaved and obscures the violence of slavery."[61] While much of Hartman's critique of hegemony circles its inadequacy, its incapacity to describe the violences of the slave system, or the ways it obscures, mystifies, and misses the truth of slavery, her project still maintains that there is something fundamentally ineffable about the terrors of enslavement.

In part, Hartman argues for the *ambiguity* of terror. As a discourse or as an account of the functioning of domination in civil society, hegemony renders practice as politics, reducing the ambivalent and ambiguous resistances and capitulations of the enslaved to the languages of agency, selfhood, and subjectivity. "Even the Gramscian model," she writes,

> with its reformulation of the relation of state and civil society in the concept of the historical bloc and its expanded definition of the political, maintains a notion of the political inseparable from the effort and the ability of a class to effect hegemony. By questioning the use of the term "political," I hope to illuminate the possibilities of practice and the stakes of these dispersed resistances. All of this is not a preamble to an argument about the "prepolitical" consciousness of the enslaved but an attempt to point to the limits of the political and the difficulty of translating or interpreting the practices of the enslaved within that framework. The everyday practices of the enslaved occur in the default of the political, in the absence of the rights of man or the assurances of the self-possessed individual, and perhaps even without a "person," in the usual meaning of the term.[62]

In her move beyond the language of rights and the figure of the person, Hartman anticipates what a decade later would be called a "politics of the impersonal."[63] In what came to be called modernity, the racialization of slavery produced the space between raw life and legal person that allowed slave regimes to call themselves democracies. The slave estate that was the basis for the liberal revolutions of the eighteenth century produced the rights-bearing subject, the legal person, and the citizen. A critique of slavery from the position of the enslaved would require another set of actors. Across *Scenes*, Hartman cultivates a practice of analysis that holds on to the ambiguous suffering and endurance of the enslaved. Her critique aims to imagine a "politics without a proper locus" and to articulate forms of resistance that might be expressed beyond the stultifying vocabularies of integration or separatism, a more perfect union or a Black nation, or the quagmire of Black citizenship.[64]

CITIZENSHIP, RIGHTS

> So much of what we're living with today is linked to that first experience in globalization where the currency of globalization was the black body. Black bodies could be taken anywhere in the world, at any point in time,

sans passport, sans visa. That was the currency of globalization then and I don't think we have had a reckoning on that yet, and this is why we keep recycling and returning to these moments, to which we will continue to return until (if ever) and unless we come to some kind of reckoning.

—M. NOURBESE PHILIP, IN SAUNDERS, "DEFENDING THE DEAD," 76

The critique of hegemony Hartman pursues leans heavily on the language of citizenship, linking her critique of hegemony to a critique of the figure of the Black citizen. This theme recurs throughout *Scenes*, as when she argues that "the self-possessed subject with his *inalienable* attributes is quite unthinkable or unimaginable in this case," or that "the slave is neither civic man nor free worker but excluded from the narrative of 'we the people' that effects the linkage of the modern individual and the state."[65] In a conference report published three years before *Scenes*, Hartman refers to "one of the founding truths of the white republic—black bodies are excluded from the 'we the people' that establishes the citizen subject."[66] And in a reflection on the book's tenth anniversary, she discussed the way the book "closes in on the liminal status of the freed subject, the ambiguity of that status, the impossibility of that status, and the crisis of citizenship."[67] By challenging the discourse of hegemony, Hartman opened space to more clearly understand the predicaments of Black subjection and the ideological work performed by the figure of the Black citizen.

The Black body, fettered or nominally free, sanctions and sanctifies the project of American citizenship. The terror of antiblackness allows America to cohere as an ideological and political project, but also as a genre of belonging. In a 2002 interview, Hartman described the dilemma of Black positionality in America as caught between two narrative possibilities: "On one hand, the slave is the foundation of the national order, and, on the other, the slave occupies the position of the unthought."[68] Black citizenship was bifurcated and functioned as what Jacques Derrida would call a "category of encircling exclusion, of exclusion encircling what it wants to neutralize or cast out."[69] Hartman remarks on the limited political and conceptual horizon available to a Black politics within this framework. "So much of our political vocabulary/imaginary/desires have been implicitly integrationist even when we imagine our claims are more radical," she said, before describing the problems of Black political aspiration after emancipation.[70] "Ultimately the metanarrative thrust is always towards an integration into the national project, and particularly when that project is in crisis, black people are called upon to affirm it."[71] The figure of the slave is the constitutive outside that makes national belonging possible, but when that belonging begins to fall apart, the demand to repair that antiblack belonging falls onto the figure of the Black citizen—a figure for whom citizenship entails certain duties and obligations and uncertain rights and privileges.

Citizenship is belonging imbued with rights, and the citizen is an effect of the terror of the slave regime. Slavery created a social order founded on terror and the pleasures of terror, on the visceral and ephemeral uses of the Black body, on the manifold possible forms of consuming Blackness.[72] The dual status of Blacks as objects and subjects of terror and consumption created a citizenship without rights. The early years of Hartman's scholarship posed a triangulation of consumption, terror, and citizenship as not only long-standing in the United States, but constitutive of the American national project. The next phase in her itinerary would expand the historical, geographic, and ontological scope of that argument.

While Hartman's project in and around *Scenes of Subjection* was unique, challenging the several fields it worked between, the wider field of cultural studies had already been circling the relations between neoliberal capitalism and belonging, between consumption and citizenship.[73] In *Transnational America: Feminisms, Diasporas, Neoliberalisms*, Inderpal Grewal distilled those tendencies within cultural studies into a critique of transnational circulations of the concept of "America" in the era of globalization. In particular, Grewal posed the figure of the consumer-citizen as the privileged subject at the nexus of neoliberal multiculturalism and globalization at the turn of the twenty-first century. In the book's final chapter, she places the figure of the multicultural consumer-citizen in the new context of the post-9/11 national security state. The emerging war on terror that Grewal's work documents would crystallize tendencies within (feminist and queer) cultural studies that had emerged, retroactively, to process all that had and hadn't changed over the last decades of the twentieth century.

Within the heterogenous enterprise called cultural studies, practitioners were reckoning with the shifting politics of cultural production and reception following the gains of the Civil Rights era. As minoritized culture workers gained access to mainstream cultural institutions, media industries, and the organs of popular and academic cultural criticism, the demands of an older cultural politics, for "inclusion" and "positive representations," began to reach predictable and unpredictable limits. "Films are not necessarily good because black people make them," observed Stuart Hall in his essay "New Ethnicities." He continued,

> They are not necessarily "right-on" by virtue of the fact that they deal with the black experience. Once you enter the politics of the end of the essential black subject you are plunged headlong into the maelstrom of a continuously contingent, unguaranteed, political argument and debate: a critical politics, a politics of criticism. You can no longer conduct black politics through a strategy of a simple set of reversals, putting in place of the bad old essential white subject, the new essentially good black subject. Now, that formulation may seem to threaten the collapse of an entire political world. Alternatively, it may be greeted with extraordinary relief at the passing away of what at one time seemed to be a necessary fiction. Namely, either that all black people are good or indeed that all black people are *the same*.[74]

Across the fields that Robyn Wiegman has called "identity knowledges," critics faced the challenge of developing new forms of cultural analysis that moved beyond the old Manichean divides, according to which the cultural productions of the oppressor class and oppressed classes could be reliably critiqued based on the social identity of the author, or on the apparatus of its production and dissemination. The essential and essentially good minority subject was reinvented through new political ambiguities. The conceptual receptacle for these new ambiguities was (neo)liberal multiculturalism.

Within some precincts of cultural studies, the era of neoliberalism was most significantly marked by the incorporation of long-excluded forms of social and cultural difference.[75] On this reading, neoliberal multiculturalism in the United States emerged from the confluence of (1) the legislative and judicial victories of the Civil Rights era and the force of the Black Power movement, (2) shifts in the horizon of political possibility emerging from the new social movements, (3) the massive growth of the national security state and dismantling of the welfare state, (4) a new era of deregulation and the liberalization of international trade, and (5) the expansion of immigration from Asia and Latin America after the Immigration and Nationality Act of 1965. The political and legal frameworks of official white supremacy lost their legitimacy as the functions of the state were increasingly privatized. At the same time, a variety of new immigrant communities established themselves across the United States and were, to different degrees in different times and places, integrated into the mainstream of American politics, industry, and culture. Outwardly, diversity was lauded as a political ideal and corporate ethos.

At the same time, the new nations of the old colonial order faced the structural adjustments of international financial institutions. Young governments were forced to abandon social programs, open their economies to Western corporations, and incentivize the emigration of local elites whose commitment to the project of decolonization had been decisive for many liberation struggles.[76] In the West, the doctrine of free trade, new communication technologies, and advances in the infrastructures of international travel created new, global networks for the exchange of goods, labor, information, and capital. Together, these dynamics were heralded as a new and unprecedented era of globalization. For the Canadian poet and novelist, M. NourbeSe Philip, the dynamics of globalization at the turn of the twenty-first century were linked in essential ways to the era of globalization inaugurated by a properly global commerce in African life. Over the course of centuries, "the currency of globalization was the black body," and "black bodies could be taken anywhere in the world, at any point in time, *sans passport, sans visa*."[77] As a form of fixed capital and speculative investment, the slave experienced a paradoxical freedom of movement across the fluctuating borders of competing imperial projects.[78] That movement kick-started what became a properly global capitalism while functioning as a kind of information technology. The surfaces of bodies became the vehicle for a transnational matrix of (economic, cultural, social, political, moral) values. For Philip, reckoning with this first experience of globalization was constantly deferred, and so the first experience of globalization returned over and again, through the symptoms of the dominant culture and the aesthetic, intellectual, and political practices of the African diaspora.

In *Transnational America*, Grewal explored the dynamics of globalization and neoliberal multiculturalism through the figure of the consumer-citizen. By the end of the twentieth century, "America" was simultaneously a national project, the "last remaining superpower" after the dissolution of the Soviet Union, and something akin to a global brand—at once a political, ideological, and marketing project. A global empire and a global product, America "came to connote both whiteness and multiculturalism within the framework of an American exceptionalism" that cut across national and cultural boundaries. This growing indeterminacy of whiteness and multiculturalism was "regulated by a discourse of the liberal democratic state and a consumer citizenship seemingly unbound from territories and races and classes."[79] For Grewal, the figure of a transnational America signified both the incorporation of an increasingly multiracial citizenry into the political, social, and cultural lives of the United States, and the ways "America" circulated globally as a kind of intellectual property and consumer identity. The "American way of life" would come "to signify a variety of affiliative practices of belonging" for immigrant communities in the United States and for the new pool of potential consumer-citizens produced by globalization.[80] The difference between earlier formations and this new, globalized idea of America, Grewal argued, "was the imbrication of changing and contingent nationalist belonging with a transnational consumer culture facilitated by new technologies of communication, production, and consumption."[81]

Changes in technology, geopolitics, and the political economy of a post-Soviet global capitalism allowed the categories of "America" and "American" to expand to incorporate a range of historically excluded populations. This was not an unalloyed good, as it might be in a liberal progress narrative, but an ambivalent challenge for feminist thought and politics. The capacious new interiors of "America" and its new forms of national and transnational belonging produced new forms of investment in American empire and capitalism. "Within transnational connectivities," Grewal writes,

> consumer culture became the medium through which discourses of race, gender, and class produced nationalism. Consumer citizenship, simultaneously transnational and national, enabled increased levels of connectivities with transnational consumer culture. This version of citizenship, in which liberal democracy could only be imagined or made possible through consumer culture and its focus on choices between alternative goods or through the work of the market, produced liberal subjects in various parts of the world. The movements of goods and capital along with changes in national economies that took place during the last decades of the twentieth century affected all kinds of cultural formations.[82]

By the turn of the century, global capitalism had not only circumscribed the political realities of the entire Global North and much of the Global South—as globalization could be weaponized to discipline any nation that strayed from the preferred policies of the international financial institutions—it also colonized the political imagination of the transnational consumer-citizen. For much of the world, the most salient choices available were between different goods, choices mediated by "the market."

In the wake of the "there is no alternative" neoliberalism of Margaret Thatcher and Ronald Reagan, the loss of the Soviet Union as a figure and funder of anticapitalist struggle, and the assassination of the Third World project by the Bretton Woods institutions, resistance to the world order of global neoliberalism took on the retrograde, spectacular form of international terrorism.

The attacks on the World Trade Center and Pentagon in September of 2001 placed terror at the center of America's psychic life in a new way. Long a leading exporter and perpetrator of political violence across the world, the United States experienced spectacular acts of political violence on its own soil. Much of *Transnational America* was written before the Bush administration declared an open-ended war on terror, but the closing chapter re-frames Grewal's theorizations of consumer citizenship within a national context that had suddenly and traumatically embraced older xenophobias and was working to create new ones. In the preceding decade, much of the emerging fields of feminist and queer cultural studies had become interested in a micropolitics of power, one most interested in the presumed political power of post–Civil Rights Black America.[83] After September 11, the official and unofficial Islamophobia, xenophobia, imperialism, and jingoism of the second Bush administration only electrified cultural studies' atmosphere of antiblackness.

For Grewal, the new national security state and its apparently permanent state of exception led to a fundamental reconfiguration of racial formation in the United States. With the figure of the terrorist, a capacious category "including 'Middle Eastern men,' 'Muslims,' and those who 'look Middle Eastern or Muslim,'" Grewal argues that "another racial formation was created that produced a new Other."[84] And as this new Other emerged, "new 'Americans' were constructed through their solidarity with those who died or suffered in the attacks and through their difference from the 'terrorists.'"[85] For Grewal, these two processes of racial (re)formation were mutually reinforcing. As the category of the terrorist is racialized around the (real or imagined) "Middle Eastern or Muslim" subject, "racism against other nonwhites does not occupy 'domestic' politics as much as it did before."[86] The racial Others of September 10 could be "mobilized to be American in order to produce the non-American, racially identifiable Middle Eastern Muslim male as a new category of visibility."[87] It may be that the new racial categories occasioned by "the events of September 11" only intensified the tendency to declare, over and over, that anti-Black racism was on the wane, to move "beyond" antiblackness, and to intimate that Black Americans had gone from victims to victimizers in America's national melodramas.

In pursuit of this argument, Grewal gathers a range of cultural artifacts of the emerging national security state. There are official exhortations from the Bush administration for Americans to return to the shopping malls. There are syndicated newspaper cartoons depicting *hyphenated* Americans becoming *just* Americans. There are advertisements for insurance companies and department stores decorated with American flags, and an array of multicultural Americans waving and wearing flags. There are also "reports" of a new support for racial profiling from communities that were once the practice's primary targets. While nearly all of these images, reports, and representations are mediated by the structures of American corporate mass media and the advertising industry, Grewal treats them as elements in a popular structure of feeling rather than as moments in the manufacture of consent. In this analysis, ideological warfare is laundered as mass culture and hegemony's production of common sense is naturalized as mass culture. In the context of Grewal's larger argument, this reversal of relations of power enables her narrative of a new Black American subject with access to citizenship, its privileges, and its investments in American empire.

On 20 September 2001, Grewal describes seeing "identical images" on the front pages of two Bay Area newspapers, "one of a black family and one of a white family, holding babies and saying goodbye. Once again, the heterosexual American family, white and multicultural, was shown to be suffering and torn apart because of an attack by the 'Middle Eastern' Other."[88] The two front pages are not reproduced in the book but appear in the article published in 2003 in *Social Identities*.[89] Contrary to Grewal's characterization, the two images are a study in contrasts. The front page of the *San Francisco Chronicle* includes a photograph of a Black family under a headline reading "U.S. Orders Ships, Jets to Persian Gulf." The Black sailor is shown from the waist up, standing in the center left of the frame, facing toward the left. His young son is in his arms, and the boy's gaze is directed up toward him. The sailor looks more tired than resolute. His wife stands behind him, holding their one-year-old daughter in her arms. The girl's gaze wanders away to the right side of the frame. The woman's face is obscured by her hand as she wipes away tears. Above the headline is a quote from President George W. Bush: "When we take action, we will take action because we know we'll be in the right." The noncoherence of Bush's declaration rubs against the matter-of-factness of the ships and jets being ordered to the Persian Gulf. The image of the Black family fills the ideological space between Bush's sentence, which repeats *we* four times in a sentence struggling to link "action" to a concept of "right," and the headline, which has ships and jets being ordered by the American state and by the collective will of the first-person plural *US*. Between the obvious hubris and incompetence of the Bush administration, and the less obvious hubris and incompetence of the machinery of the national security state, which had spent the 1990s curing itself of the American public's Vietnam syndrome, the Black family was called upon to vouchsafe America as an imperial project. In other words, the front page of the *Chronicle* documents America preparing to make war.

The headline of the smaller *West County Times* reads "U.S. Warplanes Heading to Gulf." Above the lead story are two banner stories, one on the diminishing playoff chances of the Oakland A's baseball team and one reading "Patriotic Music Soars: Nation Finds Comfort Singing Praises of America." In the photograph, the subjects are all shown from the shoulders up. The white sailor embraces his wife, with their infant son held between their bodies. The sailor is facing the right side of the frame and his right eye is directed just to the right of the camera. He is caught between the moment with his family and the moment he will have to leave them. Their son is in the center of the frame, wearing a sailor's hat much too large for his small head. The hat is falling down the side of his face, pressing against his chubby cheek. His face is pointed directly to the camera and his gaze meets the viewer directly. The family unit in their embrace creates a single shape, and a white object just behind them, far out of focus, produces the backlit halo effect of three-point cinematic lighting. The image is a portrait of the white family called to patriotic service. The front page of the *Times* naturalizes the deployment of troops to the Gulf—the "warplanes" are "heading" to the Gulf, whereas in the *Chronicle* the United States "orders" ships and planes to the Gulf. The *Times* image, by longtime photojournalist L. Todd Spencer, appears on his website as the thumbnail of a gallery titled "Serve." The image itself is titled "Like Father, Like Son." Like the patriotic music soaring after 9/11, the *Times* cover traffics in the most common tropes of white American mythmaking.

Far from "identical," the two images reflect the bifurcation of American citizenship, as both families are separated to secure an American empire that expresses itself through the figure of the white child. The image of the Black family is less an expression of a new Black citizenship than another moment in a history of Black people being "called upon to affirm" an

American national project in crisis. If Grewal collapses these disparate images into identical instances of "the heterosexual American family, white and multicultural, . . . suffering and torn apart because of the attack by the 'Middle-Eastern' Other," that collapse is, in part, a reflection of the very figure of the consumer-citizen that organizes her project.[90] By reading a newly wounded American imperial project through the scattered discursive debris of advertising circulars, local and regional newspapers, political cartoons, "reports" of shifting attitudes, and various "images" and "media representations," Grewal reduces ideology to discourse; she reduces the "values, statements and practices fixed or unified by the interests of the ruling class" to "an open-ended, polyvalent, and heterogenous assemblage of statements."[91] And by reducing the project of capitalist imperialism to the figure of the consumer-citizen, she evacuates consumption of its material relation to debt and exploitation, and citizenship of the materiality of rights, duties, and obligations. The figure of Black American citizenship only coheres analytically by detaching critical practice from ideology, capital, and the racial state.

For Saidiya Hartman, the Black citizenship brought about by emancipation and the Civil War Amendments offered the burdens of obligation without the liberty of rights. Her project, as it developed through and after *Scenes of Subjection*, has been characterized by an intensifying skepticism toward the state and the promises of liberalism. In a review published the year after *Scenes*, Hartman examined a recent work by a feminist cultural studies scholar that read nineteenth-century accounts of revolts aboard slave ships to trace the development of American racial ideologies. That author "[located] the origins of white supremacy in the shift in the discourse of national identity that occurred by the insertion of the word 'white' into state suffrage requirements that took place in the 19th century." Hartman pushed back on the argument that it was "the word 'white' [that] restricted the universalist embrace of liberalism" and "not the four million enslaved Africans outside the purview of the 'all men are created equal' of the Declaration." In effect, on Hartman's reading, the author "endorses an interpretation of the Constitution as color-blind and proceeds as if the division between slave and free is not a mode of racial differentiation already dividing the body politic."[92] Hartman took issue with the attempt to recuperate liberalism as a political ideology adequate to the task of imagining for the enslaved a freedom worthy of the name. That author "strives to establish the emancipatory potential of liberalism" and "her defense assumes that the heterogeneity and polyvalence of discourse safeguards liberty and equality."[93] The implicit or explicit reliance on liberalism's political horizon, the implicit or explicit belief that heterogeneity and polyvalence are safeguards of liberty, and the implicit or explicit faith in the rights-bearing subject of liberal democracy underlies much of the critical project and political imagination of feminist and queer cultural studies.

In the decades after *Scenes*, Hartman's work would return over and again to the limits of liberalism. Hartman challenged the credulity of a mainstream in feminist and queer cultural studies that took the liberal tradition for granted even as it pursued critiques along its edges: "Does not one need to ask if liberalism has or if it can remedy racial domination, class exploitation, and gender inequality, or if the discourse of rights is not also the purveyor of forms of domination, subjection, and exploitation?" Against the figure of the citizen, against a belonging imbued with rights, Hartman's work began from a critique of rights that would lead to the problem of sovereignty. The projects that took shape following *Scenes* were guided by another question: "Are there narratives of liberation other than those of liberalism and nationalism?"[94]

SOVEREIGNTY, POWER

> The legacy that I chose to claim was articulated in the ongoing struggle to escape, stand down, and defeat slavery in all of its myriad forms. It was the fugitive's legacy. It didn't require me to wait on bended knee for a great emancipator. It wasn't the dream of a White House, even if it was in Harlem, but of a free territory. It was a dream of autonomy rather than nationhood. It was a dream of an elsewhere, with all its promises and dangers, where the stateless might, at last, thrive.
>
> —SAIDIYA HARTMAN, *LOSE YOUR MOTHER*, 234

> What if blackness is the refusal to defer to, given in the withdrawal from the eternal delay of, sovereignty?
>
> —FRED MOTEN, "BLACKNESS AND NOTHINGNESS," 751

Around the time *Scenes of Subjection* made it to the academic community, Saidiya Hartman was beginning a Fulbright year in Accra, Ghana. In Ghana, Hartman worked on a project called "Captives, Mourners, and the Tragedy of Origins," which would become a 2002 article, "The Time of Slavery," and her 2007 book, *Lose Your Mother: A Journey Along the Atlantic Slave Route*. In an interview around the publication of *Lose Your Mother*, Hartman distanced the work of the book from the genre of critical memoir. With reference to the work of earlier Black women intellectuals like Erna Brodber, Zora Neale Hurston, and Katherine Dunham, Hartman gestured toward the ways "women often attempt to embody an archive or to be it," and that "courage and recklessness are required to be a host of history."[95] To pursue an encounter with the originary tragedies of the Atlantic world, to "write about a history that is this encounter with nothing," or "a past that has been obliterated so that even traces aren't left," and to give an account of "the enormity of violence that characterized the process of captivity and enslavements," Hartman attempted a different writing of and a different encounter with history.[96] For Hartman, this encounter with the violence of history "had to be embodied in physical story, and I was the one who had to hazard the journey."[97] The forms Hartman began to cultivate in this moment of her itinerary, critical fabulation and intimate history, were also informed by her work with Stephen Best on the Redress Project.[98]

While Hartman and Best would go on to theorize the tethers of the past in different ways, in their work together they connected the historical question of redress for enslavement to broader questions about sovereignty, subjectivity, and the state.[99] In their introduction to a 2005 special issue of *Representations*, Hartman and Best separated the work of the Redress Project from contemporaneous questions of reparations for slavery: "In posing the question of slavery in terms of the incomplete nature of abolition, we are concerned neither with 'what happened then' nor with 'what is owed because of what happened then,' but rather with the contemporary predicament of freedom, with the melancholy recognition of foreseeable futures still tethered to this past."[100] In the decades after emancipation, after legislative efforts to compensate former slaves were defeated, again and again, lawyers representing former slaves sought redress through America's courts. Their claims for redress were stymied by the legal protections afforded to governments. The proposed litigants had no standing because "the government, unlike an individual defendant, could not be sued without its consent."[101] That decision "nullified not only the specifics of the litigants' plea but also, and more important, the very conception of the government as culpable or obligated. Redress could only obtain when the state recognized itself as negligent, when it acknowledged its unjust enrichment." The doctrine of sovereign immunity would "foreclose the possibility of a discussion of the racial state, and as such . . . reinscribe the neutrality of the state."[102] Within and across her major works, Hartman rebuffs the notion of the American state, its Constitution and laws, and its animating liberalism as neutral, as capable (even if it were willing) of redressing the originary tragedy of Atlantic slavery.

Between these projects sits the question of sovereignty, as a foundation of the Euro-American political imagination, as a problem for imagining futures beyond slavery and settler colonialism, and as a challenge for imagining Black liberation. Over the past thirty years, the concept of sovereignty has been a central concern for a range of academic discourses and in response to a range of political and conceptual crises, including (1) the decline of the nation-state and the Westphalian order, (2) the rising prominence of non-governmental organizations and the influence of transnational corporate entities and international financial institutions, (3) the intensification of the United States' international criminal belligerence following 11 September 2001, alongside (4) corollary discourses regarding so-called terrorist organizations operating sub- and transnationally, (5) the global production of refugee and stateless populations, (6) renewed critiques of settler colonialism and broad interest in Indigenous knowledge production and activist formations, (7) the rise of global telecommunication networks and, later, the ascendance of social media platforms that swallowed the advertising base of traditional media conglomerates, (8) the Anglo-American reception of the works of Michel Foucault, Carl Schmitt, Giorgio Agamben, and Achille Mbembe, and (9) the related but distinct receptions of Sylvia Wynter and the late work of Jacques Derrida, whose political-theological treatments of sovereignty gesture toward both the secularization of state power and its re-enchantments in the latter twentieth century. The problem of theorizing sovereignty and an insovereign alternative are caught within this field of static. In this section, I examine the problematic of sovereignty as it interacts with the tension between Blackness and the diasporic, and I situate both terms in relation to Indigeneity.

Within settler colonial studies and critical Indigenous studies, theorizations of colonization, decolonization, and Indigenous resistance and resurgence have articulated profound critiques of the nation-state and colonial and settler sovereignties as technologies and techniques of dispossession. At the same time, they have wrestled with articulating Indigenous sovereignties as paths toward imagining alternative socialities and forms of belonging. In *Settler Colonialism: A Theoretical Overview*, the Australian historian Lorenzo Veracini traced fissures within the problematic of sovereignty, arguing that national/imperial sovereignties have historically existed in an agonistic relationship with settler sovereignties: "As settler colonial political traditions focus on the self-governance of the local community, and as imperial and national structures rarely affect settler control over local matters, colonial and settler colonial sovereignties can routinely accommodate each other."[103] Indeed, "corporate self-constituted structures can accommodate a variety of sovereign claims."[104] Veracini draws attention to the reality that "a settler sovereignty can be understood as distinct and operating in conjunction with other colonial, national, and imperial sovereignties."[105] At least three sovereign claims can be gleaned from Veracini's analysis here: state/imperial sovereignty, settler sovereignty, and indigenous sovereignty.[106]

On the surface, the coexistence of state and settler sovereignties poses a fundamental problem for the conceptual and practical lives of sovereignty. "In dominant post-Westphalian conceptions of political order," Mark Rifkin writes, "the undivided nature of such rule remains crucial to its character: spheres of sovereignty cannot overlap or they cease to constitute claims to sovereignty."[107] The right of sovereign power to undivided dominion and jurisdiction has functioned as a pretext for the displacement of Indigenous nations. Elsewhere, Rifkin argues that *sovereignty*, as a term, "functions as a placeholder that has no determinate content." At least in part, sovereignty is a story that states tell about themselves, a story about the foundations of their legitimacy, and the legitimacy of their monopoly on violence. The logic of sovereignty is "fundamentally circular and self-validating" and it "grounds the legitimacy of state rule on nothing more than the axiomatic negation of Native peoples' authority to determine or adjudicate for themselves the normative principles by which they will be governed."[108] In the context of the settler state, state sovereignty is a story that disappears Indigenous peoples, or a story in which Native people are always in the process of disappearing, as a way of sanctifying and sanctioning the settler political community's experience of itself as what Rifkin has called an "emplaced political collectivity."[109] In practice, the settler state can and does accommodate multiple sovereignties, in part because these sovereignties are stories about belonging—belonging imbued with power. These stories about belonging are, ultimately, not political but theological.

Within the discourse of critical Indigenous studies, settler and state sovereignties are frequently rendered *political* in contrast to more holistic Native sovereignties. For Audra Simpson, one goal of Indigenous critique is to "distinguish between sovereignty as western exceptionalism and dominance, and sovereignty as Indigenous belonging, dignity, and justice."[110] As a critical practice, Native sovereignties are "more than a problem of the violence to exclude, to maim, to kill in the name of jurisdiction, or a reminder of past agreements"; they are the basis of collective forms of "resistance and refusal to dispossession and encroachment" and so "are practices of care in addition to pronouncements of trespass and theft." For Simpson, "this fact renders sovereignty as a form of relationality rather than a violent claim of property, exclusion, and a right to kill."[111] Elsewhere, Leanne Simpson places even greater emphasis on the internal diversity of indigenous sovereignty. "Indigenous thought," she writes,

> which is as diverse as the land itself, roots sovereignty in good relationships, responsibilities, a deep respect for individual and collective self-determination, and honoring diversity. When indigenous peoples use the English word sovereignty in relation to our own political traditions, we use it to mean authentic power coming from a generated consensus and a respect for dissent rather than sovereignty coming from authoritarian power or power-over style of governance. We use it to refer to the self-determination of our political cultures and nonhierarchical systems of governance, and we use it to mean the maintenance of these relationships through balance, care, and nurturing rather than coercion.[112]

These critiques of settler/state sovereignties reduce them to the political, while noting their peculiarities—their circular logic, their pretextual quality, their exceptionalism and dominance. Those peculiarities might be theorized as what Wendy Brown has called a "theological remainder," the remnants of the specifically *mystical* foundations of sovereign authority.[113] The theological basis of sovereignty allows it to travel across political communities organized by various creation myths, cosmologies, and narratives of belonging. The disenchantments of the liberal revolutions and the secularization of state power were always *extensions* of this theological aspect of sovereignty. Within the psychic life of the settler state, these are also sovereignties of balance, care, and nurturing. Through the secular theology of sovereignty, the settler state reinscribes its own neutrality, the neutrality of its laws, its borders, its possession of and jurisdiction over lands and waters, and its right to place and displace peoples within its borders and under its jurisdiction.

The critique of settler colonialism attends to the discrepancy between the ideals and self-soothing fictions of the settler state and the realities of dispossession, displacement, and genocide. Those realities are extensions of the settler state's materialized conceptualization of the relations between space, being, and belonging. They are stories about "emplaced political collectivity" that presuppose the permanent and repetitive disappearance of one people to create and recreate another people. But critical Indigenous studies insists on the distinction between these forms of sovereignty when the crucial distinction may not reside within the sovereignty concept itself.[114] In Mark Rifkin's extended engagement with critical Black studies, he suggests that imagining new forms of relationality between Black and Native communities is "less about the absence of sustained communality or landedness—of claims to nation or territory—than an openness to forms of engagement and an ethics of mutual responsibility that arise out of the encounter with other people(s) and their ways of understanding themselves."[115] But if the settler state reinscribes the neutrality of conquest, Rifkin's formulation reinscribes the neutrality of *people(s)* as a genre of belonging. If Blackness throws this genre of belonging into crisis, what then is the status of a Black sovereignty? This is also to ask, is there, or can there be, something like a Black indigeneity?[116]

These questions are at the heart of the relationship between indigeneity and diaspora as forms of belonging. Marginalized within settler polities, diasporic subjects inhabit the displaced indigeneity of a deferred or delayed belonging. In *Unruly Visions: The Aesthetic Practices of Queer Diaspora*, Gayatri Gopinath recovers the queer connections between diaspora and indigeneity. While the two concepts "are, more often than not, situated in binary or oppositional relation to one another," Gopinath's project cultivates "a deep understanding of conjoined pasts, presents, and futures, and envisions (indeed, insists upon) the possibility of affiliation among nonequivalent and at times even oppositional formations."[117] Rather than foreclose, a priori, the possibility of affiliation across nonequivalent or oppositional formations, the shared territories of the diasporic and Indigenous obtain through a queer practice of critique. For Gopinath, the possibility of "fluid exchanges between the indigenous and the diasporic" relies, on one hand, on a queer critique of the nation-state and its structuring normativities, and, on the other, on a deep reckoning with the conscriptions in and complicities with settler colonial projects by non-Native diasporic populations.[118] As Gopinath's project moves toward the postcolony in Africa and the diasporas produced by Atlantic slavery, the categories of diaspora and indigeneity butt up against problems of Black indigeneity and Black sovereignty.

Across a long engagement with the visual artist Allan deSouza and a reading of Saidiya Hartman's *Lose Your Mother*, Gopinath examines the "braided and overlapping" histories of South Asian diasporic subjects before and after Kenyan independence and the Black diaspora produced by Atlantic slavery.[119] Allan deSouza's art is informed by his multiply diasporic personal history: His parents were born in Goa when it was a Portuguese colony and later became Indian citizens and British colonial subjects. They moved to British-controlled Kenya and began a family. Kenya declared independence in 1963, and sometime shortly thereafter, Allan (who was a young boy) and his family moved to England. He would later settle in California, while his parents retired to Portugal. DeSouza's artistic practice engages with these overlapping histories of colonization, settlement, and displacement, and different spatial and temporal politics of belonging to multiple diasporas: "Perhaps I was too often in the wrong place, but if your family history and childhood experience are routed through three different colonies and their colonial powers—Goa under the Portuguese, India under the British, and Kenya, again British—then being in the wrong place and at the wrong time too easily becomes habitual."[120]

For Gopinath, deSouza's photo series *The Lost Pictures* is a powerful intertext for the embodied history of Hartman's *Lose Your Mother*. In reading the works together, Gopinath is careful not to collapse the "different historical processes (of slavery, colonialism, indentureship, nationalism, migration)" that condition their projects: "While the work of Hartman and deSouza make clear that the losses that attend the legacies of slavery are distinct from those of colonialism or postcolonial nationalism, it is nevertheless worth putting these different experiences of diasporic loss into dialogue, in order to bring to the fore the common ground that they do in fact share."[121] Despite her caution, Gopinath's formulation of "different experiences of diasporic loss" reinscribes the neutrality of loss that forms common ground even as it is experienced differently. In her own formulation of Black diasporic melancholia, Sara Clarke Kaplan offers another formulation of loss when she asks, "How can we 'let go' of losses that are reproduced in marginally different forms with every generation? Because, rather than being a state of exception, black unfreedom has been integral to the production of liberal ideologies of white freedom; and because black subjugation continues to be a central means through which the nation-state reproduces itself structurally and ideologically, these losses are doubly excluded from any process of mourning and moving on."[122] In

Haunted Life, David Marriott asks, "If to be black is to reenact an impeachment that is self-obliterating, how does one exhume a loss that erases the self as a cadaverous resemblance, and, because of that renunciation, is nothing more?" That is, for Marriott, "nothing is the essence of blackness, nothing defines its drama and role," and, further, "it is only through the presence of such spectral resentment that the black can resemble anything at all."[123] This is all to say that, rather than being a distinct form of "loss" sharing a common ground with other diasporic formations, Black loss is the loss of the capacity to lose—"a memory resembling a memory of a thing that he remembered. And not so much remembered as felt. And not so much felt as a memory which held him."[124] The paradox of the Black diasporic is that Blackness names a form of deracination that obliterates the category of indigeneity; a form of permanent, ontological displacement that permanently defers the diasporic as a form of belonging. There is no indigenous Blackness and so there is no diasporic Blackness.

This paradoxical status comes into clearer view in Gopinath's treatment of postcolonial Africa. The postcolonial African nations founded across the middle of the twentieth century were shaped by the tension between Blackness and Africanness. In their self-invention, they were *African* countries, their sovereignty issued from their status as the Indigenous peoples living in relation to lands, waters, and forms of animal and plant life. But Africa does not enter Gopinath's text as a site of Indigeneity. Instead, and in line with broader tendencies within transnational feminist and queer critique, decolonized African states are *postcolonial* and *nationalist*. In part, these characterizations reflect the multiethnic character of those states and the ways territories and peoples were reshaped and displaced by European colonial projects. But it also indicates the Blackness of the postcolonial African state, and the predicament of a Black sovereignty.

DeSouza's *The Lost Pictures* were composed through a postcolonial past and a diasporic present: Prints of images from his family's archive of photographic slides and family photos, taken in Kenya in the years after independence, were placed in different spaces in his Los Angeles apartment to accumulate the accretions of his everyday life. "In their final version," Gopinath writes, "the past, in the form of the original slide images, is rendered ghostly, fading into white, barely visible, while the diasporic present asserts itself through the detritus of the artist's own body: semen, blood, hair, food, sloughed-off skin."[125] In Gopinath's telling, deSouza's diasporic present emerges from the vexed position of the Indian diaspora in postcolonial Africa: "East African Indians inhabited a 'dubious status,' situated as they were 'in a precariously liminal category between colonized and colonizer.' This liminality meant that, as historian Thomas Metcalf notes, 'Indian Africans remained vulnerable to a politics of hostility, exclusion and even, in the case of Idi Amin's Uganda, expulsion.'"[126] In this formulation of the politics of hostility, exclusion, and expulsion, Gopinath collapses the diverse political statuses of South Asian residents—occupying the position of what Shona Jackson, writing on the colonial experiences of the greater Caribbean, has called "involuntary settlers"—in the new states of Eastern Africa, generally, and the case of post-independence Kenya, specifically.[127]

Reading deSouza alongside Hartman, Gopinath presents two critiques of African nationalisms. "For Hartman," she writes, "the slogan 'Africa for Africans abroad and at home' from the anticolonial nationalist era conjures forth the seductive promise of diasporic belonging in the new nation that, forty years after independence, rings hollow; it highlights her own sense of estrangement as a black diasporic subject in postcolonial Africa. For Indian Africans such as deSouza, however, this slogan from its very inception is no seduction, but an ominous sign of what is to come, for it names a collective history of expulsion, as 'authentic Africanness' came to be defined in strictly racial terms."[128] Gopinath's characterization of African independence and "the vexed position of 'the Asian African' within Black African nationalist discourse" erases both the agency of Asian (involuntary) settlers in Africa and the history of Kenya in the years after independence.[129] When Kenya gained independence in December of 1963, "the essential distinction in the constitution was that between citizen and non-citizen, regardless of race," and "non-Africans domiciled in Kenya had two years in which to make up their minds whether to register as citizens."[130] With independence, "government leaders made no attempt to disguise their rejection of dual citizenship. They, and the African population at large, demanded total identification of the non-Africans with the newly independent state."[131] In the early years of independence, the Indian bourgeoisie in Kenya were asked to choose between British passports and Kenyan passports, between the Commonwealth and a common Africanness. It may have been the Blackness and not the State-ness of the African state, the loss of a tenuous Humanity, that posed the greatest challenge for settlers invited to relinquish passports that placed them, even in a degraded way, within the Commonwealth and within the genres of the Human. The Blackness of the post-colonial African state is the space between the British and Kenyan passports, the stain of the sovereignless within the postcolonial state. "The vast majority of Europeans and a considerable portion of the Asian population at independence left Kenya over the next fifteen years."[132]

Without ignoring the limits of postcolonial nationalisms, the politics of authenticity and xenophobia, how do we account for the fear of becoming African, of being touched by an abjection more profound than the bodily debris coating old family photos? And how do we account for the ontological space between Africanness and Blackness? The limit of African sovereignty has always been its proximity to an insovereign Blackness. There is no such thing as a Black nation. Blackness, following William C. Anderson, is the nation on no map.

The problem of an insovereign Blackness, the production of Blackness as sovereignlessness, begins in the early modern trade in captive Africans and the racialization of slavery. In his contribution to the Redress Project, the historian Herman Bennett sought to complicate the stories told about successive waves of enslavement and colonial exploitation in Africa. For Bennett, "a simplistic savage-to-slave scenario," in which "the European need for labor and its perception of Africans facilitated the transatlantic slave trade"—that is, an origin story that reduces the racialization of slavery to economic and cultural forces, ignoring the complexity of early modern politics in both Europe and Africa—"saddles social theory and our political reality with the flawed epistemological assumption about a homogenous 'black' subject."[133] In reality, early modern exchanges between Europe's Christian kingdoms and the kingdoms and empires of the West African coast were determined through complex webs of sovereign power. Bennett's analysis challenges historiographies of Atlantic slavery that read the early modern trade through the lens of those obliterations of African sovereignty that characterized the carving up of Africa at the end of the nineteenth century. Unlike the settler and franchise colonies established in the nineteenth century, the centuries of Atlantic slavery were organized around commercial and political relationships between European and African sovereigns, additionally mediated for Europeans by the regulations of the Catholic Church. "The church," Bennett writes, "in tandem with African agency and Portuguese commercial motives, curtailed wanton slave raids and established an institutional context through which some of Guinea's inhabitants assumed the status of sovereign subjects. Others, however, were considered the *herrschaftlos* (sovereignless)—both in the eyes of Africans and Europeans—and legitimately slaves."[134] The slave trade produced a split, internal to Africa, between sovereign and sovereignless, what Bennett would later call a distinction between African kings and Black slaves.[135] The sovereignless of sub-Saharan Africa became the sovereignless of the Americas, making sovereignty meaningful in new ways for both settlers and natives. By the middle of the nineteenth century, as Europe fell again upon Africa, Blackness had become sovereignlessness.[136]

In *Lose Your Mother*, Hartman takes up Bennett's formulation in the context of the slave trade in the territory that would become the nation of Ghana. Visiting what had been the central marketplace of the northern city of Salaga, Hartman encounters a retired schoolteacher and they struggle to untangle their braided histories. Hartman describes a time when the local elite, the Gonja, captured and sold people they called *grunshi*, "a pejorative term equivalent to pagan, primitive, or barbarian," "a ragtag name for the 'stateless' people living on both sides of the Ghana and Burkina Faso border and to the north and west of Gonja," "a name synonymous with defeat."[137] Those slaves "came from small-scale, non-Islamic, agricultural societies without chiefs. Aristocratic warrior states viewed them as inferior, savage, and weak. African royals and elites, like their European counterparts, envisioned the stateless and the sovereignless as suited for slavery."[138] The teacher, for his part, experienced the history of his city as a sadness, as something that happened to the warriors and merchants conducting the trade as much as it happened to their hapless, sovereignless neighbors who were captured and trafficked. In the indeterminate space between indigeneity and diaspora, we return to an endless encounter with the door of no return. We are left asking, what do we do with the history that happens to us? How do we navigate the limits of our agency? And what would it mean to inhabit a world on the other side of sovereignty?

To the extent that *Lose Your Mother* has been read through the genre protocols of memoir, as a story of Hartman's disillusionment with the dream of Pan-Africanism and her discovery of a new, diasporic belonging, an anarchist critique of the state has been lost in favor of fugitive longing and belonging otherwise. Hartman's earliest work offered a critique of the American state and its foundational liberalism, and the next stage in Hartman's itinerary expanded that critique to the African state, to what could only be misnamed as Black states. Instead, Hartman reveals the oxymoron of a Black state and poses another dream: the dream of a "struggle to escape, stand down, and defeat slavery in all of its myriad forms," the dream "of a free territory." "It was a dream of autonomy rather than nationhood. It was a dream of an elsewhere, with all its promises and dangers, where the stateless might, at last, thrive"—the insovereign dream of a feminist Black anarchism and the sovereignless wail of the anarchy of colored girls assembled in a riotous manner.[139]

THE INDETERMINATE ANARCHY OF BLACK FEMINIST THEORIZING

> Black anarchism is anarchism otherwise, and its goal is the reconstruction of everything.
>
> —SAIDIYA HARTMAN, "BLACK IN ANARCHY," xvi

In her preface to William C. Anderson's *The Nation on No Map*, Hartman points toward an old idea for new ways of imagining a radical cultural politics. "'Anarchism' is an open and incomplete word," she writes, "and in this resides its potential. It is to perceive possibilities not yet recognizable; it hints at what might be, at modes of living and relation that are unthinkable in the old frameworks."[140] In her *Wayward Lives, Beautiful Experiments*, Hartman turns to the formation of Black ghettoes in the early twentieth century to uncover wild experiments in living freely. For Hartman, the young Black women she uncovers in the archive lived a kind of lay anarchism. "Esther Brown," she writes in "The Anarchy of Colored Girls Assembled in a Riotous Manner,"

> did not write a political tract on the refusal to be governed, or draft a plan for mutual aid or outline a memoir of her sexual adventures. . . . The cardboard placards for the tumult and upheaval she incited might have said: "Don't mess with me. I am not afraid to smash things up." But hers was a struggle without formal declarations of policy, slogan, or credos. . . . She knew firsthand that the offense most punished by the state was trying to live free. To wander through the streets of Harlem, to want better than what she had, and to be propelled by her whims and desires was to be ungovernable. Her way of living was nothing short of anarchy.[141]

For Hartman, these practices of everyday rebellion were something other than mere impressions of anarchism. Instead, they shared a relation to the idea of "thought in deed," which Hartman calls "critical to anarchist practice" as well as "the foundation of a black feminist practice." For Hartman, the inchoate Black feminist practice of Black girls like Esther Brown "shares much with anarchism in its critique of state violence and struggle against enclosure on the plantation and in the city."[142] Across Hartman's recent work, she has made the insurgent freedoms of past forms of Black living available to the radical imaginations of the present.

Hartman's itinerary, as a current within the heterogenous itinerary of Black feminist theorizing, has troubled the foundational categories of feminist and queer cultural studies, which I've considered here through the discourses of transnational feminism and diasporic queer theory. Across the different discourses of cultural studies, hegemony, citizenship, and sovereignty have set the political and conceptual horizons for the critique of domination and for imagining alternative frameworks for belonging. Those foundational categories offer dreams of belonging otherwise that nonetheless naturalize and reinforce antiblackness as their condition of possibility. The limits internal to feminist and queer cultural studies' political imagination produce and reproduce Blackness as at once an anchoring point of reference and an anxious site of negative comparison. In these analyses, Black women appear as agents of the hegemony of Western feminism, as representatives of the American family torn apart by foreign terrorism, or unwitting accomplices to the racisms of Black African nationalisms.

Frank Wilderson has called this gesture "the ruse of analogy," but the theorizations of Blackness pursued in different ways by Wilderson, Hartman, and their fellow travelers, seem to reveal how the Black radical tradition itself has misapprehended antiblackness through analogy. On plantations, captive Africans suffered *like* slaves, and as sharecroppers in the ruins of the plantations, freedmen suffered like serfs. In the twentieth century, Black Americans suffered like a dishonored racial caste, like an industrial reserve army, like the Lumpenproletariat, like workers, like an internal colony, and like second-class citizens. In the tidal wave of reaction after the moment of Civil Rights and Black Power, those analogies broke against the sheer, heedless mania of antiblackness. The modulations of racial capitalism and the racist state in the latter half of the twentieth century were instructive as, over and over, white America demanded its own abandonment so that no scrap of social surplus would be redirected toward their Black neighbors—better fascism than the nightmare of "social equality."

The state was stripped of its capacity to contribute to the social welfare and what was left was the bureaucratic distribution of violence. That violence could be as subtle as hypertension and as shocking as murders distributed virally across social media platforms.[143] That violence became the atmosphere for the urban underclass and for suburban exodusters, for those warehoused in prisons and those working in the professions. The State pared itself down to the machinery of Black dying, to the morbid reinscription of hundreds of thousands of names of victims of state and state-sanctioned violence. No extant critical discourse has touched the singular, structuring irrationality of antiblackness. In its way, the movements collected under the heading of "Black Lives Matter" are placeholders for Black liberation struggle. They signal the magnitude of the problem, and gesture toward the forms of decentralization and mutual aid that might prefigure another way of being.

The material and immaterial scale of Black suffering and its apparent detachment from any particular political or economic rationality, its sheer gratuitousness, has thrown into the sharpest possible relief the limitations of both the traditional bourgeois political formations and their most radical counterparts on the Left. This was, in part, the argument made in Sam Mbah and I. E. Igariwey's *African Anarchism* and echoed by Hartman in *Lose Your Mother*: that African socialisms (to say nothing of the continent's capitalist states) had failed to deliver on their promises of political and economic democracy, of returns to the (mythical) egalitarian social forms that preceded colonialism. In a similar vein, the discourse of afropessimism that emerged in the United States at the turn of this century was first articulated through a critique of the Gramscian Left. In "Gramsci's Black Marx," Frank Wilderson argued that "slavery—the 'accumulation' of black bodies regardless of their utility as labourers, through an idiom of despotic power—is closer to capital's primal desire than is waged oppression—the 'exploitation' of unraced bodies that labour through an idiom of rational/symbolic (the wage) power: A relation of terror as opposed to a relation of hegemony."[144] Wilderson's critique of the structuring logics of the Marxist tradition was informed by an ongoing reconsideration of the history of racial slavery and the political, economic, and epistemological foundations of the world that formed in the shadow of slavery. In the early formulation of that reconsideration, Hartman wrote that "the history of the black body in the Americas is a chronicle of terror: enslavement, domination, subjection, and confinement. . . . It has withstood the unimaginable; the body has existed as an object of property, harnessed as a productive and reproductive machine, and acculturated and disciplined through monumental acts of violence. The body has been confined, despised, bestialized, and desired."[145] In this critique of antiblackness, *slavery* becomes an insufficient rubric for articulating the situation of the Black subject, those sentient objects around which a world of human beings discovered themselves as rights-bearing subjects, as chapter after chapter was added to a chronicle of terror. The critical discourses of feminist and queer cultural studies have struggled to imagine freedom from that terror.

In her recent engagements with Black anarchism, Hartman has begun to articulate the possibilities that live in an anarchist alternative, and the anarchisms internal to, but rarely considered within, the Black radical tradition. "'Anarchism,'" she writes, "is an open word whose contours and meaning are shaped by the long struggle for Black liberation, by the centuries-long resistance to racial slavery, settler colonialism, capitalism, state violence, genocide, and anti-Blackness. 'Anarchism' gathers and names the practices of mutual aid and the programs for survival that have sustained us in the face unimaginable violence. It unfolds with and as Black feminism and Indigenous struggle. It offers a blueprint for radical transformation, for the possibilities of existence beyond the world of scarcity and managed depletion, enclosure, and premature death."[146] Anarchism is the most radical imagining of a human freedom, of a freedom *for humans*. A Black anarchism is one endeavor to imagine freedom beyond humanity. A feminist Black anarchism operates in the non-space where Blackness unmakes self-determination. Part of the heterogeneity of Black anarchism obtains in the different ways that its theorists and practitioners understand the status of Blackness—as race, ethnicity, nationality, status, structural position, inheritance or disinheritance. The problem of defining Blackness recurs, in part, because the world formed from racial slavery manufactured subjectivity from the same alloy of terror and pleasure that produced Blackness. Blackness appears as the very abeyance of the coordinates of subjectivity—hegemony, citizenship, and sovereignty. The history of Black liberation struggle has been shaped by the contradictions of demanding rights that are only meaningful through relations of terror.

In the noise riot that occupies the center of the third book of *Wayward Lives, Beautiful Experiments*, Hartman imagines a new kind of demand, unfettered by the traps of racial liberalism. "The chants and cries insisted: We want to be free. The strike begged the question: Why are we locked up here? Why have you stolen our lives?" Hartman imagines a politics without a proper locus, a Black liberation struggle that begins nowhere, wants nothing, and threatens everything. The insovereign dream of a feminist Black anarchism risks the incoherence of the noise riot.

> All those listening on the outside could discern were: "gales of catcalls, hurricanes of screams, cyclones of rage, tornadoes of squalls." The sounds yielded to "one hair-raising, ear-testing Devil's chorus." Those inside the circle listened for the love and disappointment, the longing and the outrage that fueled this collective utterance. They channeled the fears and the hopes of the ones who loved them, the bad dreams and the nightmares about children stolen away by white men and lost at sea. The refrains were redolent with all the lovely plans about what they would do once they were free. These sounds traveled through the night air.[147]

From this creative destruction, the deconstruction of life itself, the otherwise and indeterminate anarchism of Black feminist theorizing, as an expression of a feminist Black radicalism, dreams the reconstruction of everything.

Epilogue

In a Burning House

> Whatever's burning in me is mine!
>
> **Toni Morrison, *Sula*, 93**

All of the answers curl back into questions.

In a Field of Static has been structured, in part, by the premise that, across academic discourses, Black feminism is overdetermined. To say "Black feminism" is to be too understood, too quickly. Its possible meanings—for academic practice, art, politics, or thought—are known in advance. A narrow set of potentialities have been appropriated by and incorporated into the institution. When we say, "Black feminism," we lose the chance to be surprised by what we find. This book has been animated by the desire for other possible relations to the pasts, presents, and futures of Black feminist theorizing. Throughout, I have insisted on the heterogeneity of Black feminist theorizing, elaborated idiosyncratic moments in the archive of Black feminist thought, pursued my own readings of the conflicts that have shaped feminist and queer cultural studies, and sought new ways of inhabiting a field of static that is, finally, irreducible. At the same time, this form of writing insists on a kind of closure: Each chapter offers a complete thought, an argument that closes down on itself and that, collectively, forms a coherent unity. These final pages will unravel some of the threads pursued across the previous chapters.

Antiblackness might name the desire to annihilate the noncoherent nothing that inhabits all living. Strategies for living with or in this incoherence have tended to be expressed in the languages of spiritual practice, in practices of invention, in shattering experiences of becoming undone—or, in the rigorous errancy of Black Study, which may be nothing other than the breath of Black feminist theorizing. It may be that all "identity knowledges" spring from this breath of Black feminist theorizing. If feminist and queer cultural studies continue to be worth pursuing, it is *because* they are missed encounters with Black feminist theorizing. In their encounters with Black feminism, they touch the potential to imagine a critique of the Human and an end of the world.

By way of ending, I want to turn, first, to one beginning of Black feminist criticism: Barbara Smith's "Toward a Black Feminist Criticism" and its signal Black lesbian reading of Toni Morrison's *Sula*. First published in 1977, Smith's essay imagined a new territory for the study of Black women's creative expression. Beyond the (massive) intervention of positing a Black feminist critical practice, Smith placed a Black lesbian sensibility at the center of this new speculative agenda. Over the next decade, a range of Black feminist critics would take issue, specifically, with Smith's Black lesbian reading of Morrison. In part, this emerging field of critical praxis was shaped by a desire to distance Black feminism from the indeterminacy of the figure of the Black lesbian introduced in Smith's essay. With "Toward a Black Feminist Criticism," and with the resistances to it that shaped the next decade of Black feminist critical practice, Black feminist criticism began as a missed encounter with itself.

Smith's essay opens with her sense of the existential problem before her: There is no precedent for a Black feminist criticism. Her essay is an act of invention. Black women writers in the United States had never yet enjoyed a "strategic audience of heightened consciousness to read and interpret" their work, so much of it had come and gone, moved in and out of fashion, without becoming part of the fabric of the national literary culture.[1] Criticism allowed literature to live on. In Smith's words, "for books to be real and remembered they have to be talked about."[2] A Black feminist criticism offered alternatives to the hostile, obfuscating, and ignorant interpretations of Black women's writing common to the time. Smith was interested in challenging those reading practices, imagining other practices, and exploring "what the existence or non-existence of Black lesbian writing reveals about the state of Black women's culture and the intensity of *all* Black women's oppression."[3] Smith would pursue this latter project through a reading of Toni Morrison's *Sula* as a lesbian text.

Smith articulates the queerness of Morrison's text in terms of its representations of heterosexuality and of the central relationship between Sula and Nel. Smith argues that "Sula's presence in her community functions much like the presence of lesbians everywhere to expose the contradictions of supposedly 'normal' life," that "Sula's feelings about sex with men are . . . consistent with a lesbian interpretation of the novel," and that "*Sula* is an exceedingly lesbian novel *in the emotions expressed, in the definition of female character* and *in the way that the politics of heterosexuality are portrayed*."[4] Smith is clear that, "obviously Morrison did not *intend* the reader to perceive Sula and Nel's relationship as inherently lesbian," but Smith's reading practice finds those particular forms of indeterminacy that open space for living differently with, within, and in relation to a normative heterosexuality.[5]

Smith relies on the burgeoning field of feminist theory to ground a theory of lesbian literary and political expression. Smith refers to the manifesto of the New York Radicalesbians, who wrote, "A lesbian is the rage of all women condensed to the point of explosion. She is the woman who . . . acts in accordance with her inner compulsion to be a more complete and freer human being than her society . . . cares to allow her."[6] Smith also points to a paper given at a meeting of the Modern Language Association by the lesbian novelist Bertha Harris, who offered that, "if in a woman writer's work a sentence refuses to do what it is supposed to do, if there are strong images of women and if there is a refusal to be linear, the result is innately lesbian literature."[7] Finally, Smith referred to comments by Wilmette Brown, cofounder of Black Women for Wages for Housework: "I have searched throughout Black history, Black literature, whatever, looking for some women that I could see were somehow lesbians. Now I know that in a certain sense they were all lesbian. But that was a very painful search."[8] Across these points of reference, a Black lesbian writing takes shape as rage and refusal, as an expression of a nonlinear inner compulsion toward completeness and freedom. With Brown, Smith introduces the possibility that there is something queer about Black femininity itself, but that point is never elaborated.[9]

The year after the essay appeared in the second issue of *Conditions*, Smith was invited to present her work at the fourth annual National Conference of Afro-American Writers, hosted by Howard University's Institute for Arts and Humanities in May of 1978. The "Black Woman Writers and Feminism" panel was moderated by June Jordan and featured Smith, the poet Sonia Sanchez, and the political scientist Acklyn Lynch. In addition to reading selections from "Toward a Black Feminist Criticism," Smith offered two keywords for an emergent Black feminist criticism: "The word that comes to my mind is 'responsible,' criticism having integrity and honesty; truth-telling as a major function for both fiction and the criticism of it. Another keyword is 'integrated.' Thus black feminist criticism is an integrated analysis just as the practice of black feminism is an integrated politics." For Smith, the integrated politics of Black feminism was "anti-capitalist, anti-sexist, anti-heterosexist and of course, anti-racist."[10] This construction of the relation between criticism and politics was common to both Black Arts and feminist criticism, and the question of the politics of literary interpretation was being debated more broadly across the profession of academic literary criticism. Smith's intervention brought those traditions together in a way that touched something essential to but missing from each discourse.

Among those in attendance that day at Howard was the psychiatrist Frances Cress Welsing, a member of the Howard faculty whose "Cress Theory of Color Confrontation," a precursor of the later "melanin studies" offshoot of Afrocentric practice, had been published in *The Black Scholar* four years earlier. Within her sprawling remarks, Welsing offered a warning, rendered in the transcript as "If we endorse homosexuality, then we have endorsed the death of our people (applause)."[11] Much of the rest of the questions and comments from the audience expressed consternation over homosexuality, generally, and lesbianism, specifically. In a 2003 interview with Loretta Ross, Smith reflected, "The crowd turned ugly. It was a free-for-all. Living theater but . . . really it was more like a horror movie than any other genre (laughs)."[12] In the conjuncture represented by a national Black writers' conference at Howard in 1978, as a new Black literary criticism was beginning to be consolidated elsewhere at formerly racially exclusive research universities, and while Black Arts criticism was still the standard, Smith's audience agreed that Black criticism and Black politics were mutually reinforcing. By and large, however, the lesbianism of Smith's Black feminism was experienced as a problem for Black art *and* politics.

With "New Directions for Black Feminist Criticism," Deborah McDowell represented an emerging scholarly consensus that problematized the premise that criticism could be an adjunct to politics. "I am not sure that either in theory or in practice Black feminist criticism will be able to alter significantly circumstances that have led to the oppression of Black women," McDowell lamented. More concretely, McDowell was troubled by Smith's reading of *Sula* as a lesbian text, writing that Smith's "definition of lesbianism is vague and imprecise," and that she had "simultaneously oversimplified and obscured the issue of lesbianism." For McDowell, "Black feminist critics who write from a lesbian perspective" faced the task of defining "lesbianism and lesbian literature precisely," and she warned that "until they can offer a definition which is not vacuous, their attempts to distinguish Black lesbian writers from those who are not will be hindered."[13] McDowell's disagreement with Smith was expressed through the concerns of canon formation as a form of literary taxonomy: What was or was not "Black feminist literature," or "lesbian literature," or "Black lesbian literature," had to be drawn as precisely as possible to demonstrate methodological rigor. This tendency assumed the existence of a discrete tradition of Black women's literary production, and concerned itself with the unearthing of a distinct *language* of Black women's writing. In other words, this critical practice experienced indeterminacy as a problem to be solved. The figure of the Black lesbian was a particularity that could not be generalized, and the potential of a Black lesbian writing had to be quarantined.

Later, Hazel Carby began her *Reconstructing Womanhood* with a discussion of the Black feminist criticism of the previous decade. For Carby, both Smith and McDowell represented approaches to Black feminist criticism reducible "to an experiential relationship that exists between black women as critics and black women as writers who represent black women's reality." She added, "Theoretically this reliance on a common, or shared, experience is essentialist and ahistorical."[14] In part, Carby's critique was informed by a tradition of Black British cultural studies grounded in historical materialism, but she also anticipated what became common critiques of essence in feminist cultural studies and the historicism that became the dominant mode of literary critical practice in the wake of Theory.[15] In the context of her larger interventions, Carby was producing an intellectual history of Black feminist thought that bracketed the work of the previous decade as theoretically unsophisticated (essentialist and ahistorical), as a necessary false start before Black feminist theory could be rearticulated through the methods of cultural studies.[16] Again, the irruptive possibility of a Black feminist criticism as one expression of a Black lesbian writing—a Black writing that avowed the queerness internal to Blackness—had to be contained for Black feminism to enter academic discourse as a coherent, bounded and bound, enterprise.

But, like *Sula* itself, these different beginnings of Black feminism are rich in contradictory possibilities. This book has engaged with Black feminist theorizing "in a field of static," but *Sula* offers another figure, of Black feminism articulated through the ambivalent possibility of a burning house. Morrison's story offers variations on burning: Plum burning in his bed; Hannah burning, spinning across the lawn; and Sula returning and burning through the marriages of the Bottom. Sula insists to her mother that whatever is burning in her is her own, and that she would "split this town in two and everything in it before" she let anyone put it out.[17] She finally warns her mother, "Maybe I'll just tip on up here with some kerosene and—who knows—you may make the brightest flame of them all."[18] Sula offers herself as an embodied critique of reproductive futurity, as the nightmare of the politics of respectability.

Sula shook the community of Black women readers, and became one of the first texts by a Black woman author to ground an analysis by Hortense Spillers. In "A Hateful Passion, a Lost Love," Spillers placed Morrison's novel and the singular figure of Sula Peace in conversation with the protagonists of Margaret Walker's *Jubilee* and Zora Neale Hurston's *Their Eyes Were Watching God*. "Toni Morrison's *Sula* is a rebel idea," she writes, and "for all its brevity and quiet intrusion on the landscape of American fiction, [it] is, to my mind, the single most important irruption of black women's writing in our era." In contrast to the literary figures of Black femininity that preceded her, Sula brings "to light dark impulses no longer contraband in the black American female's cultural address," and "the novel inscribes a new dimension of being, moving at last in contradistinction to the tide of virtue and pathos which tends to overwhelm black female characterization in a monolith of terms and possibilities." In abeyance of a narrow repertoire of moral fiber and quiet suffering, Sula presented an alternative model of Black feminine expression and invention. Spillers writes, "I regard Sula the character as a literal and figurative *breakthrough* toward the assertion of what we may call . . . new female being."[19]

Spillers never admits the figure of the lesbian into her analysis of *Sula*, the novel, or Sula, the character, and Barbara Smith appears only in a passing reference to the recent anthology, *But Some of Us Are Brave*. Nonetheless, Spillers's commentary may offer as thorough an elaboration of "Black lesbian writing" as was ever attempted. Her text teems with elements of such an elaboration, but it may be condensed, incompletely, as follows: Spillers writes that Sula "lives for Sula and has no wish to 'mother' anyone, let alone the black race in some symbolic concession to a collective need"; that "compared with past heroines of black American fiction, Sula exists foremost in her own consciousness"; that "through Sula's unalterable 'badness,' black and female are now made to appear as a *single* subject in its own right, fully aware of a plenitude of predicative possibilities, for good and ill"; that "in careful, exquisite terms Sula has been endowed with dimensions of other possibility"; that "Morrison imagines a character whose destiny is not coterminous with naturalistic or mystical boundaries"; that "Sula emerges as an embodiment of a metaphysical chaos in pursuit of an activity both proper and sufficient to herself"; that "whatever Sula has become, whatever she is, is a matter of her own choices, often ill-formed and ill-informed"; and that "we are prepared to accept her negative, naysaying freedom as a necessary declaration of independence by the black female writer in her pursuit of a vocabulary of gesture—both verbal and motor—that leads us as well as the author away from the limited repertoire of powerless virtue and sentimental pathos."[20] Finally, for Spillers, "even though she is a character in a novel, her strategic place as *potential being* might argue that *subversion* itself—law breaking—is an aspect of liberation that women must confront from its various angles, in its different guises," and "Sula's outlawry may not be the best kind, but that she has the will toward rebellion itself *is* the stunning idea. This project in liberation, paradoxically, has no particular dimension in time, yet it is for all time."[21] Across these fragmented expressions of a timeless, unbound subjectivity, of an outlaw existence, Spillers articulates without articulating the Black lesbian writing that Barbara Smith began to express in "Toward a Black Feminist Criticism," and that became the hard kernel of contradiction in the Black feminist criticism that followed. From this missed encounter with itself, we might imagine Black feminist theorizing as the poiēsis of the very indeterminacy that is the shared and unshareable condition of all living.

In the foreword to *Sula*, Morrison placed the novel in the context of a time and place that offered alternative scripts for a feminist or feminine living: "In 1969, in Queens, snatching liberty seemed compelling. Some of us thrived; some of us died. All of us had a taste."[22] In their different fashions and in their contradictory approaches, Smith and Morrison and Spillers and McDowell and Carby articulate Black feminisms that reckon with the disparate ends of the desire to snatch liberty. In this way, Black feminist theorizing may be a way of reckoning with those ambivalent desires, for freedom and unfreedom, for living and dying, that characterize our misery and our ordinary unhappiness. We might find that Black feminist theorizing, in its heteroglot and heterogenous richness, offers different relationships to the promiscuous possibility and uncertain ends of a burning house. And that, in our missed encounters with Black feminism, we might "not only know better how to live, but how to dream."[23]

OTHER BEGINNINGS

We have a right to burn what we cultivate.

—C. L. R. JAMES, *THE BLACK JACOBINS*, 361

In the weeks before the 2024 US presidential election, the online literary magazine *n+1* published an essay by Saidiya Hartman that, at once, articulated the cul de sac faced by progressive politics in the wake of fifty years of neoliberal structural adjustments, and reckoned with the complicities of Black women across the professional managerial class and the elite strata of political, economic, and academic institutions. The essay, "Crow Jane Makes a Modest Proposal: A Solution to the Problem of Race Relations," is an unsparing provocation for a moment when a Black woman was a candidate for the highest office in the land, and at a moment when Black women held, tenuously (sometimes unsuccessfully), the presidencies of elite universities by articulating Black feminist positions against unionization drives and student protests against apartheid and genocide.

Without pursuing an extended reading of Hartman's essay, which should come to be regarded as one of her major statements, I want to explore briefly some of the ways it challenges and exemplifies the Black feminist theorizing that has been central to this project. What does it mean, fifty years after the Combahee River Collective formed in Boston, Massachusetts, for a small number of Black women to hold positions of nominal power at corporations that exploit workers, wreck the environment, and profit from death? What do we make of the tendency to celebrate as progress the presence of Black women at the top of an org chart at institutions of tertiary education that, otherwise, remain committed to reproducing and intensifying social inequality? And how do we square the circle of a Black woman's candidacy for the presidency of a settler empire? These questions can be asked in bad faith—as facile, rhetorical questions that individualize and moralize the operations of systems, structures, and institutions that deal in exploitation, dispossession, and death, no matter the social identities of the participants.[24]

In "Crow Jane," Hartman pursues another kind of judgment, a critique informed by and expressed through a Black feminist anarchism. With its "modest proposal," Hartman's essay invokes the modern history of satire, but the appellation *Crow Jane* is so unabashed and freighted with meaning, the piece is so laden with references, its rhythm is so bludgeoning, that it breaks through the generic conventions of satire.[25] In the piece,

Hartman uses the formal conventions of the litany, the rhetorical form that uses repetition in ways that resemble a prayer or supplication. In this way, "Crow Jane" echoes other moments in Hartman's recent work, including her closing remarks at the *Scenes* at 20 Conference held at Rutgers University in October of 2017, and her essay on *Antigone*, "Litany for Grieving Sisters."[26] In those texts, or performances of texts, Hartman used the form of the litany to explore gratitude and tragedy, to catalog her appreciation for the care of her students, readers, colleagues, and co-conspirators, and to name the routinized forms of violence that link Sophocles's Athens to the American present. "Crow Jane," on the other hand, is an incendiary indictment of an antiblackness, a will to empire, and a desire to inhabit Humanity as a genre of being that is internal to the very traditions of Black feminism that inform Hartman's project.

"Crow Jane" catalogs the debasement, the mendacious sincerity, the smiling nihilism, the hope against hope of the Talented Tenth who've breached the One Percent. Hartman begins, "Crow Jane doesn't say *the sun's gonna shine in her back door someday* or lament motherless children or keen for those murdered in the streets, but she does assure us that a better day is coming, that the arc of empire bends toward justice."[27] The piece caricatures the noxious positivity necessary for living in the dead end of racial capitalism, in the financialized afterlife of the real economy. It represents the speech of those joyful warriors who discipline the voting public's meager demands for change, who offer "there is no alternative" as a celebration of an always unfolding catastrophe. Hartman writes,

> Crow Jane's lecture is a composition deracinated from the field and choked with the language of the covenant. It is reasoned, measured, never strident, to ensure its reception by those who are not inclined to heed any truths dropped from *sooty* lips, who prefer to talk about the weather as we are dying, who espouse civility as the tanks roll into the city, who demand the exchange of ideas without antagonism or unrest, those for whom conquest is encounter and slavery a training school for Negroes, those who are accustomed to dictating the terms of address, those who possess the power to deaccession your ass in a minute. Yet, in her case, they prove willing to suspend, if only temporarily, the rules of engagement, the visceral disbelief in any worldview but their own, in any standpoint hostile to their *determined chains* of meaning, and cede to the native informant's predictable babble. Fortunately, she has been educated at the most elite schools, so the master's episteme is her own. Like the quiet storm, her modest proposal

> is easy listening, nothing but legible speech without any discordant tones or ugly feelings; it is assimilable, digestible, delectable as good Negroes are wont to be. The *so articulate* delivery extends the reassuring comfort of the familiar, mammy fascism, statecraft in black- and brownface. No hue and cry. No *fuck it*, no *burn it down*, no *program of complete disorder*, no rebellion, no unrepentant destruction. Just this metaphorical aptitude, this figurative capacity or talent for becoming whatever is required, or nobody at all. Just the tender gift of reproductive labor *in service of* the order, the welcome of her beautiful humiliation, the betrayal of her volition, the dulcet tones of submission, the vow to wait, to keep waiting and waiting until oblivion. The propensity to endure until hardly any of us is left standing, just the appeal, father may I, master may I, man may I, which is so much better than any pledge of allegiance.[28]

Through the figure of Crow Jane, Hartman articulates the irreducible incompleteness of Black freedom struggle. Put differently, though it may be *perverse* to hear empire defended in the name of Black feminism, the will toward empire is not a *perversion* of Black feminism. The heterodox heterogeneity of Black feminist thought holds slavery and its emancipation, empire and its abolition, capitalism and its collapse. Black feminism is a contested terrain, a field of static, and it is only as radical as the struggles pursued in its name.[29]

The present project has endeavored to make space for the counterintuitive questions enabled by Black feminist theorizing, to find new answers in old debates. But all of its answers curl back into questions. Every ending holds another beginning. Black feminism cannot guarantee a radical politics. It can, however, enable questions that get to the core of both our present contradictions, and the irreducible impasses of being in common, touching the anarchism internal to Black feminist theorizing and still-unfolding traditions of feminist Black radicalisms. It can, as well, as Hartman has demonstrated across her itinerary, offer new ways to give further expression to *fuck it*, to *burn it down*, to *I will no longer be complicit in genocide*, to *the only thing in the world that's worth the effort of starting*, to *we have a right to burn what we cultivate*.

"Crow Jane," the essay, may be a not-so-distant relative to Jamaica Kincaid's short story "Ovando," her 1989 allegory of the history of colonialism. Kincaid's story unfolds as a century-spanning inventory of an unnamed Native narrator's encounter with and entrance into History.[30] By the end of her encounter with the at once real and allegorical figure of

Frey Nicolas de Ovando, whose name is shared with an early colonial governor of Hispaniola, Kincaid's narrator understands that Ovando "cannot pass judgment on himself" because "he loves himself beyond measure."[31] Ovando, as a figure for the spirit of colonialism, as an expression of the imperial project, "loved himself so that all other selves and all other things became nothing to him."[32] Kincaid's narrator warns that "such a love is a worm asleep in every heart, and must never be awakened; such a love lies like kindling in every heart, and must never be lit."[33] Like Kincaid, Hartman wards against the moralism that launders complicity, that insists on an impossible innocence in the face of the crimes of history. The history issuing forth from the Door of No Return only offers the burning house of racial capitalism, and no heart is free from those desires that destroy life. Ovando cannot pass judgment on himself, but neither can Kincaid's narrator, the figure of the colonized: "A true and just sentence would be imbued with love for Ovando. The sentence must bear within it sympathy and identification, for only if the judge resides in Ovando and Ovando resides in the judge can an everlasting judgment be passed."[34] Hartman resides in Crow Jane and Crow Jane resides in Hartman. Crow Jane, after all, is but one of many names.[35] Both Hartman and her Crow Jane are daughters of the desires called Black feminism. The exquisite rage of "Crow Jane" gestures precisely toward the love, the sympathy and identification, that make it possible to imagine other ways of being, of being in common, caught in a burning house.

From this relation between love and rage, Hartman's late colleague at Berkeley, June Jordan, once offered, "We are not all that is possible. None of us has ever really experienced justice. None of us has known enough tenderness."[36] The desire for justice can only be impatient, because justice is always too late, because justice has never yet arrived. But the love which might become justice, the tenderness waiting on the other side of justice, is an impossible patience and an exorbitant grace. And all of these endings are other beginnings.

Acknowledgments

The path this project took was much longer than I intended, full of false starts, interruptions, and digressions. I'm grateful for that path now, because I could not have written this book in this way without all the years, failures, joys, frustrations, and surprises. The book has benefited from many forms of community over the course of its development—from Irvine to Chicago, back to Irvine, and then to Ontario and New Orleans.

In my first stay at Irvine, the mentorship of Karen Kim and Jared Sexton changed the direction of my life. I also met friends and interlocutors who helped shape my engagement with Black studies and feminist theory, among them: Rachal Burton, Ryan Sinclaire Davis, Jerome Dent, Emmeline Domingo, Asia Hodges, Angela Kyomugisa, Jessica Lee, Millie Lein, Theresa Miller, Krithika Santhanam, Noelle Sepina, Indar Smith, Selamawit Terrefe (1970–2024), Samiyyah Tillman, and Jaye Austin Williams. Karen and Jared also led me to a major in African American studies that put me in classrooms with Tiffany Willoughby-Herard and Frank B. Wilderson III, who showed me the possibilities of rigorous, engaged, and ethical teaching and scholarship.

In Chicago, Adrienne Brown gave me space to "make the theory my object" and helped me to develop what would become the first versions of the chapters included here. Chicago was a time of being wildly broke, broken-toothed, and insomniac, but I made a dearest, lifelong friend in Annise Moy and met fellow travelers like Huey Copeland, Brittnay Proctor-Habill, Sam Tenorio, Cecilio Cooper, and Mai'a Williams. It was also in Chicago that I began a correspondence with Jennifer Nash, who, along with Samantha Pinto, has offered unfailing support and encouragement through all the stages of this project.

When I returned to Irvine, Jared Sexton, Sora Han, and Rei Terada shaped this work through their engagement, encouragement, and example. Over those years in Irvine, I enjoyed the intellectual community and friendship of R. M. Aranda, A. J. Baginski, Laycee Barragato-Gibson, Cristina Benitez (1989–2017), Sonia Desai, Letty Garcia, Garrett Bridger Gilmore, Williston Chase, Patrice Douglass, Katy Escobar, Shasta Gilmore, Katrina Goudey, Beth Kopacz, Meredith Lee, Shadee Malaklou, Taija Mars McDougall, Julian Nykolak, Judy Rodriguez, sabine stxrm, Robert Wood, and Annie Yaniga. At Irvine, these chapters were strengthened by the engagement of two writing groups; the first consisted of Diana Leong, Sara-Maria Sorentino, Christopher Chamberlin, Minky Malone, and Linette Park, and the second consisted of Morgan Slade, Amanda Peterson, Justin Strong, and Ernest Chavez. Those groups included some of the best writers and most formidable thinkers at Irvine, and also dear friends.

After my time at Irvine ended, I lived for a year in a spare room at the home of my grandmother, Shirley Apostolides (1939–2025). I shared in caring for my grandmother with my brother, Joshua (1981–2024), who helped me protect time for the hard work of deconstructing and reconstructing these chapters, planning revisions, and finding gigs to make ends meet. In 2022, I became a visiting assistant professor in the Department of Communication at Tulane University, a rare outpost of cultural studies teaching and scholarship. The faculty at Tulane fought to keep my contract renewed and found teaching for me when I needed it most. At Tulane, I also got to work with students like Caleb, Lucy, Bre, Joe, Karrington, and Gabe, who truly made the work worthwhile. My time in New Orleans was also shaped in the best ways by friends like Victoria Le and Emily Miller. In the final months of completing the manuscript, when my employment was up in the air (again), I was happy to participate in a writing group convened by Sarah Jane Cervanek and Camille DuBose that helped me across the finish line.

Near the end of my time in Irvine, I began working with Elizabeth Ault at Duke University Press. Along with Ben Kossak, Elizabeth patiently and persistently guided me through the publication process. Two anonymous reviewers offered the gift of serious and rigorous engagement, and the present work is stronger for it.

Over the years of writing this book, Cristina Visperas and Sarah Richter have been dear partners in thought and ideal readers. Jet Vanderlee reminds me to breathe, to relax my jaw, to lower my shoulders, and to open my heart. Adrian Trujillo Centeno, my oldest friend, reminds me what really matters. I'm grateful to my mother, Brenda, and my stepfather,

Robert; my father, Ronald; my sister, Jessie; and the Wylers, Nielsens, and Davises, who are always there to welcome me home, wherever that happens to be. Lorna Krabill is singularly dear, brilliant, open, and kind; the music of her words is my favorite song; and I'm glad to have finished this book in the home we share, in the world we make together.

Notes

INTRODUCTION

1 Spillers et al., "Whatcha Gonna Do?," 301.

2 Without *fixing* the meaning of Black feminist theorizing, we might say that it names one activity of Black feminism, it is one expression of Black feminism, it is the breath or the pulse or the energy of Black feminism. Insofar as the terms are mutually co-constitutive, there is some overlap in how I deploy them throughout the book.

3 Douglass, *Engendering Blackness*, 2.

4 It may be that scholarship has taken on an outsized role in the production and dissemination of radical discourses because the academy is one of vanishingly few sites in the contemporary United States where creative and scholarly writing are even minimally subsidized. The consolidation of the creative industries by monopoly capitalism and the open ideological warfare against the remnants of the academic humanities are two sides of an attack on our capacity to collectively articulate alternative visions for our shared existence.

5 Spillers, "Afterword," 249.

6 Spillers, "Afterword," 250.

7 Spillers, *Black, White, and in Color*, xvi.

8 Spillers, *Black, White, and in Color*, 13.

9 Spillers et al., "Whatcha Gonna Do?," 301.

10 Spillers, *Black, White, and in Color*, 12–13.

11 From Davis's introductory remarks at Spillers's lecture "To the Bone: Some Speculations on the Problem of Touch," given at Northwestern University, Evanston, IL, 15 November 2018.

12 On writing as a practice of thinking, see Chandler, "Figure of W. E. B. Du Bois."

13 In "Theory as a Body of Work," the longtime editor William Germano discusses the difficult journey from essay to book that remains a feature of the academic career path.

14 In a recent Festschrift honoring Spillers, Nicole Spigner writes that "Spillers's essays are literary not only because essays *are* literary production, but because of her dedication to and use of poetics in her writing. Her academic work is criticism, theory, and literature, simultaneously" ("All the Things," 192n1).

15 Spillers, *Black, White, and in Color*, 13.

16 Spillers, *Black, White, and in Color*, 153.

17 In "The 'Beached Whale,'" Sharon Holland raises some of these questions in relation to the methodological space between gender studies and sexuality studies.

18 On the place of the Spillersian lexicon in feminist theory, see Pinto, "Black Feminist Literacies."

19 Nash, "Strange Bedfellows," 58.

20 This is true even for the writing that predates her engagements with poststructuralism, as well as her book reviews and, indeed, her short fiction.

21 J. Hillis Miller is instructive here. Remarking on the state of literary study at the turn of the millennium, Miller offered a set of aphorisms that ended with the following: "Though a given critical theory or methodology is universalizable, able to be appropriated by others, institutionalized, or translated, what is most valuable in a given critic or scholar is a distinctive tone or note that is unique to him or her and cannot be successfully imitated. This means other critics should be read as literature, with the same care, the same attention to detail. Any critic not worth such careful reading is not worth reading" ("Literary Study," 66). The present project is, in part, an experiment in reading Black feminist theorizing *as literature*.

22 As one aspect of Black feminist theorizing, "static" is a kind of "strategic device, opening onto its own abyss," and Black feminist theorizing is "an unclosed, unenclosable, not wholly formalizable ensemble of rules for reading, interpretation, and writing" (Derrida, "Time of a Thesis," 40).

23 Wilderson, "Gramsci's Black Marx," 231.

24 González, "Indigenous Acts," 133.

25 Wagner, *Disturbing the Peace*, 1.

26 Wagner, *Disturbing the Peace*, 2.

27 In *Critique of Black Reason*, Achille Mbembe offers an expansive overview of the cultural, intellectual, and geopolitical histories of slavery in relation to what he calls the "becoming black of the world."

28 As I understand it, this has been one throughline of Fred Moten's itinerary across his poetry, criticism, and his thinking-in-common with Stefano Harney.

29 Wilderson, "Gramsci's Black Marx," 232.

30 These readings of Blackness as deathliness build from the work of David Marriott, especially his *Haunted Life*.

31 Spillers, "Quarrels into Ploughshares," 236.

32 In Alderfer et al., *Diary of a Conference*, 42.

33 Rapaport, *Theory Mess*, 2.

34 Rapaport, *Theory Mess*, 3–4.

35 DuCille, "Occult of True Black Womanhood," 603, quoted in Rapaport, *Theory Mess*, 2.
36 Rapaport, *Theory Mess*, 2; emphasis added.
37 See Alexander-Floyd, "Disappearing Acts."
38 DuCille, "Short Happy Life," 33.
39 Griffin, "That the Mothers May Soar," 484.
40 See McKay, "Naming the Problem," and Painter, "Black Studies, Black Professors."
41 Boyce Davies, *Black Women, Writing and Identity*, 55.
42 McDowell, *Changing Same*, 157–58.
43 Exemplary readings here include Abel, "Black Writing, White Reading," and duCille, "Occult of True Black Womanhood."
44 Vance, *Pleasure and Danger*, xiv.
45 "Contributors," *boundary 2* 23, no. 3 (1996): 258.
46 "Contributors," *boundary 2* 20, no. 2 (2003): 222. "The Idea of Black Culture" remains one of the works Spillers intends to publish.
47 Christian, "Race for Theory," 53.
48 Christian, "Race for Theory," 52.
49 An earlier version of the present project included a chapter on the moment that produced "The Race for Theory." That chapter grew into its own manuscript project, "A Race, for Theory: Critical Theory, Black Studies, and the Beginnings of Black Feminism."
50 Christian, "Race for Theory," 53.
51 Spillers et al., "Whatcha Gonna Do?," 308.
52 For an extended theorization of the ways race operates on the surfaces of the body, see Visperas, *Skin Theory*.
53 Sexton, *Amalgamation Schemes*, 9.
54 Sexton, "Curtain of the Sky," 16.
55 Spillers, *Black, White, and in Color*, 179.
56 Spillers, *Black, White, and in Color*, 179. The opening epigraph of Frank Wilderson's doctoral dissertation attributes to Spillers the following: "Every generation of African Americans must rediscover the institution of slavery for themselves. It's never finished." The epigraph echoes arguments Spillers makes in her paper for the English Institute, as well as her long-standing interest in the matter of the generational in the African diaspora. The line Wilderson attributes to Spillers indicates another kind of species division in modernity—between those subjects for whom slavery is a primal scene that must always be rediscovered, and those subjects for whom slavery is a primal scene that must always be repressed and that returns in the form of different psychic and social symptoms.
57 Spillers, *Black, White, and in Color*, 17, 215.
58 Žižek, *In Defense of Lost Causes*, 17.
59 Wilderson, *Red, White and Black*, 58.

60 Combahee River Collective, "Black Feminist Statement," 276.

61 Toni Cade Bambara opens *The Salt Eaters* with this problematic, as her Minnie Ransom asks, "Are you sure, sweetheart, that you want to be well?" (3). As the opening chapter unfolds and the theme is formulated and reformulated, Ransom warns, "Wholeness is no trifling matter. A lot of weight when you're well" (10). Put differently, the problem of freedom and our necessarily mixed feelings and conflicting desires should not be reduced to bad politics and false consciousness.

62 Kaplan, *Black Reproductive*, 3.

63 Kaplan, *Black Reproductive*, 25.

64 Elsewhere, I treat the question of theorizing freedom and unfreedom in relation to the anarchist tradition and contemporary abolition feminisms. See Bliss, "To Strive and Fail."

65 Spillers, *Black, White, and in Color*, 20.

66 Spillers, *Black, White, and in Color*, 20. In chapter 4, especially, I trace the obscurity of Black unfreedom across the itinerary of Saidiya Hartman, as well as in the symptomatic appearances of figures of Blackness, in their relation to the figure of the slave, within the transnational and diasporic turns in feminist and queer cultural studies.

67 Here, my method works at an angle to Clare Hemmings's *Why Stories Matter*, and her practice of citation that emphasized the ways ideas circulated across feminist discourses and minimized the individual author. Engaging with ideas as though they belong under a single and singular signature can lead to intellectual scapegoating, to the negative construction of some thinkers as racist, heterosexist, and retrograde. My own process relies on an intimacy with the "voice" of the writer.

68 Elizabeth Bruss's posthumous *Beautiful Theories: The Spectacle of Discourse in Contemporary Criticism* remains a remarkable analysis of this shift in the life of criticism. I consider Bruss's work in relation to contemporary Black feminist and queer studies in Bliss, "Defense, Redemption, Care."

69 In *Object Lessons*, Robyn Wiegman explores in a nonjudgmental way the tactics by which cultural studies scholarship (or those corners of cultural studies Wiegman calls "identity knowledges") has attempted to express radical political commitments in the form and content of scholarly prose. The "daunting hope," as Wiegman calls it, is that "if only we find the right discourse, object of study, or analytic tool, our critical practice will be adequate to the political commitments that inspire it" (3). Over the last several years, the political commitments rendered through cultural studies scholarship have expanded from the traditional range (from radical to left-liberal) to include politics that are alternatively precious and exhausted, bedraggled and optimistic. These texts have tended to aim for various otherwise experiences of a world beyond repair or redemption. After decades of this kind of work, decades that have coincided with a general de-democratization and the

emergence of new fascisms in the United States, it may be time to reevaluate the efficacy of critical cultural studies as a genre of political intervention. We might, like Wiegman, allow ourselves to be interested in the desires given shape by these discourses and by these forms of academic practice.

70 See Jameson, "On 'Cultural Studies.'"

71 Morrison, *Beloved*, 3.

72 Clifton, *Good News About the Earth*, 1.

73 Alice Walker, letter to the editor, *New York Times Book Review*, 20 January 1974, 27.

74 Nash, "Writing Black Beauty," 103; emphasis added. This line of thought is expanded in Nash's *How We Write Now*. The question of loss will be taken up again in chapter 4.

75 King, "Post-Identitarian and Post-Intersectional Anxiety," 116. King's distinction between "anxious" reading and "loving" reading recalls the stakes of a queer feminist criticism that pitted "paranoid" reading against "reparative" reading. Eve Kosofsky Sedgwick is the key figure here, though the most useful reading of the *distinction itself* might be found in Tim Dean and Robyn Wiegman's "What Does Critique Want?"

76 To be sure, if I were less opaque to myself, I might write a book that *reads* my own anxieties—rather than a book that *catalogs* them.

77 Freud, *Standard Edition*, 16:403–4. Freud, of course, revised this position at different moments in his thought.

78 See Lacan, *Four Fundamental Concepts*, 41.

79 I borrow *socionom* from Spillers, who has built the concept out across several of the essays collected in *Black, White, and in Color*.

80 Fanon, *Black Skin, White Masks*, 117.

81 Judy, "Fanon's Body," 79.

82 Judy, "Fanon's Body," 54.

83 In "The Psychopharmacology of Everyday Life," Jamieson Webster puts it this way: "The problem here, or maybe even the solution, is that we anxious people do know the truth: we are all going to die alone, others do what they like, something in sexuality inevitably fails, who even knows what anyone is thinking, I don't know what I want, I don't know how to give you what you want, and I certainly don't know what is going to happen, between us, or at all. Anxiety is always the signal of a truth that is calling you."

CHAPTER ONE. OPEN LETTERS, AND THE IRRELATIONAL EROTICS OF A BLACK FEMINIST NEGATIVITY

1 Lorde, *I Am Your Sister*, 83.

2 Hemmings, *Why Stories Matter*, 48.

3 Gumbs, "Speculative Poetics," 132. With her recent biography of Lorde, *Survival Is a Promise*, Gumbs, at once, documents the various forms of Lorde's

survival into the present and cultivates a creative practice from the archives of Lorde's life and work.

4 Halberstam, *Queer Art of Failure*, 6.

5 Around this time, I remember going on a first (and only) date with a librarian in Chicago. We were talking about our work over lunch, and when I mentioned working in histories of Black feminist theorizing, she asked, with genuine concern, if I was afraid of Black women "getting mad" at me for doing that work. From what I could tell, she was not a terminally online person. It was common sense that Black women were both territorial and threatening, beyond rationality.

6 A year later, he tweeted a long list of new "confessions," which led to the termination of his employment and a prolonged retreat from public life. His erstwhile contemporaries, who may or may not have been behind the *Feminist X* experiment a year before, responded with a concern that inspired the Black feminist author Mikki Kendall to coin the hashtag #solidarityisforwhitewomen.

7 "Professional feminism" describes a particular commercialization and professionalization of feminism by primarily young, elite-educated, white women, (less than) tacitly premised upon the exclusion of women-of-color feminists. Professional feminism was not the high theory of research universities, but an attempt to mainstream and monetize feminist movement. The teleology of the professional feminist's career involved a journey from online journalism, publication in feminist presses, and adoption onto the syllabi of women's studies courses at teaching and liberal arts colleges, to the promised land of the paid lecture circuit, advisory boards of nonprofit organizations, feminist marketing and public relations consulting firms, and appearances paneling on MSNBC.

8 The statement also highlights the limits of working through collective political or conceptual problems on social media platforms—platforms that are "social" yet privately owned (and effectively private, even when they're publicly traded) and that promise to be tools for free and open communication but are designed for trolls and provocateurs.

9 This is not to argue that the "true" Lorde is singularly antirelational in her political and theoretical orientation. Rather, it is to argue that there does exist an antirelational Lorde among the many Audre Lordes. The value of *this* Lorde lies in how apparently counterintuitive she appears against her monolithic representation as an embodiment of relationality, solidarity across difference, and desire for multiracial coalition.

10 Telling, "Quite Contrary," 34–35.

11 De Veaux, *Warrior Poet*, 236.

12 Daly, *Gyn/Ecology* (1990), xxx.

13 De Veaux, *Warrior Poet*, 246. The conference was the occasion for Lorde's most famous and most scathing public indictment of white women's racism, "The Master's Tools Will Never Dismantle the Master's House," an immanent

critique of the conference, its organizers, and its participants. And, perhaps more than any other speech by Lorde, a source for her reputation among white feminists as angry, guilt-provoking, disrupting, and divisive (248–51).

14 Daly, *Gyn/Ecology* (1990), xxx. These passages were republished with slight changes in her 1992 intellectual autobiography, *Outercourse: The Be-Dazzling Voyage.*

15 De Veaux, *Warrior Poet*, 248.

16 Quoted in Bulkin, "Racism and Writing," 10.

17 Quoted in Bulkin, "Racism and Writing," 10–11.

18 In the "New Intergalactic Introduction" written for the 1990 republication of *Gyn/Ecology*, Daly offered an account of the beginnings of *Gyn/Ecology* within the business of the university. Following the publication of her second book, *Beyond God the Father*, in 1973, Daly applied for promotion to full professor in the fall of 1974. Five years earlier, she had been denied tenure and placed on a definite contract, a move meant to end her career at Boston College. After backlash from students and attention from the national press, the college backtracked and granted Daly a tenured post as associate professor. At the beginning of 1975, Boston College denied her promotion to full professor. This time, the outpouring of support from students and the larger community of feminists did not reverse the college's decision. She would remain an associate professor until she was, in her description, forced into retirement. But Daly describes the denied promotion at the beginning of 1975 as a moment that "unleashed my powers and hurled me further on my Intergalactic Voyage" (*Gyn/Ecology* [1990], xiv). Because her previous work "had been superscholarly and yet had been called 'unscholarly' by the cynical and deceptive fathers of reversal, I was now liberated into the possibility of qualitatively Other Daring Deeds" (xv).

19 Daly, *Gyn/Ecology* (1990), 59.

20 De Veaux, *Warrior Poet*, 233.

21 By 1988, Daly's project would be reduced to a retrograde "cultural feminism" by Linda Martín Alcoff ("Cultural Feminism Versus Post-Structuralism"). For an extended discussion of this cultural and intellectual context, see Katherine, "Too Early Morning," and Monagle, "Mary Daly's *Gyn/Ecology*."

22 See Hemmings, *Why Stories Matter*.

23 In the lesbian-feminist print culture of 1979, Daly was beyond reproach. In a critical essay that appeared in *Sinister Wisdom* in 1980, Elly Bulkin described the critical consensus as crazy-making. "Only my discussions with other lesbian-feminists . . . prevent me from discounting my own perceptions—my own decision *not* to 'gynuflect'—as some sort of craziness" ("Racism and Writing," 11).

24 Lorde, "Open Letter" (*Top Ranking*), 89.

25 Lorde, "Sister, Morning Is a Time for Miracles," in *Collected Poems of Audre Lorde*, 347.

26 Lorde, "Open Letter" (*Top Ranking*), 90.

27 Lorde, "Open Letter" (*Top Ranking*), 90.

28 Lorde, "Open Letter" (*Top Ranking*), 88, 92.

29 Lorde, "Open Letter" (*Sister Outsider*), 66.

30 Levitt, "Letter to Mary Daly," 110.

31 Levitt, "Letter to Mary Daly," 111.

32 At least some of the women close to Daly saw a wounded, vulnerable person in the face of criticism. In a letter to Lorde, Adrienne Rich said of Daly: "I know Mary's rigidities, her self-protections, her tendency to see all criticisms as onslaught, as pure attack (so that she could not really read your letter as written). But also I know that . . . nothing comes easy for Mary nor does she make anything easy; 'false transcendence' was her phrase and she is repulsed by glib 'feelings'" (quoted in De Veaux, *Warrior Poet*, 248).

33 Katherine, "Too Early Morning," 267.

34 Katherine, "Too Early Morning," 294.

35 For Katherine, "the letter calls, not for the end of radical feminism, but for an antiracist, antiethnocentric radical feminism, for a radical *white European American* feminism. This sort of politic is not born out of a particular theoretical framework, it is achieved through interaction fueled by a desire to make connections under complex systems of oppression, the desire to show you hear" ("Too Early Morning," 294).

36 Daly, "New Intergalactic Introduction," xxix–xxx.

37 Daly, "New Intergalactic Introduction," xxx.

38 Daly, "New Intergalactic Introduction," xxxi.

39 Daly, "New Intergalactic Introduction," xxxi.

40 Bersani, "Sociality and Sexuality," 656.

41 Daly, "New Intergalactic Introduction," xxxi.

42 Daly, *Outercourse*, 233n.

43 Ironically, as Clare Monagle observes, Lorde herself was no less invested in a feminist mysticism than Daly. In Monagle's words, "Lorde desired a mystical feminism and was not wary that it be universalizing, as long as it was capaciously so" ("Mary Daly's *Gyn/Ecology* ," 343–44).

44 Amber Katherine's essay takes into account Daly and Lorde's meeting, less so the content of her remarks in the republication of *Gyn/Ecology* and *Outercourse*, and makes a distinction between a response and a response "in kind." "While this is a reply to Lorde," she writes, "it is not a reply in kind, since it was not part of an open, community dialogue" (296n18). The challenge with Katherine's assessment of the private meeting at the conference is that at the time it happened, Lorde's letter was also, effectively, a private matter.

45 Lorde, *Cancer Journals*, 12.

46 Lorde et al., "Lit from Within," 3.

47 Lorde et al., "Lit from Within," 3.

48 On "Signifyin(g)," see Jablon, *Black Metafiction*, and Judy, "Irony and the Asymptotes."

49 One might also mention Hortense Spillers's articulation of "reading" as a critical practice, what she describes as an interest in "*reading* as a method, period." A practice that constitutes "a repertory of attitudes committed to the discursive and the semiotic analysis" (*Black, White, and in Color*, 6). This critical practice is also an affective practice or disposition toward language as a site of meaning-making and also a site laden with power relations. On this score, see also Akasha Hull's reading of Toni Cade Bambara's *The Salt Eaters*, "What It Is I Think She's Doing Anyhow."

50 Spillers, *Black, White, and in Color*, 156.

51 De Veaux, *Warrior Poet*, 251.

52 In the period between *The Black Unicorn* in 1978 and *Our Dead Behind Us* in 1986, Lorde describes struggling with poetry. Much time and energy went into her recovery from breast cancer, her teaching load at John Jay College and then Hunter College, and the travel connected to presentations at conferences, lectures, and poetry readings. Additionally, she gave much time over to the writing of her biomythography, *Zami: A New Spelling of My Name*, published in 1983, and the work collected in *Sister Outsider* in 1984.

53 Lorde, *Collected Poems*, 347.

54 Lorde, *Collected Poems*, 347.

55 Quoted in De Veaux, *Warrior Poet*, 248.

56 Lorde, *Collected Poems*, 347.

57 De Veaux, *Warrior Poet*, 252–53.

58 Lorde, *Collected Poems*, 347.

59 Brooks, *Report from Part One*, 68.

60 On the specifically political aspects of relationality, I am indebted to my conversations with Kevin Rigby Jr.

61 Lorde, *Collected Poems*, 347.

62 Lorde, *Cancer Journals*, 12.

63 Aimé Césaire, quoted in Fanon, *Black Skin, White Masks*, 71.

64 Lorde, *Cancer Journals*, 12.

65 For Lorde, this is not at all a quietism, it is not resignation. In the next line she writes, "I can never accept this," before linking back to the scale of the personal, "like I can't accept that turning my life around is so hard, eating differently, sleeping differently, moving differently, being differently" (*Cancer Journals*, 13). In Lorde's thought, this thinking across registers is a form of "integrity," the integration of different scales of experience, the personal and the political, living and dying.

66 Wilderson, *Red, White and Black*, 58.

67 On the reception of afropessimism in the context of Black feminist and queer studies, see Bliss, "Forgetting."

68 Wilderson, *Red, White and Black*, 58–59.

69 In the acknowledgments to both *Red, White and Black* and Wilderson's doctoral dissertation, he thanks Amanda Lashaw, an anthropologist of education

and then a graduate student at UC Berkeley, for offering him the question, "What does it mean to suffer?," which he describes as radically altering the guiding questions of his research. Much of the critique of afropessimism, it seems, argues that afropessimism *limits* Blackness to suffering, when it might be more apt to say that Wilderson is interested in the ways suffering defines *all life* and all living. The matter or the stuff of suffering, then, remains an open question despite the certainty read into Wilderson's prose. (We might also note the resonances between this aspect of afropessimism and certain traditions of Buddhist thought.) In an interview conducted by Denise Ferreira da Silva in 2022, Hortense Spillers, who by then had distanced herself from the project of afropessimism in no uncertain terms, invokes suffering as she distinguishes between Black persons and Black subjects. For Spillers, "a Black Subject reads the world in a certain way, and if that is the case, then you might occupy the position of one who suffers, and I mean by that one who sees; you need not necessarily have had the experience, historically speaking, of Middle Passage in order to come to a certain viewpoint" (Ferreira da Silva, "Sending Language into Battle," 36). In other words, we might note the central importance of suffering as a feature of Blackness while also holding onto the promiscuity and indeterminacy of suffering.

70 Wilderson, *Red, White and Black*, 89.

71 Among others, see Solow, "Capitalism and Slavery"; Sweet, "Iberian Roots"; and Vaziri, "On 'Saidiya.'"

72 Wilderson, "Biko and the Problematic of Presence," 104.

73 Wilderson, "Biko and the Problematic of Presence," 104–5.

74 Wilderson, "Biko and the Problematic of Presence," 105.

75 Wilderson, "Biko and the Problematic of Presence," 112.

76 Indeed, in the interview from *Off Our Backs* during which Lorde claimed to have "talked" with Mary Daly, the interview shifted immediately to the interviewer's own anxieties about race.

77 Lorde, *Sister Outsider*, 125.

78 Lorde, *Sister Outsider*, 127.

79 Palmer, "Otherwise than Blackness," 249.

80 Palmer, "Otherwise than Blackness," 249.

81 Jackson, "Theorizing in a Void," 630.

82 Palmer, "Otherwise than Blackness," 272.

83 One running theme of the present text is that every embrace holds some equivocation, at the very least as the consequence of being beings possessed by the unconscious, and usually much less heroically than being thwarted by the unconscious. In a suggestive response to Calvin Warren's *Ontological Terror*, Jared Sexton challenges certain versions of the prescription to "end the world." "Human life is not *all* life," he offers, "and the world, such as it is, is not the earth. All of *existence* is finite, whether it is living or nonliving, human or nonhuman, but imagining it without Being does not require imagining it

destroyed. It entails imagining it in and as the ruins of Being, after the end of the world, in an entirely other relation to the nothing from whence it comes" (Sexton, "Response"). We might ask in good faith whether the recurrent formulation of the end of the world is a symptom of a more general impasse—theoretical, economic, political, ecological—in which it's hard to imagine the world continuing anyway. The "end of the world" becomes a place-name for that horizon beyond which life, or living, is unimaginable. In bad faith, we might suspect that these formulations of desiring the end of the world are an alibi for quietism, fatalism, accelerationism, and so on—a type of giving up, or a gift to the forces of ecological destruction. It's useful to remember that at least one of our functions as academics is to read and write on behalf of the ownership class, who run our institutions. Rich people will always steal our best ideas and repackage them as evil caricatures of themselves. Whether it's intersectionality or assemblage, which I discuss in the next chapter, there is no idea so radical or so pure that the capitalist class can't repurpose it against us. It is the price of this particular ticket.

84 Karera, "Blackness and the Pitfalls," 47.

85 Karera, "Blackness and the Pitfalls," 48.

86 Patterson, *Slavery and Social Death*, 1.

87 Patterson, *Slavery and Social Death*, 1; emphasis added.

88 Karera's argument in "Blackness and the Pitfalls of Anthropocene Ethics" finds an angular path between some early disagreements between Frank Wilderson and Jared Sexton, working to articulate afropessimism, and Fred Moten, working in a more "optimistic" vein of Black cultural studies. For each of these three theorists, despite their other real differences, there is a certain embrace of the figure of the enslaved. That is, they each refuse to pathologize or demean *being a slave*—even, or especially in the case of Moten, if being or becoming a slave is the risk of relationality.

For Moten, this is one central feature of his disagreements with Orlando Patterson. Patterson's demeaning commentary on American slaves is, like his detestable commentary on Anita Hill after her testimony before the US Senate Judiciary Committee in 1991, a stain on his conceptual apparatus—a conservatism difficult to square against the radical potential of his text. Though absent from *Slavery and Social Death*, Patterson's commentary in a 1974 review of Eugene Genovese's *Roll, Jordan, Roll* haunts his later work. Two moments from Patterson's text merit close engagement. First, Patterson saw in Genovese's study a desire to find resistance among the Black slaves of the antebellum United States that, for Patterson, is sadly absent from the historical record. "The house servants, the drivers, the mechanics, the free Negroes, the mammies, the mulattoes, the black soldiers and the mass of field Negroes who pass through these pages I find, as a class, morally degraded and utterly wanting in their reluctance to resist, even when the system was crumbling around them. They chose devious paths to salve their battered egos, and evolved a limited creed—indulgently pedestrian and immediate in its concerns, lacking in prophetic idealism, a total betrayal of the profound eschatology and heroic ideals of their African ancestors" ("Peculiar Institution Again," 37).

A moment later in the text, Patterson takes his critique a step further. "A people, to deserve the respect of their descendants," he writes, "must do more than merely survive spiritually and physically. *There is no intrinsic virtue in survival, no virtue in the reflexes of a cornered rat*" (38; emphasis added). Patterson's disdain for Black American slaves stands in stark contrast to Moten, Sexton, and Wilderson. It also sits as a rebuke of Patterson's contemporary, Angela Davis, who lionizes the work, borne so often by Black women, of so-called mere survival. In "Reflections on the Black Woman's Role in the Community of Slaves," Davis describes the work of survival as "the prerequisite of all higher forms of resistance" (7). Through all this, we are left with the thorny question, what is wrong with being or embodying what Patterson calls generalized dishonor?

89 Bersani, "Science of Literature," 547.

90 Lorde, *Cancer Journals*, 46.

91 The figure of "sensation without feeling" comes from Lorde in "The Uses of the Erotic." See Lorde, *Sister Outsider*.

92 Lorde, *Cancer Journals*, 46.

93 Lorde, *Cancer Journals*, 48.

94 Lorde, *Cancer Journals*, 49.

95 Though Kant is less present in contemporary cultural studies, the project Terada pursues in *Metaracial: Hegel, Antiblackness, and Political Identity* traces the ways antiblackness shaped the Enlightenment (and, later, Romantic) projects of Kant, Hegel, Rousseau, and Marx—in other words, the source waters of most contemporary Western critical practice. See also Judy, "Kant and the Negro."

96 Terada, "Racial Grammar," 275.

97 Terada, "Scruples," 252.

98 Derrida, "Faith and Knowledge," 64.

99 Terada, "Frailty of the Ontic," 41.

100 In "On the Beginning of the World," Jennifer Nash suggests that some articulations of afropessimism travel a similar path as earlier dominance feminisms in their theorizations of sexuality. Such a tradition of dominance feminism would include obvious figures like Catherine MacKinnon and Andrea Dworkin, but also Mary Daly and certain moments in the work of Audre Lorde.

101 Lorde, *Sister Outsider*, 53.

102 Lorde, *Sister Outsider*, 56.

103 Lorde, *Cancer Journals*, 47.

CHAPTER TWO. BURIED SUBJECTS, AND THE LINES FROM INTERSECTIONALITY TO ABOLITION

1 Here I am nodding to Hortense Spillers's afterword to *Conjuring*, which opens with reference to the "community of black women writing in the United States" as "a vivid new fact of national life." Her formulation of "black women *writing*" signals both "the palpable and continuing urgency of black women writing themselves into history" and "the variety of aims that accompany their project" ("Afterword," 249). The choice of verb over noun anticipates the strategy deployed by Barbara Christian in "The Race for Theory," choosing *theorizing* over *theory*. I follow this strategy in my discussions of "Black feminist theorizing" throughout the present text. Likewise, my use of *tradition* follows Spillers, signifying that traditions "are not, like objects of nature, here to stay, but survive as *created social events* only to the extent that an audience cares to intersect them" (250). My hope with these formulations is to foreground the capaciousness and contingency of a field of inquiry called Black feminist theorizing while signaling also the political and intellectual work of its practitioners.

2 Bambara, *Black Woman*, 4.

3 Morrison, "What the Black Woman Thinks," 27, 29.

4 Lorde, "Role of Difference," 5. Lorde's remarks were later revised and anthologized as "The Master's Tools Will Never Dismantle the Master's House." The importance of this moment in Lorde's work is taken up in chapter 1.

5 Around the late 1990s, the uneasy relation between feminist practice and the institutional life of women's studies became an issue of collective inquiry, in the "Women's Studies on the Edge" special issue of *differences* (Fall 1997) edited by Joan W. Scott, and across multiple essays by Robyn Wiegman, including "Academic Feminism Against Itself" and "Feminism, Institutionalism, and the Idiom of Failure." For a profile on Kendall that provides background on the hashtag as well as her artistic-intellectual-political practice, see Ross, "Mikki Kendall."

6 May, *Pursuing Intersectionality*.

7 Nash, "Feminist Originalism."

8 Rapaport, *Theory Mess*, 18.

9 Spillers, *Black, White, and in Color*, 7.

10 Too often, critiques performing close readings of single texts or authors are dismissed with the suggestion that if one simply reads another author or text, the argument collapses. The impulse to dismiss antiblackness as the limitation of particular authors, rather than as a structuring energy in (at least) Western intellectual practice, as such, is beyond the scope of the present chapter. However, for a reading of the "post-intersectional" moment that engages with the atmosphere or atmospherics of the critique

of intersectionality, see Tiffany Lethabo King's recent work on the contemporary push toward the post-identitarian ("Post-Identitarian and Post-Intersectional Anxiety").

11 Hemmings, *Why Stories Matter*, 44.

12 Wiegman, *Object Lessons*, 240.

13 See Nash, "Re-Thinking Intersectionality," "Un-Disciplining Intersectionality," "On Difficulty," "'Home Truths' on Intersectionality," "Institutionalizing the Margins," and *Black Feminism Reimagined*.

14 Nash, "On Difficulty."

15 DuCille, "Occult of True Black Womanhood," 600.

16 Nash, "Institutionalizing the Margins," 60.

17 Nash, "Institutionalizing the Margins," 46.

18 Nash, "Institutionalizing the Margins," 60–61.

19 Nash, "Institutionalizing the Margins," 61.

20 Puar, "Cyborg," 50.

21 Puar, "Cyborg," 63, 50.

22 Puar, "Cyborg," 63. Puar's engagement with the figure of the assemblage, or with what in Deleuze and Guattari is called *agencement*, makes recourse centrally to *A Thousand Plateaus* and Guattari's "I Am an Idea-Thief," an interview published the same year *A Thousand Plateaus* was published in French. What is striking, at first, about Puar's reading of Deleuze and Guattari is the introduction of a strange certainty with regard to the meaning of their work. In part, Puar follows here the (mostly white, mostly male) Anglo-American community of Deleuzians and Guattarians (and the two in combination), which has produced a robust and occasionally dizzying body of writing out of the network of concept-metaphors at work (at play) in Deleuze and Guattari's collectively authored works. That Puar's engagement with Deleuze and Guattari fits so comfortably with the high theory avant garde's consensus is notable insofar as their work has, in a few short decades, become the stuff of academic consensus-building. That is, Puar follows an Anglo-American tradition of reducing the seemingly irreducible.

Nonetheless, Puar opens the 2012 piece with Brian Massumi's observation in *Parables for the Virtual* that "grids happen." That is, "social and cultural determinations feed back into the process from which they arose" (8). Grids appear to make sense, to produce moments of sense-making, within what Puar calls "the endless affirmative becomings of movement, flux, and potential" ("Cyborg," 49). For Massumi, determination and indeterminacy are "inseparable and always actually coincide while remaining disjunctive in their modes of reality," a premise that, we will see, is considerably more supple and labile than the direction toward which Puar moves (*Parables for the Virtual*, 8). The opening figure of the grid is noteworthy also for its resonance with the art theorist Rosalind Krauss's exploration of grids in modernist art. For Krauss, it is precisely because grids *don't happen* that their ubiquity in modernist visual art requires attention: "Flattened, geometricized, ordered, [the grid] is antinatural, antimimetic, antireal. It is what art looks like when it turns its back on nature. In the flatness that results from its coordinates, the grid is the means of crowding out the dimensions of the real and replacing them with the spread of a single surface. In the overall regularity of its organization, it is the result not of imitation, but of aesthetic decree" ("Grids," 51). But in the symbolic economy of Puar's work, the identitarian feminist goddess is the figure of the grid, while the intersection of *techne* and *bios* at the figure of the cyborg, circuit boards implied if not themselves diagrammed, represents flux and becoming.

This confused alignment is not peculiar to Puar. There is, after all, a "cultural subject . . . concealed beneath the overwhelming debris of the itemized account, [and] between the lines of the massive logs of commercial enterprise" that set in motion what we now call modernity (Spillers, *Black, White, and in Color*, 210). Hortense Spillers offers us more on the figure of the grid in her "Notes on an Alternative Model—Neither/Nor": "The world according to captives and their captors strikes the imagination as a grid of identities running at perpendicular angles to each other: *things* in serial and lateral array; beings in hierarchical and vertical array. On the serial grid, the captive—the chattel property—is the equivalent of inanimate and other living things" (*Black, White, and in Color*, 314). In the ledgers of the slave trade, enslaved people are ordered alongside "other" commodities, barrels of gunpowder, baled cotton, gallons of rum. For Spillers, "those subjects located at this juncture of saturated elements are both more and less than human, the former because they enter into a wider ecumenicalism with named and claimed things, or vocabularies of experience; the latter because it is their destiny by virtue of Christ's church, by whom the country swears, and the spirit of national insurgence and constitutionality to be human first and only" (315). These are the grids that haunt Puar's project, or Massumi's project, or the project of modernist art, or the project of the nation-state from the moment of its historical emergence—more and less than human, propertized human being, the capacity for the production of value.

23 Puar, "Cyborg," 63.

24 Gilmore, *Golden Gulag*, 28.

25 Deleuze, "Postscript," 7. The potential here to read Deleuze as a student of Black Study, and the fact that Puar resists such a reading, says something about Puar's practice of reading and her engagement with Deleuze (and Guattari). Along these lines, one might read Deleuze and Claire Parnet's 1977 essay "Many Politics" as a precursor to Puar's critiques of intersectionality that is notably absent from Puar's several engagements with intersectionality. Writing in the space between the publication of the two volumes of *Capitalism and Schizophrenia*, Deleuze and Parnet open with an observation that would seem to be disallowed according to the protocols of Puar's critique of

Crenshaw: "Whether we are individuals or groups, we are made up of lines and these lines are very varied by nature." Across this brief essay, Deleuze and Parnet detail three types of lines: molar lines "of rigid segmentarity," molecular lines "with thresholds or quanta," and lines of flight. Without disappearing too far into their jigsaw of metaphors, Deleuze and Parnet's molar lines most closely resemble the categories associated with intersectional analysis, while molecular lines are the stuff of Puar's iteration of assemblage theory: "They trace out little modifications, they make detours, they sketch out rises and falls," and they are home to becomings and micro-becomings, all of the stuff of the critique of intersectionality (*Dialogues II*, 93). But Deleuze and Parnet never prioritize one line over another, writing that "there is no assemblage which does not include" molar lines (96), because "what we call an assemblage is, precisely, a multiplicity," and "any assemblage necessarily includes lines of rigid and binary segmentarity, no less than molecular lines, or lines of border, of flight or slope" (99). That Puar's appropriation of Deleuze eclipses the openness of these formulations speaks to the political and affective investments animating her encounter with Crenshaw specifically, and Black feminist theorizing generally.

On the third type of line, the line of flight, see Koerner, "Line of Escape," which adjusts the translation more literally to "line of escape," which Deleuze and Parnet (and Deleuze and Guattari) take from the Black revolutionary, George Jackson. This is another encounter between Deleuze and the Black radical tradition that Puar's analysis scrupulously avoids. For a radical revision of the line of flight, see McDougall, "Untitled #2."

26 For a pathbreaking challenge to the critique of rights discourses, see Han, *Letters of the Law*, especially chapter 1.

27 Puar, "Queer Times, Queer Assemblages," 128; emphasis added.

28 Puar, "Queer Times, Queer Assemblages," 127.

29 Puar, "Queer Times, Queer Assemblages," 127.

30 Puar, "Queer Times, Queer Assemblages," 128.

31 Puar, "Queer Times, Queer Assemblages," 128.

32 Puar, "Queer Times, Queer Assemblages," 127.

33 Puar, *Terrorist Assemblages*, 213; emphasis added.

34 The production of an animate "queerness" at this point in Puar's analysis returns us to Deleuze and Parnet's "Many Politics." "The second line," the molecular line which is the stuff of Puar's assemblage, they write, "has its own dangers," adding that "it is certainly never sufficient to trace out a molecular line, to be carried along a supple line" (*Dialogues II*, 103). Specifically, the danger of molecular lines obtains in the possibility of lionizing the figure of the marginal. "Some have said that we see the schizophrenic as the true revolutionary. We believe, rather, that schizophrenia is the descent of a molecular process into a black hole. Marginals have always inspired fear in us, and a slight horror. They are not clandestine enough" (104). The figure of a

screaming queerness, too, would seem counter to their formulation. Reiterating this point, it is here in the text that Deleuze himself appears in parentheses, bearing his initials, to offer his own misgivings about the marginal. "In any case," he writes,

> they scare me. There is a molecular speech of madness, or of the drug addict or the delinquent *in vivo* which is no more valid [than] the great discourses of the psychiatrist *in vitro*. There is as much self-assurance on the former's part as certainty on the latter's part. It is not the marginal who create the lines; they install themselves on these lines and make them their property, and this is fine when they have that strange modesty of men of the line, the prudence of the experimenter, but it is a disaster when they slip into a black hole from which they no longer utter anything but the micro-fascist speech of their dependency and their giddiness: "We are the avant-garde," "We are the marginals." (104)

35 Puar, "Cyborg," 51–52.

36 Puar, "Cyborg," 52.

37 Puar, "Cyborg," 52; emphasis added.

38 Certainly, *women of color* is a slippery signifier. Historically, however, it has been deployed by nonwhite, nonblack women to simultaneously parasitize Black women's political energy and displace Black women's political demands. We might consider one genealogy of the term *women of color* as a contingent political identification in the context of the 1977 National Women's Conference in Houston, Texas, as does Loretta Ross in a talk posted to YouTube by the Western States Center, an Oregon-based progressive political organization. Ross notes that the identification was born of nonblack women's desire to be included in the plan of action put forth by the Black Women's Caucus. See "The Origin of the Phrase 'Women of Color,'" 15 February 2011, by Western States Center, YouTube, https://www.youtube.com/watch?v=82vl34mi4Iw. Whether this is parasitism or coalition politics depends on one's perspective. While Ross leans toward the latter, we note that another member of the Washington, D.C., contingent, Terri Clark, warned at the time against "a false sense of security" produced by the "appearance of great unity" at the conference for which "much optimism has been vented in the feminist press." "We think that the connections between single issues and the oppression of women have been made," she cautioned, "we think that coalitions have been formed" ("Houston," 2).

39 Puar, "Cyborg," 52.

40 Puar, "Cyborg," 53.

41 This desire also finds expression in Puar's formulation of "sexual citizenship" arising from her reading of *Lawrence v. Texas* (2003). For Puar, the overturning of antisodomy statutes in *Lawrence*, "the annexing of a black-white sodomy duo to civilization," has two principal implications. First, "as

the ascendancy of whiteness achieved through the sexual and racial hybrid couple, a token of tolerance . . . that now invites homosexuals despite or perhaps even because of national identity becoming more hegemonic than ever" (*Terrorist Assemblages*, 137). That is, an expression of white supremacist homonationalism in the service of the national security state. Second, "as a surrogate citizenship to black subjects who remain economically disenfranchised to the extent of their exclusion from the model minority ethnic, proffering sexual citizenship in the face of the failures of racial inclusion" (136–37). That is, the cynical inclusion of Black Americans into the national project by expanding the range of the sexually (if not racially) normative. The flimsy assertion that the recognition of Black citizenship (itself a disingenuous premise) is the counterpart to or precondition for state repression against nonblacks (especially in the post-9/11 moment) is endemic to transnational feminist and queer theorizing, a theme taken up in chapter 4.

42 Puar, *Terrorist Assemblages*, 215.

43 Weizman, *Hollow Land*, 200–201.

44 See Puar, *Terrorist Assemblages*, 216.

45 Cho et al., "Toward a Field," 791–92.

46 Crenshaw, "Demarginalizing," 140.

47 Crenshaw, "Demarginalizing," 160.

48 See Holland, *Erotic Life of Racism*.

49 Gordon, *Her Majesty's Other Children*, 76.

50 Sexton, *Amalgamation Schemes*, 9.

51 Jackson, "Waking Nightmares," 359.

52 Scott, *Fantasy of Feminist History*, 6.

53 Dean, "Lacan and Queer Theory," 247.

54 Crenshaw, "Demarginalizing," 140.

55 Crenshaw, "Mapping the Margins," 1244.

56 Crenshaw, "Mapping the Margins," 1244n9.

57 This returns us a final time to Deleuze and Parnet, whose critical practice resonates here with Crenshaw in a way we would not expect from Puar's readings. The final section of "Many Politics" opens with the practical observation that "it is in concrete social fields, at specific moments, that the comparative movements of deterritorialization, the continuums of intensity and the combinations of flux they form must be studied" (*Dialogues II*, 101). That is, where Crenshaw's location in legal studies is frequently marshaled as evidence for the fixity of intersectionality—some variation on "intersectionality loses its explanatory power outside of an analysis of the law"—it would seem that Deleuze and Parnet insist on the concrete and specific context as the necessary site for theorization. When they arrive at something like a prescription for critical practice, they situate their position with the claim that "differences pass between the lines, even though they are all immanent to one another, all entangled in one another" (107). "This is why," for Deleuze and Parnet, "the

question of schizoanalytics or pragmatics, micro-politics itself, never consists in interpreting, but merely in asking what are your lines, individual or group, and what are the dangers on each. 1) What are your rigid segments, your binary and overcoding machines? . . . 2) What are your supple lines, what are your fluxes and thresholds? . . . 3) What are your lines of flight, where the fluxes are combined, where the thresholds reach a point of adjacence and rupture?" (107–8).

While my reading of Crenshaw does not aim to reconcile her formulations with those of Deleuze, Parnet, Guattari, or their Anglo-American communities of reception, the resonances between these discourses point toward a gap in Puar's critique of intersectionality. Puar's conclusions reflect a failure to read both Crenshaw and Deleuze and company with the generosity on which Deleuze would seem to insist.

58 Crenshaw, "Mapping the Margins," 1243n4.

59 Crenshaw, "Mapping the Margins," 1242; emphasis added.

60 Puar, "Queer Times, Queer Assemblages," 128.

61 On the figure of the "vocal critic" of intersectionality, see Nash, *Black Feminism Reimagined*, especially chapter 1.

62 A preliminary overview of the field would include Davis, *Are Prisons Obsolete?* and *Abolition Democracy*, Davis and Rodriguez, "The Challenge of Prison Abolition," Kaba, *We Do This 'til We Free Us*, Gilmore, *Abolition Geography*, and Davis et al., *Abolition. Feminism. Now.*

63 Wacquant, "From Slavery to Mass Incarceration," 60.

64 Crenshaw, "Race, Reform, and Retrenchment," 1348.

65 Crenshaw, "Race, Reform, and Retrenchment," 1349.

66 Crenshaw, "Race, Reform, and Retrenchment," 1384.

67 Crenshaw, "Race, Reform, and Retrenchment," 1383–84.

68 Crenshaw, "Race, Reform, and Retrenchment," 1387.

69 *Political ontology* is an imperfect name for a genre of existence that arises from within history, from a politics (and "available to historic challenge through collective struggle"), but that functions *as if* it is transhistorical, *as if* it is not available to political challenge (Sexton, "People-of-Color-Blindness," 37). Not for nothing, different theorists have moved between (at least) *ontological*, *political ontological*, *para-ontological*, and *quasi-ontological* to give a name to these dynamics. Throughout, there is a sense that, at some indeterminate moment, something *within* history *broke history open*. And we live on the other side of a rupture that cannot (and *ought not*) be returned to some prior state of affairs.

70 Spillers, *Black, White, and in Color*, 13.

71 Spillers, *Black, White, and in Color*, 155.

72 Spillers, *Black, White, and in Color*, 156.

73 Spillers, *Black, White, and in Color*, 14.

74 Spillers, *Black, White, and in Color*, 156.

75 Spillers et al., "Whatcha Gonna Do?," 300.

76 Spillers, *Black, White, and in Color*, 11.

77 Spillers, *Black, White, and in Color*, 203.

78 Spillers, *Black, White, and in Color*, 209.

79 Spillers, *Black, White, and in Color*, 36.

80 Spillers, *Black, White, and in Color*, 209.

81 Spillers, *Black, White, and in Color*, 214–15.

82 Spillers, *Black, White, and in Color*, 20.

83 Cover, "Violence and the Word," 1601.

84 Cover, "Violence and the Word," 1609.

85 Benjamin, "Critique of Violence," 242. In a recent commentary on this moment in Benjamin's "Critique," Başak Ertür extends Benjamin's point here: "The seemingly law-preserving implementation of capital punishment is in fact a reenactment and reiteration of law-positing violence. The law is renewed and reinforced through the reenactment of the violence at its origin on the body of the condemned" ("Conscription and Critique," 276).

86 Cover refers to "a recent explosion of legal scholarship placing interpretation at the crux of the enterprise of law" ("Violence and the Word," 1601–2n2). Echoing Cover, in "Race, Reform, and Retrenchment" Crenshaw refers to "a recent explosion of literature on legal texts and their interpretation" (1344n54).

87 Cover, "Violence and the Word," 1602n2.

88 Crenshaw engaged with Jacques Derrida's work around binary oppositions, as well as Antonio Gramsci's theorizations of hegemony. The late Italian Marxist had been the subject of a renewed scholarly interest since the 1970s, cutting across (at least) the Birmingham School of cultural studies and the Essex School of discourse analysis. Emerging from the latter, Ernesto Laclau and Chantal Mouffe's *Hegemony and Socialist Strategy* is a key unspoken interlocutor of Crenshaw's thought.

89 Cover, "Violence and the Word," 1606–7.

90 Cover, "Violence and the Word," 1606n15. Cover's argument here operates contrapuntally to Hortense Spillers's contemporaneous argument from "Mama's Baby, Papa's Maybe" that "sticks and bricks *might* break our bones, but words will most certainly *kill* us" (68).

91 Crenshaw, "Race, Reform, and Retrenchment," 1382; emphasis added.

92 See Gilmore, "Globalisation and US Prison Growth," and "What Is to Be Done?" On this era in global racial capitalism, see Wang, *Carceral Capitalism*, and on how the punishment bureaucracy of the United States functions to extract revenues from differently vulnerable populations, see Karakatsanis, "Punishment Bureaucracy."

93 On the features of governance after legitimacy, see Passavant, *Policing Protest*.

94 Agamben, *Creation and Anarchy*, 75. On this formulation of an-archē in the context of Black studies, and especially in its connections to a feminist Black speculative philosophy, see Carter, "Anarchē," and *Anarchy of Black Religion*.

95 As mentioned earlier, there are in fact robust reactionary movements that claim the name of abolition. There are even conservative iterations of prison abolition. Both Cover and Crenshaw acknowledge that the word of the law, the appropriate legal and rhetorical incantations, are only one part of a larger story.

96 Spillers, *Black, White, and in Color*, 206.

97 Spillers, *Black, White, and in Color*, 203.

98 Spillers, *Black, White, and in Color*, 228.

99 Spillers, *Black, White, and in Color*, 229.

100 Morrison, "What the Black Woman Thinks," 24.

101 Derrida, "Psyche," 44. I refer here to Jasbir Puar and Amit Rai's figure of the "monster-terrorist-fag" as what Jacques Derrida has called a "normal monstrosity." "Monsters cannot be announced," Derrida writes. "One cannot say: 'Here are our monsters,' without immediately turning those monsters to pets" ("Some Statements," 80). The terrorist in Puar's work, to the extent that it relies on the figure of the Black citizen-subject, is just such a monster-turned-pet, a supposed figure of the unrepresentable that is a symptom for the refusal to reckon with the problematic of a global antiblackness.

102 DuCille, "Occult of True Black Womanhood," 603.

CHAPTER THREE. HOPE AGAINST HOPE, AND THE QUEER NEGATIVITY OF A BLACK FEMINIST POIĒSIS

1 Caserio, "Antisocial Thesis."

2 Bersani, *Homos*, 181.

3 Muñoz, *Cruising Utopia*, 18.

4 On queer-of-color critique, see Ferguson, *Aberrations in Black*, for its initial formulations, and Holland, *Erotic Life of Racism*, for an intellectual history of work in the field as well as an analysis of its relation to Black queer studies.

5 Morrison, "Slow Walk," 9–10.

6 Morrison, "Slow Walk," 10.

7 Morrison, "Slow Walk," 3.

8 Morrison, "Slow Walk," 4.

9 Morrison, "Slow Walk," 6.

10 Douglass, *Engendering Blackness*, 2.

11 In Sharon Holland's *an other*, the human animal is productively reimagined as the *hum:animal*.

12 Baldwin, *Nobody Knows My Name*, 116.

13 Morrison, "Slow Walk," 8.

14 Morrison, "Slow Walk," 4.

15 Morrison, "Slow Walk," 5.

16 West, "Reconstructing the American Left," 10–11.

17 West, "Reconstructing the American Left," 10. Nihilism in Black America would be elaborated in West's *Race Matters*.

18 Dean, "Antisocial Homosexual," 827.

19 Edelman, *No Future*, 3.

20 Edelman, *No Future*, 29.

21 Edelman, *No Future*, 31.

22 Keeling, "Looking for M—," 567–68.

23 For some of the former criticisms, see Snediker, *Queer Optimism*; Dean, "Impossible Embrace"; and Halberstam, "Anti-Social Turn."

24 Muñoz describes anti-antiutopianism as "not about a merely affirmative or positive investment in utopia," adding that "gay and lesbian studies can too easily snap into the basically reactionary posture of denouncing a critical imagination that does not short-sightedly deny anything but the here and now," and describing antirelational and antiutopian orientations as "failures of imagination in queer critique" ("Thinking Beyond Antirelationality," 825–26).

25 Dinshaw et al., "Theorizing Queer Temporalities," 194.

26 Dinshaw et al., "Theorizing Queer Temporalities," 195.

27 Muñoz, *Cruising Utopia*, 95.

28 Spillers, *Black, White, and in Color*, 204.

29 Patterson, *Slavery and Social Death*, 7.

30 Patterson, *Slavery and Social Death*, 5.

31 Patterson, *Slavery and Social Death*, 5.

32 Edelman, *No Future*, 27.

33 Morrison, "Slow Walk," 8.

34 Morrison, "Slow Walk," 12.

35 Smith, "Diane," 59.

36 Smith, "Diane," 67. The "Diane" of the text, Diane Sabin, later moved to California's Bay Area, where she maintained a chiropractic practice and met and eventually married the Black feminist poet, essayist, critic, novelist, and activist Jewelle Gomez.

37 Smith, "Wedding," 103.

38 Smith, "Diane," 59–62.

39 Smith, "Diane," 62.

40 Smith, "Diane," 63.

41 Dean, "What's the Point," 150; Dean, "Sex and the Aesthetics of Existence," 387.

42 Dean, "What's the Point," 150.

43 See, for instance, Bersani's 1972 essay for *the Partisan Review*, "Is There a Science of Literature?"

44 Bersani, *Future for Astyanax*, ix.

45 Bersani, *Future for Astyanax*, x.

46 Bersani, *Future for Astyanax*, x; emphasis added.

47 Bersani, *Future for Astyanax*, xi. See also Bersani and Dutoit, "Merde Alors."

48 By this time, Bersani is already connecting these questions to the insovereign sovereignty of the aesthetic object. In "The Subject of Power," he writes,

The literary work is ontologically slippery (in the undecidable relation of literary language to the subjects it proposes to describe) and yet unable not to stay in place (the book cannot flee from our scrutiny). It is limitlessly coercive (the book speaks to the reader's silence; it allows for his responses only in its own anticipatory formulations of them) and yet it has no power to resist our violations of it. The literary work simultaneously, and paradoxically, immobilizes and disorients being; it is a permanently shifting (and shifty) inert object. Finally, literature is always an image of the frictional differentiations which constitute power; even when it does not explicitly treat the social operations of power, writing can't help but be a procession of verbal differences. And yet the writer also uses the system of differences which is language as the "other" in which he more or less secretly works to appropriate a self, to perpetuate the same. (21)

49 Bersani, "Subject of Power," 2.

50 Wacquant, "Great Penal Leap Backward," and Davis, *Are Prisons Obsolete?*, both offer accounts of where the community of experts imagined prisons to be heading in the 1970s, and the explosion of racialized mass incarceration in the decades that followed.

51 Bersani, "Subject of Power," 20.

52 Bersani, "Subject of Power," 21.

53 Bersani, *Freudian Body*, 4.

54 Žižek, *Sublime Object of Ideology*, 132.

55 Smith, "Diane," 63.

56 Smith, "Diane," 64–65.

57 Smith, "Diane," 65.

58 See Bliss, "Arranging Flowers," for an extended reading of the relation between mourning and desire.

59 Smith, "Diane," 66

60 Bersani, *Freudian Body*, 38.

61 Phillips, "Magical Act."

62 In "The Paradoxes of the Symptom in Psychoanalysis," Colette Soler writes, "There is no subject without a symptom, since the symptom signals an individual manner of confronting sexuality. It is through the symptom that everyone has access to his or her jouissance, supplying the lack proper to language via the forgeries of the unconscious" (90).

63 Bersani, "Sociality and Sexuality," 647.

64 Bersani, "Sociality and Sexuality," 647. In "Sex *Instead* of Shattering" and *Homo Psyche*, Gila Ashtor argues that Bersani misreads Laplanche around the meanings of *ébranlement*. While I find her readings of Laplanche persuasive, I might place the accent differently: not that Bersani misread Laplanche, but that Bersani had a *motivated* reading of Laplanche, one that bent the latter's work toward what Bersani sought to explore for himself. Put differently, it isn't clear to me that Bersani's goal was fidelity to the letter of Laplanche's text.

65 Bersani, "Sociality and Sexuality," 647–48.

66 This iteration of seduction theory was challenged for finding widespread abuse among the respectable bourgeoisie. The abandonment of seduction theory, on the grounds that child abuse could not possibly be as common as neurotic symptoms, has been read by feminist theorists like the late Florence Rush as a failure of the psychoanalytic imagination and an instance of sexism that derailed a major set of interventions.

67 Bersani, "Sociality and Sexuality," 646.

68 Dean, "Uses of Perversity," 273.

69 Bersani, "Rejoinder to Walter Benn Michaels," 163.

70 Bersani, "Rejoinder to Walter Benn Michaels," 163.

71 Bersani, "Sociality and Sexuality," 656.

72 Bersani, "Sociality and Sexuality," 656. Early in "Diane," Smith recalls a conversation with her sister Barbara, during which they "had a discussion of Diane's fuzzy, wrong hair and of Barbara's wrong hair. (Also there was some totally irrelevant mention of my own hair if I remember correctly)" (60). Desire is one of the ways we find ourselves reoccurring differently everywhere.

73 Bersani, "Psychoanalysis and the Aesthetic Subject," 174.

74 Bersani, "Psychoanalysis and the Aesthetic Subject," 174.

75 Bersani, "Is the Rectum a Grave?," 222.

76 Edelman, "*Ce n'est pas ça*," 129.

77 Bersani, "Is the Rectum a Grave?," 222.

78 Smith, "Diane," 65.

79 Smith, "Diane," 66.

80 Smith, "Diane," 67.

81 Smith, "Boston Murders," 319.

82 See Douglass, *Engendering Blackness.*

83 Smith, "Boston Murders," 319.

84 Lorde, *Sister Outsider*, 54.

85 See Edelman, "Ethics of Desubjectivation?"

86 Bersani, "Is the Rectum a Grave?," 203–4.

87 Adam Geary's *Antiblack Racism and the AIDS Epidemic: State Intimacies* offers an account of the forms of state violence that produced the AIDS epidemic as a racialized phenomenon.

88 Bersani, "Is the Rectum a Grave?," 199, 200.

89 Bersani, "Is the Rectum a Grave?," 205; emphasis added.

90 Bersani, "Is the Rectum a Grave?," 205.

91 Bersani, "Is the Rectum a Grave?," 208.

92 Bersani, "Is the Rectum a Grave?," 209.

93 See Wang, *Carceral Capitalism.*

94 See Martinot and Sexton, "Avant-Garde of White Supremacy."

95 Gumbs, "Speculative Poetics," 141.

96 Gumbs, "Speculative Poetics," 133.

97 Edelman, *No Future*, 16; Gumbs, "Speculative Poetics," 132.
98 Dienstag, *Pessimism*, 3.
99 Gumbs, "Speculative Poetics," 131.
100 Roderick Ferguson's *Aberrations in Black* offers an extended engagement with the career of "the Black family" in both sociology and literature.
101 Gumbs, "Speculative Poetics," 142.
102 Muñoz, "Thinking Beyond Antirelationality," 826.
103 Muñoz, *Cruising Utopia*, 1.
104 Baraka, *"The Baptism" and "The Toilet,"* 56.
105 In an interesting slip, after describing the action of the play, Muñoz reverses the action of this scene, writing of "Karolis cradling Foots' head" (*Cruising Utopia*, 92). In the 2007 article version of the chapter, Muñoz would write of "Ray cradling Foots's head" in the final gesture of the play ("Cruising the Toilet," 361). This strange set of mistakes is interesting in light of Muñoz's construction of Foots as an aggressor in the scene, rather than his shared victimization alongside Karolis.
106 Muñoz, *Cruising Utopia*, 94.
107 Muñoz, *Cruising Utopia*, 95.
108 Edelman, "On Solidarity," 104n9.
109 Edelman, "Learning Nothing," 166–67n1.
110 Edelman, "Learning Nothing," 167n1.
111 Edelman, "On Solidarity," 104n10.
112 Edelman, *Bad Education*, xiii.
113 Milner quoted in Adrian Johnston, *Adventures in Transcendental Materialism*, 261–62.
114 Edelman, *Bad Education*, xiv.
115 Edelman, *Bad Education*, xv; Edelman, "*Ce n'est pas ça*," 129.
116 Desideri and Harney, "Fate Work," 169.
117 Desideri and Harney, "Fate Work," 170.
118 Gumbs, "Speculative Poetics," 132. With her recent biography of Lorde, *Survival Is a Promise*, Gumbs cultivates an archival and literary practice that recontextualizes the rhizomatic unfolding of Lorde's life and work as an ecological and ecopoetic practice of reimagining the ways life might be lived.
119 Gumbs, "Shape of My Impact."
120 Keeling, "Looking for M—," 578.
121 Morrison, "Slow Walk," 13.
122 Baldwin, *Fire Next Time*, 23.
123 Morrison, "Slow Walk," 13–14.
124 Keeling, *Queer Times, Black Futures*, ix.
125 Keeling, *Queer Times, Black Futures*, xi.
126 As Beverly Smith processes her anguish over being rejected by Diane, she imagines telling Diane how badly the rejection has hurt her: "I feel like she never really took that into herself. There was something I wanted from her

that she wasn't willing to give, wasn't able to give." Smith seems to realize immediately that she is describing a fantasy of obliterating the agency of her love object. The next sentence reads, "Volition is very tricky in this area, as if it wasn't in every other human relating" ("Diane," 66). To be sure, there is nothing unique about this fantasy, except that Smith chose not to self-censor it prior to publication. Our deepest desires are not, by virtue of being *ours*, immune to (a potential for) violence and cruelty.

127 I refer here to Jacques Lacan's formulation from his seminar *The Ethics of Psychoanalysis*: "The only thing one can be guilty of is giving ground relative to one's desire" (321).

128 Keeling, *Queer Times, Black Futures*, xiv. That Bartleby's famous formula "I would prefer not to" is queer does not make his refusal heroic. Keeling disentangles resistance from heroism. It has been a common, and convenient, refrain in recent scholarship to describe one's presence within "the institution" of academia as being "in it, but not of it" (as if to say that there is an outside to institutionality). Keeling pursues the freedom dreams of an emancipatory politics or Black freedom struggle from the insight that the institution, no matter how we feel we are not *of it*, is *of us*. Bartleby's existence, like ours, is inextricable from the ways of being we must refuse. His resistance is not guaranteed to generate a better world simply by springing from him.

129 Melville, "Bartleby, the Scrivener," 54.

130 Keeling, *Queer Times, Black Futures*, 35.

131 Keeling, *Queer Times, Black Futures*, 35–36.

132 Keeling, *Queer Times, Black Futures*, 37–38.

133 Keeling, *Queer Times, Black Futures*, 38.

134 Keeling, *Queer Times, Black Futures*, 176; emphasis added.

135 Keeling, *Queer Times, Black Futures*, 176.

136 Elsewhere in *Queer Times, Black Futures*, Keeling refers to Black existence as "a historical sensibility anchored in the ongoing transformation of the world [in the wake of transatlantic slavery], related but not bound to genetic or otherwise biological categories premised on the continuity of specific bloodlines," that thus "confounds the epistemological certainty vis-à-vis race that presently is widely assumed to be guaranteed by specific phenotypical and other perceptible cues" (66). Blackness in this formulation is both a historically situated knowledge of freedom and also a type of information technology, a medium through and upon which knowledges have circulated globally for centuries.

137 Keeling, *Queer Times, Black Futures*, 155.

138 Keeling, *Queer Times, Black Futures*, 155.

139 Morrison, "Slow Walk," 14.

140 James, "Afrarealism and the Black Matrix," 129n6, 128.

141 From James's comments after a talk by Frank Wilderson, "The Vengeance of Vertigo: Aphasia and Abjection in the Political Trials of Black Insurgents,"

John L. Warfield Center for African and African American Studies, University of Texas at Austin, 17 February 2012.

142 For an articulation of the Lacanian Real along these lines, see Žižek, "Holding the Place": "The Lacanian Real is . . . not simply a technical term for the neutral limit of conceptualization. . . . The Real is neither pre-social nor a social effect—the point is, rather, that the Social itself is *constituted* by the exclusion of some traumatic Real. What is 'outside the Social' is not some positive a priori symbolic form/norm, merely its negative founding gesture itself" (311).

143 Spillers, *Black, White, and in Color*, 156.

CHAPTER FOUR. NOWHERE, AND NOTES TO NOT BELONGING

1 The slippage or discrepancy between the social and the political has been a point of contention in the recent history of Black studies. In particular, the question of whether the condition posed by antiblackness is captured accurately by an analytic of "social death," or if some other framework, like civic or political death, better describes Blackness as a subject position. See Sexton, "Social Life of Social Death," and Moten, "Notes on Passage."

2 On Black sociality, see especially Williamson, *Scandalize My Name*.

3 See duCille, *Skin Trade*; Matsuda, "Beyond, and Not Beyond"; Holloway, "Cruel Enough"; Hong, "Future of Our Worlds"; and Soto, "Where in the Transnational World."

4 Matsuda, "Beyond, and Not Beyond," 395.

5 Holland, *Erotic Life of Racism*, 28–29.

6 Holland, *Erotic Life of Racism*, 14.

7 Falcón and Nash, "Shifting Analytics and Linking Theories," 3.

8 See Sexton, "People-of-Color-Blindness," and Han, "Slavery as Contract."

9 Patterson, *Slavery and Social Death*, 7.

10 Patterson, *Slavery and Social Death*, 7–8.

11 Patterson, *Slavery and Social Death*, 337.

12 Spillers, *Black, White, and in Color*, 226.

13 Marx, *Capital*, 169. On Blackness, antiblackness, and Marxian theories of value, see also Sorentino, "Abstract Slave."

14 Hartman, *Scenes of Subjection*, 92.

15 Hartman, *Scenes of Subjection*, 93.

16 In *Becoming Human: Matter and Meaning in an Antiblack World*, Zakiyyah Iman Jackson calls this indeterminate space between the positions of the human, the slave, and the animal, between life and matter, a kind of plasticity. The enslaved folds around and spreads across modernity's partitioning of being.

17 Sexton, *Black Men, Black Feminism*, 19–20.

18 Nagar and Swarr, introduction to *Critical Transnational Feminist Praxis*, 9.

19 Grewal and Kaplan, "Transnational Practices," 75.

20 Grewal and Kaplan, "Transnational Practices," 73.

21 Grewal and Kaplan, "Transnational Practices," 74.

22 Grewal and Kaplan, "Introduction," 7.

23 E.g., "Without an analysis of transnational scattered hegemonies that reveal themselves in gender relations, feminist movements will remain isolated and prone to reproducing the universalizing gestures of dominant Western cultures" (Grewal and Kaplan, "Introduction," 17); "We need to articulate the relationship of gender to scattered hegemonies such as global economic structures, patriarchal nationalisms, 'authentic' forms of tradition, local structures of domination, and legal-juridical oppression on multiple levels" (17); "The issue of who counts as a feminist is much less important than creating coalitions based on the practices that different women use in various locations to counter the scattered hegemonies that affect their lives" (18); and "Feminists can begin to map these scattered hegemonies and link diverse local practices to formulate a transnational set of solidarities" (19).

24 See Paul Gilroy's commentary in Smith, "State of Cultural Studies," especially 20–22.

25 Beasley-Murray, *Posthegemony*, 40.

26 Anderson, "Antinomies of Antonio Gramsci."

27 Laclau, *Politics and Ideology*, 141.

28 Laclau, *Politics and Ideology*, 141. This bifurcation of class sectarianism and social-democratic opportunism is an unspoken reference to Georges Sorel's theorization of the general strike, taken up directly in Laclau and Mouffe, *Hegemony and Socialist Strategy*. The mostly silent influence of anarchist thought across cultural studies is later given expression in the work of Saidiya Hartman and contributes in important ways to contemporary abolitionist thought. See Bliss, "To Strive and Fail."

29 Laclau, *Politics and Ideology*, 141.

30 Laclau, *Politics and Ideology*, 141n56.

31 Laclau, *Politics and Ideology*, 142n56.

32 Mouffe, "Hegemony and Ideology in Gramsci," 178–79.

33 Mouffe, "Hegemony and Ideology in Gramsci," 179.

34 Mouffe, "Hegemony and Ideology in Gramsci," 181.

35 Laclau and Mouffe, *Hegemony and Socialist Strategy*, 139.

36 Grewal and Kaplan, "Introduction," 19.

37 Grewal and Kaplan, "Global Identities," 644.

38 Grewal and Kaplan, "Warrior Marks," 8.

39 Walker and Parmar, *Warrior Marks*, 15–19.

40 Grewal and Kaplan, "Warrior Marks," 11.

41 Grewal and Kaplan, "Warrior Marks," 11–12.

42 The most extended collection of Walker's writing on meditation is her *Cushion in the Road: Meditation and Wandering as the Whole World Awakens*

to Being in Harm's Way, published in 2013. She has also published conversations between herself and teacher-practitioners such as Sharon Salzberg and Pema Chödrön. Consider the literary critic Yoshinobu Hakutani's chapter on Walker in his *Cross-Cultural Visions in African American Modernism*, Pamela Smith's essay on Walker's "ecospirituality" ("Green Lap"), or a 2016 special section on Buddhism and womanist thought in the journal *Buddhist-Christian Studies*.

43 See Nhất Hạnh, *Interbeing*. We might also consider Leo Bersani's insight from the previous chapter, "Each subject reoccurs differently everywhere" ("Sociality and Sexuality," 656).

44 A more extended consideration of the relation between different traditions of Buddhist thought and practice and a feminist and queer Black radicalism is beyond the scope of this study, but there have been moments of overlap in the recent work of Sora Han and Stefanie Dunning. See Han, *Mu*, and Dunning, *Black to Nature*.

45 See Abu-Lughod, "Gender, Religion, and Rights"; Anidjar, "Secularism"; Mufti, "Critical Secularism"; and Asad, *Formations of the Secular*.

46 Grosz, "Criticism, Feminism, and the Institution," 184.

47 Grewal and Kaplan, "Transnational Feminist Cultural Studies," 440.

48 Grewal and Kaplan, "Transnational Feminist Cultural Studies," 445n28.

49 Dhareshwar, "Toward a Narrative Epistemology," 152.

50 See Han, "Slavery as Contract," and Moten, *Stolen Life*.

51 Hartman and Wilderson, "Position of the Unthought," 186.

52 Hartman and Wilderson, "Position of the Unthought," 185.

53 Hartman and Wilderson, "Position of the Unthought," 185–86.

54 Hartman, "Excisions of the Flesh," 55; emphasis added.

55 Hartman, *Scenes of Subjection*, 3. See also Sharpe, *In the Wake*.

56 Hartman's opening gesture choice to withhold "Aunt Hester's scream" has been a point of discussion since Fred Moten's review of *Scenes* in the *Drama Review*, which he expanded in the opening chapter of his *In the Break*.

57 Saidiya Hartman, in Saunders, "Fugitive Dreams of Diaspora," 10.

58 Wilderson, "Gramsci's Black Marx," 234.

59 Hartman, *Scenes of Subjection*, 53.

60 Hartman, *Scenes of Subjection*, 53.

61 Hartman, *Scenes of Subjection*, 53.

62 Hartman, *Scenes of Subjection*, 65.

63 See Esposito, *Third Person*.

64 Hartman, *Scenes of Subjection*, 51.

65 Hartman, *Scenes of Subjection*, 53, 65; emphasis added.

66 Hartman, "Territory Between Us," 441.

67 In Saunders, "Fugitive Dreams of Diaspora," 8.

68 Hartman and Wilderson, "Position of the Unthought," 184–85.

69 Derrida, *Points . . . Interviews*, 67.

70 Hartman and Wilderson, "Position of the Unthought," 185.

71 Hartman and Wilderson, "Position of the Unthought," 185. Hartman's interlocutor in that conversation, Frank Wilderson, would later argue that the American national project is always already a crisis for Blacks, and that America can only hold on to its (fictive) coherence through terror: "From the incoherence of black death, America generates the coherence of white life" (Wilderson, "Gramsci's Black Marx," 232).

72 For two recent, celebrated studies, see Woodard, *Delectable Negro*, and Tompkins, *Racial Indigestion*.

73 The early reception of *Scenes* made clear that Hartman's project did not represent the mainstream of Black literary and cultural studies or Black feminist historiography. The literary critic Anita Patterson called *Scenes* "profoundly pessimistic" and "bleak" and found herself "unpersuaded" by Hartman's critique of the discourses of liberty, democracy, and civil rights: "We should always remember the extent to which the legacy of slavery and the failures of Reconstruction live on. But in doing so, we cannot forget that, without the discourse of rights, the Civil Rights Movement would never have happened" (Patterson, "Review of *Scenes of Subjection*," 683, 686). In her *Black Subjects*, Arlene Keizer called Hartman's critiques of agency "strikingly anomalous" compared to the strategies deployed in contemporary narratives of slavery (16). Striking a more idiosyncratic note, the historian Nell Irvin Painter found much to recommend in *Scenes*, "a new way of seeing the southern past, through careful investigation of texts together with critical race theory's insights about rights," but Hartman's references to critical theory "intervene so often they threaten to become the book's real subject" ("Review of *Scenes of Subjection*," 680). "The clutter of their [Michel de Certeau's and Hortense Spillers's] names and words really gets on my nerves" she offered, by way of closing (681). It would be the work of another intellectual history to trace how Hartman's interventions became more or less conventional in the span of twenty-five years.

74 Hall, "New Ethnicities," 443–44.

75 The intellectual history of this tendency could be told through a reading group based around the La Jolla campus of the University of California. The members of Ruby's Reading Group—among them, Roderick Ferguson, Grace Kyungwon Hong, Chandan Reddy, Ruby Tapia, and Gayatri Gopinath—and fellow travelers like Helen Jun, Lisa Cacho, and Jodi Melamed, have been at the forefront of queer-of-color-critique (coined by Ferguson) and the recent history of the critiques of racial capitalism and neoliberal multiculturalism. See especially Ferguson, *Aberrations in Black* and *Reorder of Things*; Hong, *Death Beyond Disavowal*; Cacho, *Social Death*; Reddy, *Freedom with Violence*; and Melamed, *Represent and Destroy*.

76 See Prashad, *Darker Nations*.

77 Philip, quoted in Saunders, "Defending the Dead," 76.

78 On the ways Blackness circulated across and generated the political economy of the early modern era, see, among others, Baucom, *Spectres of the Atlantic*; Carney, *Black Rice*; and Mills, *Racial Contract*.

79 Grewal, *Transnational America*, 7.

80 Grewal, *Transnational America*, 8.

81 Grewal, *Transnational America*, 13.

82 Grewal, *Transnational America*, 81.

83 Consider the work of Grewal and Kaplan in the previous section, the work of Leo Bersani and the traditions of queer negativity and queer futurity that responded to Bersani in chapter 3, the critique of intersectionality in chapter 2, and the project of a sisterhood feminism in chapter 1.

84 Grewal, *Transnational America*, 197, 208.

85 Grewal, *Transnational America*, 208.

86 Grewal, *Transnational America*, 208–9.

87 Grewal, *Transnational America*, 209.

88 Grewal, *Transnational America*, 217.

89 See Grewal, "Transnational America," 557.

90 Grewal, *Transnational America*, 217.

91 Hartman, "Review of *The Slumbering Volcano*," 260–61.

92 Hartman, "Review of *The Slumbering Volcano*," 260.

93 Hartman, "Review of *The Slumbering Volcano*," 261.

94 Hartman, "Review of *The Slumbering Volcano*," 261.

95 In Saunders, "Fugitive Dreams of Diaspora," 5.

96 In Saunders, "Fugitive Dreams of Diaspora," 4. Within the interdisciplinary humanities, some of the reception of Hartman's critical practice between *Lose Your Mother* and her subsequent essay, "Venus in Two Acts," occasionally ventured from celebrating (or rebuking) Hartman's projects in order to rebuke (or celebrate) the academic practice of history, ignoring Hartman's own admiring commentaries on the work of historians of Atlantic slavery like Stephanie Smallwood, Vincent Brown, and Jennifer Morgan. In other words, if *Hartman's* encounter with the archive could not be written *as history*, that is not to say that historiography had nothing to offer.

97 In Saunders, "Fugitive Dreams of Diaspora," 5.

98 The Redress Project consisted of a year-long Sawyer Seminar at the University of California, Irvine in 2002–3 (headed by David Theo Goldberg, then the director of the University of California's Humanities Research Institute), a working group convened by Hartman and Best at Berkeley in the fall of 2004, and a seminar at Berkeley the next fall, some of the proceedings of which were published in the journal *Representations* shortly thereafter.

99 For a commentary on this aspect of Best's later work, see Bliss, "Defense, Redemption, Care."

100 Best and Hartman, "Fugitive Justice," 5.

101 Best and Hartman, "Fugitive Justice," 6.

102 Best and Hartman, "Fugitive Justice," 7.

103 Veracini, *Settler Colonialism*, 65. For a critique of a politics of citation that has tended to emphasize the work of white theorists of settler colonialism, especially the work of Veracini and the late Patrick Wolfe, see Arvin, "Indigenous Feminist Notes."

104 Veracini, *Settler Colonialism*, 65.

105 Veracini, *Settler Colonialism*, 66.

106 Another set of questions arise here with respect to the increasing sovereignty of global capital. See Brown, "Sovereignty."

107 Rifkin, *Fictions of Land and Flesh*, 38.

108 Rifkin, "Indigenizing Agamben," 91.

109 Rifkin, *Fictions of Land and Flesh*, 51–52. On disappearance, see Arvin et al., "Decolonizing Feminism," Simpson, "Sovereignty of Critique," and Byrd, "*Loving* Unbecoming."

110 Simpson, "Sovereignty of Critique," 686.

111 Simpson, "Sovereignty of Critique," 689.

112 Simpson, "Place Where We All Live," 19.

113 Brown, "Sovereignty," 252.

114 The crucial distinction would be a contest between competing practices of collective existence, practices that are—on both sides—both concrete and aspirational, different practices of collective existence in the past, present, and future.

115 Rifkin, *Fictions of Land and Flesh*, 226.

116 In *Beyond Constraint*, Shona Jackson offers a critique of racial capitalism in which Indigeneity is reimagined in its relations to Blackness, an intervention that challenges both critical Indigenous studies and received understandings of the Black radical tradition.

117 Gopinath, *Unruly Visions*, 87, 88. Gopinath's project in *Unruly Visions* extends the work of her first book, *Impossible Desires: Queer Diasporas and South Asian Public Cultures*, as well as two essays on diasporic queer art as a practice of "re-vision." See Gopinath, "Chitra Ganesh's Queer Re-Visions," and "Archive, Affect, and the Everyday."

118 Gopinath, *Unruly Visions*, 89.

119 Gopinath, *Unruly Visions*, 129.

120 DeSouza, quoted in Gopinath, *Unruly Visions*, 126.

121 Gopinath, *Unruly Visions*, 132.

122 Kaplan, "Souls at the Crossroads," 514–15.

123 Marriott, *Haunted Life*, 43.

124 Brand, *Door of No Return*, 121.

125 Gopinath, *Unruly Visions*, 133.

126 Gopinath, *Unruly Visions*, 137.

127 On the figure of the involuntary settler, see Jackson, *Creole Indigeneity*.

128 Gopinath, *Unruly Visions*, 137–38.

129 Gopinath, *Unruly Visions*, 138.
130 Kyle, *Independence of Kenya*, 202.
131 Maxon, "Social and Cultural Changes," 112.
132 Maxon, "Social and Cultural Changes," 112.
133 Bennett, "Sons of Adam," 18.
134 Bennett, "Sons of Adam," 18.
135 See Bennett, *African Kings and Black Slaves*.
136 "In general," Bennett writes, "the Portuguese manifested little marvel in their encounter with Guinea and loosely ascribed to the continents' 'black' inhabitants a corporate place as the sovereignless, which distinguished them from the sovereign Moors—a gesture that eventually confined some 'Ethiops,' 'Negros,' 'blacks,' and 'Black Moors' to the condition of slaves" ("Sons of Adam," 35).
137 Hartman, *Lose Your Mother*, 189.
138 Hartman, *Lose Your Mother*, 190.
139 Hartman, *Lose Your Mother*, 234.
140 Hartman, "Black in Anarchy," xv–xvi.
141 Hartman, *Wayward Lives*, 229–30.
142 Hartman, *Wayward Lives*, 365.
143 On excess mortality, see Caraballo et al., "Excess Mortality," and Satcher et al., "What if We Were Equal?"
144 Wilderson, "Gramsci's Black Marx," 229–30. Here Wilderson covers a similar territory as Gayatri Spivak when she writes that "the abusive constitution of the body in chattel slavery is *not* the socialization of the body in exploitation" under capital (Spivak, *Critique of Postcolonial Reason*, 389; emphasis added).
145 Hartman, "Excisions of the Flesh," 55.
146 Hartman, "Black in Anarchy," xiii.
147 Hartman, *Wayward Lives*, 286.

EPILOGUE

1 Spillers, "Afterword," 250.
2 Smith, "Toward a Black Feminist Criticism" (1977), 27. Subsequent citations refer to this source unless noted otherwise.
3 Smith, "Toward a Black Feminist Criticism," 26.
4 Smith, "Toward a Black Feminist Criticism," 36, 37, 39; emphasis added.
5 Smith, "Toward a Black Feminist Criticism," 39.
6 Quoted in Smith, "Toward a Black Feminist Criticism," 36.
7 Quoted in Smith, "Toward a Black Feminist Criticism," 33.
8 Quoted in Smith, "Toward a Black Feminist Criticism," 40. For a powerful engagement with Brown's thought and activism, see Capper, "Domestic Unrest."
9 In *Aberrations in Black*, Roderick Ferguson argues that "Smith deploys 'lesbian' outside the boundaries of identity," that she defines it "in terms of

a set of critiques of heterosexuality and patriarchy" and "a set of social relations that point to the instability of heteropatriarchy and to a possible critical emergence within that instability" (127).

10 Smith, "Toward a Black Feminist Criticism," in Bowles, *In the Memory*, 32.

11 In Bowles, *In the Memory*, 53. Welsing was finally interrupted by June Jordan after speaking for eight of the session's fifteen allotted minutes for questions and answers.

12 Barbara Smith, interview by Loretta Ross, 7–8 May 2003, transcript of video recording, Voices of Feminism Oral History Project, Sophia Smith Collection, Smith College, 63.

13 McDowell, "New Directions," 155.

14 Carby, *Reconstructing Womanhood*, 16.

15 See Colebrook, *New Literary Histories*.

16 Elsewhere, around the same time, the Black literary critics Henry Louis Gates Jr. and Houston Baker Jr. were articulating similar critiques of Black feminist criticism from the perspective of a Black poststructuralism.

17 Morrison, *Sula*, 93.

18 Morrison, *Sula*, 94.

19 Spillers, "Hateful Passion," 293.

20 Spillers, "Hateful Passion," 294–97; emphases in original.

21 Spillers, "Hateful Passion," 320.

22 Morrison, *Sula*, xvii.

23 Smith, "Toward a Black Feminist Criticism," 42.

24 See Edwards, *Other Side of Terror*.

25 The name "Crow Jane" derives from a blues song of unknown origin, but can be traced to the Piedmont region of the American South in the 1920s. See John Kessler, "The Piedmont Blues of 'Crow Jane,'" KNKX Public Radio, 25 October 2013, https://www.knkx.org/jazz-and-blues/2013-10-25/the-piedmont-blues-of-crow-jane. In the song "Crow Jane," the titular figure is warned not to "hold her head so high" because "someday . . . you know you got to die." A blues iteration on the older form of the murder ballad, the song's narrative persona describes killing and burying Crow Jane, then missing her and wishing she had heeded his warnings. Hartman's appellation also carries resonances to "Jane Crow," coined by the Black legal scholar Pauli Murray in the middle of the twentieth century to articulate the continuities between the legal doctrine of Jim Crow and the legal status of women as a class in the United States.

26 A video recording of Hartman's remarks is available from the Rutgers Center for Historical Analysis, accessed 12 September 2024, https://rcha.rutgers.edu/past-projects/past-project-black-bodies/48-past-events/133-scenes-at-20. "Litany for Grieving Sisters" appeared in a special issue of *Representations*, "Proximities: Reading with Judith Butler."

27 Hartman, "Crow Jane."

28 Hartman, "Crow Jane."

29 See James, *Shadowboxing*, especially her chapter "Radicalizing Feminisms from 'The Movement' Era." For an earlier consideration that raised similar considerations in the early years of the development of a contemporary Black feminism, see Smith, "Black Feminism."

30 Elsewhere, Kincaid would ask, "What to call the thing that happened to me and all who look like me? Should I call it history?" ("In History," 1). In recent years, Hartman has gestured toward Kincaid as an inspiration for the projects she has pursued since *Scenes of Subjection*, and much more might be said about their encounters with the archives of slavery and colonialism, and how those have informed their different practices of writing Black life.

31 Kincaid, "Ovando," 82.

32 Kincaid, "Ovando," 83.

33 Kincaid, "Ovando," 82–83.

34 Kincaid, "Ovando," 82.

35 "'Peaches' and 'Brown Sugar,' 'Sapphire' and 'Earth Mother,' 'Aunty,' 'Granny,' God's 'Holy Fool,' a 'Miss Ebony First,' or 'Black Woman at the Podium'" (Spillers, "Mama's Baby, Papa's Maybe," 65).

36 Quoted in Gould, *Earthquake Weather*, 13.

Bibliography

Abel, Elizabeth. "Black Writing, White Reading: Race and the Politics of Feminist Interpretation." *Critical Inquiry* 19, no. 3 (1993): 470–98.

Abu-Lughod, Lila. "The Debate About Gender, Religion, and Rights: Thoughts of a Middle East Anthropologist." *PMLA* 121, no. 5 (2006): 1621–30.

Agamben, Giorgio. *Creation and Anarchy: The Work of Art and the Religion of Capitalism.* Stanford University Press, 2019.

Alcoff, Linda Martín. "Cultural Feminism Versus Post-Structuralism: The Identity Crisis in Feminist Theory." *Signs* 13, no. 3 (1988): 405–36.

Alderfer, Hannah, Beth Jaker, and Marybeth Nelson. *Diary of a Conference on Sexuality.* Barnard Women's Center/Faculty Press, 1982.

Alexander, M. Jacqui, and Chandra Talpade Mohanty, eds. *Feminist Genealogies, Colonial Legacies, Democratic Futures.* Routledge, 2006.

Alexander-Floyd, Nikol. "Disappearing Acts: Reclaiming Intersectionality in the Social Sciences in a Post–Black Feminist Era." *Feminist Formations* 24, no. 1 (2012): 1–25.

Anderson, Carol S., and Thomas Cattoi, eds. "Old Buddhist Texts: New Womanist Thought." Special issue, *Buddhist-Christian Studies* 36 (2016).

Anderson, Perry. "The Antinomies of Antonio Gramsci." *New Left Review* 1, no. 100 (1976): 5–78.

Anidjar, Gil. "Secularism." *Critical Inquiry* 33, no. 1 (2006): 52–77.

Arvin, Maile. "Indigenous Feminist Notes on Embodying Alliance Against Settler Colonialism." *Meridians* 18, no. 2 (2019): 335–57.

Arvin, Maile, Eve Tuck, and Angie Morrill. "Decolonizing Feminism: Challenging Connections Between Settler Colonialism and Heteropatriarchy." *Feminist Formations* 25, no. 1 (2013): 8–34.

Asad, Talal. *Formations of the Secular: Christianity, Islam, Modernity.* Stanford University Press, 2003.

Ashtor, Gila. *Homo Psyche: On Queer Theory and Erotophobia.* Fordham University Press, 2021.

Ashtor, Gila. "Sex *Instead* of Shattering: A Critical Exploration of Bersani and Laplanche." *Studies in Gender and Sexuality* 20, no. 4 (2019): 249–62.

Baldwin, James. *The Fire Next Time*. Dial Press, 1963.

Baldwin, James. *Nobody Knows My Name: More Notes of a Native Son*. Dell, 1962.

Bambara, Toni Cade, ed. *The Black Woman: An Anthology*. Washington Square, 2005.

Bambara, Toni Cade. *The Salt Eaters*. Vintage, 1992.

Bambara, Toni Cade. "What It Is I Think I'm Doing Anyhow." In *The Writer and Her Work*, edited by Janet Sternburg. W. W. Norton, 1980.

Baraka, Amiri. *"The Baptism" and "The Toilet."* Grove Press, 1967.

Baucom, Ian. *Spectres of the Atlantic: Finance, Capital, Slavery, and the Philosophy of History*. Duke University Press, 2005.

Beasley-Murray, Jon. *Posthegemony: Political Theory and Latin America*. University of Minnesota Press, 2010.

Benjamin, Walter. "Critique of Violence." In *Walter Benjamin: Selected Writings*, vol. 1, *1913–1926*, edited by Marcus Bullock and Michael W. Jennings. Belknap Press, 2004.

Bennett, Herman L. *African Kings and Black Slaves: Sovereignty and Dispossession in the Early Modern Atlantic*. University of Pennsylvania Press, 2019.

Bennett, Herman L. "'Sons of Adam': Text, Context, and the Early Modern African Subject." *Representations* 92 (2005): 16–41.

Bersani, Leo. *The Freudian Body: Psychoanalysis and Art*. Columbia University Press, 1986.

Bersani, Leo. *A Future for Astyanax: Character and Desire in Literature*. Little, Brown, 1976.

Bersani, Leo. *Homos*. Harvard University Press, 1995.

Bersani, Leo. "Is There a Science of Literature?" *Partisan Review* 39, no. 4 (1972): 535–53.

Bersani, Leo. "Is the Rectum a Grave?" *October* 43 (1987): 197–222.

Bersani, Leo. "Psychoanalysis and the Aesthetic Subject." *Critical Inquiry* 32, no. 2 (2006): 161–74.

Bersani, Leo. "Rejoinder to Walter Benn Michaels." *Critical Inquiry* 8, no. 1 (1981): 158–64.

Bersani, Leo. "Sociality and Sexuality." *Critical Inquiry* 26, no. 4 (2000): 641–56.

Bersani, Leo. "The Subject of Power." *Diacritics* 7, no. 3 (1977): 2–21.

Bersani, Leo, and Ulysse Dutoit. "Merde Alors." *October* 13 (1980): 22–35.

Best, Stephen, and Saidiya Hartman. "Fugitive Justice." *Representations* 92 (2005): 1–15.

Bethel, Lorraine. "What Chou Mean *We*, White Girl? Or, The Cullud Lesbian Feminist Declaration of Independence (Dedicated to the Proposition That All Women Are Not Equal, i.e., Identical/ly Oppressed)." *Conditions* 2, no. 2 (1979): 86–92.

Bliss, James. "Arranging Flowers." *Palimpsest* 8, no. 2 (2019): 1–9.

Bliss, James. "Defense, Redemption, Care: Black Feminist and Queer Studies." *Feminist Studies* 47, no. 1 (2021): 34–61.

Bliss, James. "Forgetting: Loss, Invention, and Unbearable Life." *Women's Studies Quarterly* 52, no. 3–4 (2024): 53–67.

Bliss, James. "To Strive and Fail: Voltairine de Cleyre and Abolition Feminism." *CR: The New Centennial Review* 24, no. 1 (2025): 213–39.

Bowles, Juliette, ed. *In the Memory and Spirit of Frances, Zora, and Lorraine: Essays and Interviews on Black Women and Writing.* Institute for the Arts and Humanities, Howard University, 1979.

Boyce Davies, Carole. *Black Women, Writing and Identity: Migrations of the Subject.* Routledge, 1994.

Brand, Dionne. *A Map to the Door of No Return: Notes to Belonging.* Vintage Canada, 2001.

Brooks, Gwendolyn. *Report from Part One.* Broadside Press, 1972.

Brown, Wendy. "Sovereignty and the Return of the Repressed." In *The New Pluralism: William Connolly and the Contemporary Global Condition*, edited by David Campbell and Morton Schoolman. Duke University Press, 2008.

Bulkin, Elly. "Racism and Writing: Some Implications for White Lesbian Critics." *Sinister Wisdom* 13 (1980): 3–22.

Byrd, Jodi A. "*Loving* Unbecoming: The Queer Politics of the Transitive Native." In *Critically Sovereign: Indigenous Gender, Sexuality, and Feminist Studies*, edited by Joanne Barker. Duke University Press, 2017.

Cacho, Lisa. *Social Death: Racialized Rightlessness and the Criminalization of the Unprotected.* New York University Press, 2012.

Capper, Beth. "Domestic Unrest: Social Reproduction and the Temporalities of Struggle in Lizzie Borden's *Born in Flames.*" *Third Text* 31, no. 1 (2017): 97–116.

Caraballo, César, Daisy S. Massey, Chima D. Ndumele, et al. "Excess Mortality and Years of Potential Life Lost Among the Black Population in the US, 1999–2020." *Journal of the American Medical Association* 329, no. 19 (2023): 1662–70.

Carby, Hazel. *Reconstructing Womanhood: The Emergence of the Afro-American Woman Novelist.* Oxford University Press, 1987.

Carney, Judith. *Black Rice: The African Origins of Rice Cultivation in the Americas.* Harvard University Press, 2002.

Carter, J. Kameron. "Anarchē; or, The Matter of Charles Long and Black Feminism." *American Religion* 2, no. 2 (2021): 103–35.

Carter, J. Kameron. *The Anarchy of Black Religion: A Mystic Song.* Duke University Press, 2023.

Caserio, Robert L. "The Antisocial Thesis in Queer Theory." *PMLA* 121, no. 3 (2006): 819–21.

Chandler, Nahum D. "The Figure of W. E. B. Du Bois as a Problem for Thought." *CR: The New Centennial Review* 6, no. 3 (2006): 29–55.

Chandler, Nahum. "Originary Displacement." *boundary 2* 27, no. 3 (2000): 249–86.

Cho, Sumi, Kimberlé Crenshaw, and Leslie McCall. "Toward a Field of Intersectionality Studies: Theory, Applications, and Praxis." *Signs* 38, no. 4 (2013): 785–810.

Christian, Barbara. "The Race for Theory." *Cultural Critique* 6, no. 1 (1987): 51–63.

Clark, Terri. "Houston: A Turning Point?" *Off Our Backs* 8, no. 3 (1978): 2.

Clifton, Lucille. *Good News About the Earth: New Poems*. Random House, 1972.

Colebrook, Claire. *New Literary Histories: New Historicism and Contemporary Criticism*. Manchester University Press, 1997.

Combahee River Collective. "A Black Feminist Statement." *Women's Studies Quarterly* 42, no. 3/4 (2014): 271–80.

Cover, Robert. "Violence and the Word." *Yale Law Journal* 95 (1986): 1601–29.

Crenshaw, Kimberlé. "Demarginalizing the Intersection of Race and Sex: A Black Feminist Critique of Antidiscrimination Doctrine, Feminist Theory, and Antiracist Politics." *University of Chicago Legal Forum* 139 (1989): 139–67.

Crenshaw, Kimberlé. "Mapping the Margins: Intersectionality, Identity Politics, and Violence Against Women of Color." *Stanford Law Review* 43, no. 6 (1991): 1241–99.

Crenshaw, Kimberlé. "Race, Reform, and Retrenchment: Transformation and Legitimation in Antidiscrimination Law." *Harvard Law Review* 101, no. 7 (1988): 1331–87.

Daly, Mary. *Amazon Grace: Re-Calling the Courage to Sin Big*. Palgrave Macmillan, 2006.

Daly, Mary. *Gyn/Ecology: The Metaethics of Radical Feminism*. Beacon Press, 1978. Rev. ed., 1990.

Daly, Mary. "New Intergalactic Introduction." In *Gyn/Ecology: The Metaethics of Radical Feminism*. Beacon Press, 1990.

Daly, Mary. *Outercourse: The Be-Dazzling Voyage*. HarperCollins, 1992.

Davis, Angela. *Abolition Democracy: Beyond Empire, Prisons, and Torture*. Seven Stories Press, 2005.

Davis, Angela. *Are Prisons Obsolete?* Seven Stories Press, 2003.

Davis, Angela. "Reflections on the Black Woman's Role in the Community of Slaves." *Black Scholar* 3, no. 4 (1971): 2–15.

Davis, Angela, Gina Dent, Erica Meiners, and Beth Richie. *Abolition. Feminism. Now*. Haymarket, 2022.

Davis, Angela, and Dylan Rodriguez. "The Challenge of Prison Abolition: A Conversation." *Social Justice* 27, no. 3 (2000): 212–18.

Dean, Tim. "The Antisocial Homosexual." *PMLA* 121, no. 3 (2006): 826–28.

Dean, Tim. "An Impossible Embrace: Queerness, Futurity, and the Death Drive." In *A Time for the Humanities: Futurity and the Limits of Autonomy*, edited by James J. Bono, Tim Dean, and Ewa Plonowska Ziarek. Fordham University Press, 2008.

Dean, Tim. "Lacan and Queer Theory." In *Cambridge Companion to Lacan*, edited by Jean-Michel Rabaté. Cambridge University Press, 2003.

Dean, Tim. "Sex and the Aesthetics of Existence." *PMLA* 125, no. 2 (2010): 387–92.

Dean, Tim. "Uses of Perversity: Commentary on Saketopoulou's 'To Suffer Pleasure.'" *Studies in Gender and Sexuality* 15, no. 4 (2014): 269–77.

Dean, Tim. "What's the Point of Psychoanalytic Criticism?" *Oxford Literary Review* 20, no. 1–2 (1998): 143–62.
Dean, Tim, and Robyn Wiegman. "What Does Critique Want? A Critical Exchange." *English Language Notes* 51, no. 2 (2013): 107–22.
Deleuze, Gilles. "Postscript on the Societies of Control." *October* 59 (1992): 3–7.
Deleuze, Gilles, and Claire Parnet. *Dialogues II*. Continuum, 2006.
Derrida, Jacques. "Faith and Knowledge: The Two Sources of 'Religion' at the Limits of Reason Alone." In *Religion*, edited by Jacques Derrida and Gianni Vattimo. Polity Press, 1998.
Derrida, Jacques. *Points . . . Interviews, 1974–1994*. Stanford University Press, 1995.
Derrida, Jacques. "Psyche: Invention of the Other." In *Psyche: Inventions of the Other*, vol. 1, edited by Peggy Kamuf and Elizabeth Rottenberg. Stanford University Press, 2007.
Derrida, Jacques. "Some Statements and Truisms About Neo-Logisms, Newisms, Postisms, Parasitisms, and Other Small Seismisms." In *The States of "Theory": History, Art, and Critical Discourse*, edited by David Carroll. Stanford University Press, 1994.
Derrida, Jacques. "The Time of a Thesis: Punctuations." In *Philosophy in France Today*, edited by Alan Montefiore. Cambridge University Press, 1983.
Desideri, Valentina, and Stefano Harney. "Fate Work: A Conversation." *Ephemera: Theory and Politics in Organization* 13, no. 1 (2013): 159–76.
De Veaux, Alexis. *Warrior Poet: A Biography of Audre Lorde*. W. W. Norton, 2007.
Dhareshwar, Vivek. "Toward a Narrative Epistemology of the Postcolonial Predicament." *Inscriptions* 5 (1989): 135–57.
Dienstag, Joshua. *Pessimism: Philosophy, Ethic, Spirit*. Princeton University Press, 2006.
Dinshaw, Carolyn, Lee Edelman, Roderick A. Ferguson, et al. "Theorizing Queer Temporalities: A Roundtable Discussion." *GLQ* 13, no. 2–3 (2007): 177–95.
Douglass, Patrice. *Engendering Blackness: Slavery and the Ontology of Sexual Violence*. Stanford University Press, 2025.
duCille, Ann. "The Occult of True Black Womanhood: Critical Demeanor and Black Feminist Studies." *Signs* 19, no. 3 (1994): 591–629.
duCille, Ann. "The Short Happy Life of Black Feminist Theory." *differences* 21, no. 1 (2010): 32–47.
duCille, Ann. *Skin Trade*. Harvard University Press, 1996.
Dunning, Stefanie K. *Black to Nature: Pastoral Return and African American Culture*. University of Mississippi Press, 2021.
Edelman, Lee. "Antagonism, Negativity, and the Subject of Queer Theory." *PMLA* 121, no. 3 (2006): 821–23.
Edelman, Lee. *Bad Education: Why Queer Theory Teaches Us Nothing*. Duke University Press, 2022.
Edelman, Lee. "*Ce n'est pas ça*: Blackness, Sex, and the Set of Illegibles." *differences* 36, no. 1 (2025): 115–32.
Edelman, Lee. "An Ethics of Desubjectivation?" *differences* 27, no. 3 (2016): 106–18.

Edelman, Lee. "Learning Nothing: *Bad Education*." *differences* 28, no. 1 (2017): 124–73.

Edelman, Lee. *No Future: Queer Theory and the Death Drive*. Duke University Press, 2004.

Edelman, Lee. "On Solidarity." *Representations* 158 (2022): 93–105.

Edwards, Erica. *The Other Side of Terror: Black Women and the Culture of US Empire*. New York University Press, 2021.

Ertür, Başak. "Conscription and Critique." *Critical Times* 2, no. 2 (2019): 270–84.

Esposito, Roberto. *Third Person: Politics of Life and Philosophy of the Impersonal*. Polity, 2012.

Falcón, Sylvanna, and Jennifer Nash. "Shifting Analytics and Linking Theories: A Conversation About the 'Meaning-Making' of Intersectionality and Transnational Feminism." *Women's Studies International Forum* 50 (2015): 1–10.

Fanon, Frantz. *Black Skin, White Masks*. Translated by Charles Lam Markmann. Pluto Press, 2008.

Farrow, Kenyon. "Audre Lorde and I Were Once Enemies." *Black Perspectives* (blog), AAIHS, 16 February 2021. https://www.aaihs.org/audre-lorde-and-i-were-once-enemies/.

Ferguson, Roderick. *Aberrations in Black: Toward a Queer of Color Critique*. University of Minnesota Press, 2003.

Ferguson, Roderick. *The Reorder of Things: The University and Its Pedagogies of Minority Difference*. University of Minnesota Press, 2012.

Ferreira da Silva, Denise. "Sending Language into Battle: Interview with Hortense J. Spillers." *boundary 2* 51, no. 1 (2024): 3–37.

Freud, Sigmund. *The Standard Edition of the Complete Psychological Works of Sigmund Freud*. Vol. 16. Edited by James Strachey. Macmillan, 1964.

Geary, Adam. *Antiblack Racism and the AIDS Epidemic: State Intimacies*. Palgrave Macmillan, 2014.

Germano, William. "Theory as a Body of Work." *Symplokē* 27, no. 1–2 (2019): 451–58.

Gilmore, Ruth Wilson. *Abolition Geography: Essays Towards Liberation*. Verso, 2023.

Gilmore, Ruth Wilson. "Globalisation and US Prison Growth: From Military Keynesianism to Post-Keynesian Militarism." *Race and Class* 40, no. 2–3 (1997): 145–57.

Gilmore, Ruth Wilson. *Golden Gulag: Prison, Surplus, Crisis, and Opposition in Globalizing California*. University of California Press, 2007.

Gilmore, Ruth Wilson. "What Is to Be Done?" *American Quarterly* 63, no. 2 (2011): 245–65.

González, Anita. "Indigenous Acts: Black and Native Performances in Mexico." *Radical History Review* 103 (2009): 131–41.

Gopinath, Gayatri. "Archive, Affect, and the Everyday: Queer Diasporic Re-Visions." In *Political Emotions*, edited by Janet Staiger, Ann Cvetkovich, and Ann Reynolds. Routledge, 2010.

Gopinath, Gayatri. "Chitra Ganesh's Queer Re-Visions." *GLQ* 15, no. 3 (2009): 469–80.

Gopinath, Gayatri. *Impossible Desires: Queer Diasporas and South Asian Public Cultures.* Duke University Press, 2005.

Gopinath, Gayatri. *Unruly Visions: The Aesthetic Practices of Queer Diaspora.* Duke University Press, 2018.

Gordon, Lewis. *Her Majesty's Other Children: Sketches of Racism from a Neocolonial Age.* Rowman and Littlefield, 1997.

Gould, Janice. *Earthquake Weather: Poems.* University of Arizona Press, 1996.

Grewal, Inderpal. *Transnational America: Feminisms, Diasporas, Neoliberalisms.* Duke University Press, 2005.

Grewal, Inderpal. "Transnational America: Race, Gender, and Citizenship After 9/11." *Social Identities* 9, no. 4 (2003): 535–61.

Grewal, Inderpal, and Caren Kaplan. "Global Identities: Theorizing Transnational Studies of Sexuality." *GLQ* 7, no. 4 (2001): 663–79.

Grewal, Inderpal, and Caren Kaplan, eds. *An Introduction to Women's Studies: Gender in a Transnational World.* McGraw Hill, 2005.

Grewal, Inderpal, and Caren Kaplan. "Introduction: Transnational Feminist Practices and Questions of Postmodernity." In Grewal and Kaplan, *Scattered Hegemonies.*

Grewal, Inderpal, and Caren Kaplan, eds. *Scattered Hegemonies: Postmodernity and Transnational Feminist Practices.* University of Minnesota Press, 1994.

Grewal, Inderpal, and Caren Kaplan. "Transnational Feminist Cultural Studies: Beyond the Marxism/Poststructuralism/Feminism Divides." *Positions* 2, no. 2 (1994): 430–45.

Grewal, Inderpal, and Caren Kaplan. "Transnational Practices and Interdisciplinary Feminist Scholarship: Refiguring Women's and Gender Studies." In *Women's Studies on Its Own*, edited by Robyn Wiegman. Duke University Press, 2002.

Grewal, Inderpal, and Caren Kaplan. "*Warrior Marks*: Global Womanism's Neo-Colonial Discourse in a Multicultural Context." *Camera Obscura* 13, no. 3 (1996): 4–33.

Griffin, Farah Jasmine. "That the Mothers May Soar and the Daughters May Know Their Names: A Retrospective of Black Feminist Literary Criticism." *Signs* 32, no. 2 (2007): 483–507.

Grosz, Elizabeth. "Criticism, Feminism, and the Institution: An Interview with Gayatri Chakravorty Spivak." *Thesis Eleven* 10/11 (1984/85): 175–87.

Gumbs, Alexis Pauline. "The Shape of My Impact." *Feminist Wire*, 29 October 2012. https://thefeministwire.com/2012/10/the-shape-of-my-impact/.

Gumbs, Alexis Pauline. "Speculative Poetics: Audre Lorde as Prologue for Queer Black Futurism." In *The Black Imagination: Science Fiction, Futurism and the Speculative*, edited by Sandra Jackson and Julie E. Moody Freeman. Peter Lang, 2011.

Gumbs, Alexis Pauline. *Survival Is a Promise: The Eternal Life of Audre Lorde*. Farrar, Straus and Giroux, 2024.

Hakutani, Yoshinobu. *Cross-Cultural Visions in African American Modernism: From Spatial Narrative to Jazz Haiku*. Ohio State University Press, 2006.

Halberstam, Jack. "The Anti-Social Turn in Queer Studies." *Graduate Journal of Social Science* 5, no. 2 (2008): 140–56.

Halberstam, Jack. *The Queer Art of Failure*. Duke University Press, 2011.

Hall, Stuart. "Gramsci's Relevance for the Study of Race and Ethnicity." *Journal of Communication Inquiry* 10, no. 2 (1986): 5–27.

Hall, Stuart. "New Ethnicities." In *Stuart Hall: Critical Dialogues in Cultural Studies*, edited by David Morley and Kuan-Hsing Chen. Routledge, 1996.

Hall, Stuart. "The Toad in the Garden: Thatcherism Among the Theorists." In *Marxism and the Interpretation of Culture*, edited by Cary Nelson and Lawrence Grossberg. University of Illinois Press, 1988.

Han, Sora Y. *Letters of the Law: Race and the Fantasy of Colorblindness in American Law*. Stanford University Press, 2015.

Han, Sora Y. *Mu: 49 Marks of Abolition*. Duke University Press, 2024.

Han, Sora Y. "Slavery as Contract: *Betty's Case* and the Question of Freedom." *Law and Literature* 27, no. 3 (2015): 395–416.

Hartman, Saidiya. "Black in Anarchy." In *The Nation on No Map*, by William C. Anderson. AK Press, 2021.

Hartman, Saidiya. "Crow Jane Makes a Modest Proposal: A Solution to the Problem of Race Relations." *n+1* 48 (2024). https://www.nplusonemag.com/issue-48/politics/crow-jane-makes-a-modest-proposal/.

Hartman, Saidiya. "Excisions of the Flesh." In *Lorna Simpson: For the Sake of the Viewer*, edited by Beryl J. Wright and Saidiya Hartman. Universe, 1992.

Hartman, Saidiya. "Litany for Grieving Sisters." *Representations* 158 (2022): 39–44.

Hartman, Saidiya. *Lose Your Mother: A Journey Along the Atlantic Slave Route*. Farrar, Straus and Giroux, 2007.

Hartman, Saidiya. Review of *The Slumbering Volcano: American Slave Ship Revolts and the Production of Rebellious Masculinity*, by Maggie Montesinos Sale. *Labour/Le Travail* 42 (1998): 260–61.

Hartman, Saidiya. *Scenes of Subjection: Terror, Slavery, and Self-Making in Nineteenth-Century America*. Oxford University Press, 1997.

Hartman, Saidiya. "The Territory Between Us: A Report on 'Black Women in the Academy: Defending Our Name: 1894–1994.'" *Callaloo* 17, no. 2 (1994): 439–49.

Hartman, Saidiya. "The Time of Slavery." *South Atlantic Quarterly* 101, no. 4 (2002): 757–77.

Hartman, Saidiya. "Venus in Two Acts." *small axe* 26 (2008): 1–14.

Hartman, Saidiya. *Wayward Lives, Beautiful Experiments: Intimate Histories of Social Upheaval*. W. W. Norton, 2019.

Hartman, Saidiya, and Frank B. Wilderson III. "The Position of the Unthought: An Interview by Frank B. Wilderson III." *Qui Parle* 13, no. 2 (2003): 183–201.

Hemmings, Clare. *Why Stories Matter: The Political Grammar of Feminist Theory.* Duke University Press, 2011.

Holland, Sharon. "The 'Beached Whale.'" *GLQ* 17, no. 1 (2010): 89–95.

Holland, Sharon. *The Erotic Life of Racism*. Duke University Press, 2012.

Holland, Sharon. *an other: a black feminist consideration of animal life*. Duke University Press, 2023.

Holloway, Karla FC. "'Cruel Enough to Stop the Blood': Global Feminisms and the U.S. Body Politic, or 'They Done Taken My Blues and Gone.'" *Meridians* 7, no. 1 (2006): 1–18.

Hong, Grace Kyungwon. *Death Beyond Disavowal: The Impossible Politics of Difference*. University of Minnesota Press, 2015.

Hong, Grace Kyungwon. "'The Future of Our Worlds': Black Feminism and the Politics of Knowledge in the University Under Globalization." *Meridians* 8, no. 2 (2008): 95–115.

Hull, Akasha Gloria. "'What It Is I Think She's Doing Anyhow': A Reading of Toni Cade Bambara's *The Salt Eaters*." In *Conjuring: Black Women, Fiction, and Literary Tradition*, edited by Marjorie Pryse and Hortense Spillers. Indiana University Press, 1985.

Jablon, Madelyn. *Black Metafiction: Self-Consciousness in African American Literature*. University of Iowa Press, 1997.

Jackson, Shona N. *Beyond Constraint: Middle/Passages of Blackness and Indigeneity in the Radical Tradition*. Duke University Press, 2024.

Jackson, Shona N. *Creole Indigeneity: Between Myth and Nation in the Caribbean*. University of Minnesota Press, 2012.

Jackson, Zakiyyah Iman. *Becoming Human: Matter and Meaning in an Antiblack World*. New York University Press, 2020.

Jackson, Zakiyyah Iman. "'Theorizing in a Void': Sublimity, Matter, and Physics in Black Feminist Poetics." *South Atlantic Quarterly* 117, no. 3 (2018): 617–48.

Jackson, Zakiyyah Iman. "Waking Nightmares—on David Marriott." *GLQ* 17, no. 2–3 (2011): 357–63.

James, C. L. R. *The Black Jacobins: Toussaint L'Ouverture and the San Domingo Revolution*. Vintage, 1989.

James, Joy. "Afrarealism and the Black Matrix: Maroon Philosophy at Democracy's Border." *Black Scholar* 43, no. 4 (2013): 124–31.

James, Joy. *Shadowboxing: Representations of Black Feminist Politics*. St. Martin's Press, 1999.

Jameson, Fredric. "On 'Cultural Studies.'" *Social Text* 34 (1993): 17–52.

Johnston, Adrian. *Adventures in Transcendental Materialism: Dialogues with Contemporary Thinkers*. Edinburgh University Press, 2014.

Judy, Ronald A. T. "Fanon's Body of Black Experience." In *Fanon: A Critical Reader*, edited by Lewis Gordon, T. Denean Sharpley-Whiting, and Renée T. White. Blackwell, 1996.

Judy, Ronald A. T. "Irony and the Asymptotes of the Hyperbola." *boundary 2* 25, no. 1 (1998): 169–90.

Judy, Ronald A. T. "Kant and the Negro." *Surfaces* 1 (1991): 1–64.

Kaba, Mariame. *We Do This 'til We Free Us: Abolitionist Organizing and Transformative Justice*. Haymarket, 2021.

Kaplan, Sara Clarke. *The Black Reproductive: Unfree Labor and Insurgent Motherhood*. University of Minnesota Press, 2021.

Kaplan, Sara Clarke. "Souls at the Crossroads, Africans on the Water: The Politics of Diasporic Melancholia." *Callaloo* 30, no. 2 (2007): 511–26.

Karakatsanis, Alex. "The Punishment Bureaucracy: How to Think About 'Criminal Justice Reform.'" *Yale Law Journal Forum* 128, no. 8 (2019): 848–935.

Karera, Axelle. "Blackness and the Pitfalls of Anthropocene Ethics." *Critical Philosophy of Race* 7, no. 1 (2019): 32–56.

Katherine, Amber L. "'A Too Early Morning': Audre Lorde's 'An Open Letter to Mary Daly' and Daly's Decision Not to Respond in Kind." In *Feminist Interpretations of Mary Daly*, edited by Sarah Lucia Hoagland and Marilyn Frye. Pennsylvania State University Press, 2000.

Keeling, Kara. "Looking for M—: Queer Temporality, Black Political Possibility, and Poetry from the Future." *GLQ* 15, no. 4 (2009): 565–82.

Keeling, Kara. *Queer Times, Black Futures*. New York University Press, 2019.

Keizer, Arlene. *Black Subjects: Identity Formation in the Contemporary Narrative of Slavery*. Cornell University Press, 2004.

Kincaid, Jamaica. "In History." *Callaloo* 20, no. 1 (1997): 1–7.

Kincaid, Jamaica. "Ovando." *Conjunctions* 14 (1989): 75–83.

King, Tiffany Lethabo. "Post-Identitarian and Post-Intersectional Anxiety in the Neoliberal Corporate University." *Feminist Formations* 27, no. 3 (2015): 114–38.

Koerner, Michelle. "Line of Escape: Gilles Deleuze's Encounter with George Jackson." *Genre* 44, no. 2 (2011): 157–80.

Krauss, Rosalind. "Grids." *October* 9 (1979): 50–64.

Kyle, Keith. *The Politics of the Independence of Kenya*. St. Martin's Press, 1999.

Lacan, Jacques. *The Ethics of Psychoanalysis, 1959–1960*. Book 7 of *The Seminar of Jacques Lacan*, translated by Dennis Porter. W. W. Norton, 1992.

Lacan, Jacques. *The Four Fundamental Concepts of Psychoanalysis*. Book 11 of *The Seminar of Jacques Lacan*, translated by Alan Sheridan. W. W. Norton, 1998.

Laclau, Ernesto. *Politics and Ideology in Marxist Theory: Capitalism—Fascism—Populism*. New Left Books, 1977.

Laclau, Ernesto, and Chantal Mouffe. *Hegemony and Socialist Strategy: Towards a Radical Democratic Politics*. 2nd ed. Verso, 2001.

Levitt, Laura. "A Letter to Mary Daly." *Journal of Feminist Studies in Religion* 28, no. 2 (2012): 109–12.

Livingston, Jennie, dir. *Paris Is Burning*. Miramax Films, 1990.

Lorde, Audre. "A Burst of Light: Living with Cancer." In *I Am Your Sister: Collected and Unpublished Writings of Audre Lorde*, edited by Rudolph P. Byrd, Johnette Betsch Cole, and Beverly Guy-Sheftall. Oxford University Press, 2009.

Lorde, Audre. *The Cancer Journals*. Aunt Lute Books, 1980.

Lorde, Audre. *Chosen Poems, Old and New*. W. W. Norton, 1982.

Lorde, Audre. *The Collected Poems of Audre Lorde*. W. W. Norton, 1997.

Lorde, Audre. "An Open Letter to Mary Daly." In *This Bridge Called My Back: Writings by Radical Women of Color*, edited by Cherríe Moraga and Gloria Anzaldúa. Kitchen Table: Women of Color Press, 1983.

Lorde, Audre. "An Open Letter to Mary Daly." In *Top Ranking: A Collection of Articles on Racism and Classism in the Lesbian Community*, edited by Joan Gibbs and Sara Bennett. February 3rd Press, 1980.

Lorde, Audre. "The Role of Difference." *Off Our Backs* 9, no. 11 (1979): 5, 27.

Lorde, Audre. *Sister Outsider: Essays and Speeches*. Crossing Press, 2000.

Lorde, Audre, Marge Piercy, Fran Moira, and Lorraine Sorrel. "Interview: Audre Lorde: Lit from Within." *Off Our Backs* 12, no. 4 (1982): 2–3, 11.

Marriott, David. *Haunted Life: Visual Culture and Black Modernity*. Rutgers University Press, 2007.

Martinot, Steve, and Jared Sexton. "The Avant-Garde of White Supremacy." *Social Identities* 9, no. 2 (2003): 169–81.

Marx, Karl. *Capital: A Critique of Political Economy. Volume One*. Translated by Ben Fowkes. Vintage, 1977.

Massumi, Brian. *Parables for the Virtual: Movement, Affect, Sensation*. Duke University Press, 2002.

Matsuda, Mari. "Beyond, and Not Beyond, Black and White." In *Crossroads, Directions, and a New Critical Race Theory*, edited by Francisco Valdes, Jerome McCristal Culp, and Angela P. Harris. Temple University Press, 2002.

Maxon, Robert M. "Social and Cultural Changes." In *Decolonization and Independence in Kenya, 1940–93*, edited by Bethwell A. Ogot and William R. Ochieng'. James Currey, 1995.

May, Vivian. *Pursuing Intersectionality, Unsettling Dominant Imaginaries*. Routledge, 2015.

Mbembe, Achille. *Critique of Black Reason*. Duke University Press, 2017.

McDougall, Taija Mars. "Untitled #2." *Propter Nos* 4 (2020): 52–66.

McDowell, Deborah. *"The Changing Same": Black Women's Literature, Criticism, and Theory*. Indiana University Press, 1995.

McDowell, Deborah. "New Directions for a Black Feminist Criticism." *Black American Literature Forum* 14, no. 4 (1980): 153–59.

McKay, Nellie Y. "Naming the Problem That Led to the Question 'Who Shall Teach African American Literature?'; or, Are We Ready to Disband the Wheatly Court?" *PMLA* 113, no. 3 (1998): 359–69.

Melamed, Jodi. *Represent and Destroy: Rationalizing Violence in the New Racial Capitalism*. University of Minnesota Press, 2011.

Melville, Herman. "Bartleby, the Scrivener." In *Billy Budd, Bartleby, and Other Stories*. Penguin Classics, 2016.
Miller, J. Hillis. "Literary Study Among the Ruins." *Diacritics* 31, no. 3 (2001): 57–66.
Mills, Charles. *The Racial Contract*. Cornell University Press, 1997.
Monagle, Clare. "Mary Daly's *Gyn/Ecology*: Mysticism, Difference, and Feminist History." *Signs* 44, no. 2 (2019): 333–53.
Morrison, Toni. *Beloved*. Alfred A. Knopf, 1987.
Morrison, Toni. "A Slow Walk of Trees (as Grandmother Would Say), Hopeless (as Grandfather Would Say)." In *What Moves at the Margin: Selected Nonfiction*, edited by Carolyn C. Denard. University Press of Mississippi, 2008.
Morrison, Toni. *Sula*. Vintage, 2004.
Morrison, Toni. "What the Black Woman Thinks About Women's Lib." In *What Moves at the Margins: Selected Nonfiction*, edited by Carolyn C. Denard. University Press of Mississippi, 2008.
Moten, Fred. "Blackness and Nothingness (Mysticism in the Flesh)." *South Atlantic Quarterly* 112, no. 4 (2013): 737–80.
Moten, Fred. *In the Break: The Aesthetics of the Black Radical Tradition*. University of Minnesota Press, 2003.
Moten, Fred. "Knowledge of Freedom." *CR: The New Centennial Review* 4, no. 2 (2004): 269–310.
Moten, Fred. "Notes on Passage (The New International of Sovereign Feelings)." *Palimpsest* 3, no. 1 (2014): 51–74.
Moten, Fred. *Stolen Life*. Duke University Press, 2018.
Mouffe, Chantal, ed. *Gramsci and Marxist Theory*. Routledge and Kegan Paul, 1979.
Mouffe, Chantal. "Hegemony and Ideology in Gramsci." In *Gramsci and Marxist Theory*. Routledge and Kegan Paul, 1979.
Mouffe, Chantal. "Introduction: Gramsci Today." In *Gramsci and Marxist Theory*. Routledge and Kegan Paul, 1979.
Mufti, Aamir R. "Critical Secularism: A Reintroduction for Perilous Times." *boundary 2* 31, no. 2 (2004): 1–9.
Muñoz, José Esteban. "Cruising the Toilet: LeRoi Jones/Amiri Baraka, Radical Black Traditions, and Queer Futurity." *GLQ* 13, no. 2–3 (2007): 353–67.
Muñoz, José Esteban. *Cruising Utopia: The Then and There of Queer Futurity*. New York University Press, 2009.
Muñoz, José Esteban. "Thinking Beyond Antirelationality and Antiutopianism in Queer Critique." *PMLA* 121, no. 3 (2006): 825–26.
Nagar, Richa, and Amanda L. Swarr, eds. *Critical Transnational Feminist Praxis*. State University of New York Press, 2010.
Nash, Jennifer C. *Black Feminism Reimagined: After Intersectionality*. Duke University Press, 2019.
Nash, Jennifer C. "Feminist Originalism: Intersectionality and the Politics of Reading." *Feminist Theory* 17, no. 1 (2016): 3–20.

Nash, Jennifer C. "'Home Truths' on Intersectionality." *Yale Journal of Law and Feminism* 23, no. 2 (2011): 445–70.

Nash, Jennifer C. *How We Write Now: Living with Black Feminist Theory*. Duke University Press, 2024.

Nash, Jennifer C. "Institutionalizing the Margins." *Social Text* 32, no. 1 (2014): 45–65.

Nash, Jennifer C. "On Difficulty: Intersectionality as Feminist Labor." *Scholar and Feminist Online* 8, no. 3 (2010). http://sfonline.barnard.edu/polyphonic/nash_01.htm.

Nash, Jennifer C. "On the Beginning of the World: Dominance Feminism, Afropessimism, and the Meanings of Gender." *Feminist Theory* 23, no. 4 (2022): 556–74.

Nash, Jennifer C. "Re-Thinking Intersectionality." *Feminist Review* 89 (2008): 1–15.

Nash, Jennifer C. "Strange Bedfellows: Black Feminism and Antipornography Feminism." *Social Text* 26, no. 4 (2008): 51–76.

Nash, Jennifer C. "Un-Disciplining Intersectionality." *International Feminist Journal of Politics* 11, no. 4 (2009): 587–93.

Nash, Jennifer C. "Writing Black Beauty." *Signs* 45, no. 1 (2019): 101–22.

Nhất Hạnh, Thích. *Interbeing: Fourteen Guidelines for Engaged Buddhism*. Rev. ed. Parallax Press, 1993.

Painter, Nell Irvin. "Black Studies, Black Professors, and Struggles for Perception." In *A Companion to African-American Studies*, edited by Lewis R. Gordon and Jane Anna Gordon. Blackwell, 2006.

Painter, Nell Irvin. Review of *Scenes of Subjection: Terror, Slavery, and Self-Making in Nineteenth-Century America*, by Saidiya V. Hartman. *Journal of American History* 85, no. 2 (1998): 680–81.

Palmer, Tyrone. "Otherwise than Blackness: Feeling, World, Sublimation." *Qui Parle* 29, no. 2 (2020): 247–83.

Passavant, Paul A. *Policing Protest: The Post-Democratic State and the Figure of Black Insurrection*. Duke University Press, 2021.

Patterson, Anita. Review of *Scenes of Subjection: Terror, Slavery, and Self-Making in Nineteenth-Century America*, by Saidiya V. Hartman. *African American Review* 33, no. 4 (1999): 683–86.

Patterson, Orlando. "The Peculiar Institution Again." *New Republic*, 9 November 1974, 37–38.

Patterson, Orlando. *Slavery and Social Death: A Comparative Study*. Harvard University Press, 1982.

Phillips, Adam. "The Magical Act of a Desperate Person." *London Review of Books* 35, no. 5 (2013). https://www.lrb.co.uk/the-paper/v35/n05/adam-phillips/the-magical-act-of-a-desperate-person.

Pinto, Samantha. "Black Feminist Literacies: Ungendering, Flesh, and Post-Spillers Epistemologies of Embodied and Emotional Justice." *Journal of Black Sexuality and Relationships* 4, no. 1 (2017): 25–45.

Prashad, Vijay. *The Darker Nations: A People's History of the Third World*. New Press, 2008.

Puar, Jasbir K. "'I Would Rather Be a Cyborg than a Goddess': Becoming-Intersectional in Assemblage Theory." *PhilosoPHIA* 2, no. 1 (2012): 49–66.

Puar, Jasbir K. "Queer Times, Queer Assemblages." *Social Text* 23, no. 3–4 (2005): 121–39.

Puar, Jasbir K. *Terrorist Assemblages: Homonationalism in Queer Times.* Duke University Press, 2007.

Puar, Jasbir K., and Amit Rai. "Monster-Terrorist-Fag: The War on Terror and the Production of Docile Patriots." *Social Text* 20, no. 3 (2002): 117–48.

Rapaport, Herman. *The Theory Mess: Deconstruction in Eclipse.* Columbia University Press, 2001.

Reddy, Chandan. *Freedom with Violence: Race, Sexuality, and the US State.* Duke University Press, 2011.

Rifkin, Mark. *Fictions of Land and Flesh: Blackness, Indigeneity, Speculation.* Duke University Press, 2019.

Rifkin, Mark. "Indigenizing Agamben: Rethinking Sovereignty in Light of the 'Peculiar' Status of Native Peoples." *Cultural Critique* 73 (2009): 88–124.

Ross, Theodore. "Mikki Kendall and Her Online Beefs with White Feminists." *Vice*, 29 May 2014. https://www.vice.com/en/article/their-eyes-were-watching-twitter-0000317-v21n5/.

Satcher, David, George E. Fryer Jr., Jessica McCann, et al. "What if We Were Equal? A Comparison of the Black-White Mortality Gap in 1960 and 2000." *Health Affairs* 24, no. 2 (2005): 459–64.

Saunders, Patricia J. "Defending the Dead, Confronting the Archive: A Conversation with M. NourbeSe Philip." *Small Axe* 12, no. 2 (2008): 63–79.

Saunders, Patricia J. "Fugitive Dreams of Diaspora: Conversations with Saidiya Hartman." *Anthurium: A Caribbean Studies Journal* 6, no. 1 (2008): art. 7.

Scott, Joan W. *The Fantasy of Feminist History.* Duke University Press, 2011.

Sexton, Jared. *Amalgamation Schemes: Antiblackness and the Critique of Multiracialism.* University of Minnesota Press, 2008.

Sexton, Jared. *Black Men, Black Feminism: Lucifer's Nocturne.* Palgrave, 2018.

Sexton, Jared. "'The Curtain of the Sky': An Introduction." *Critical Sociology* 36, no. 1 (2010): 11–24.

Sexton, Jared. "People-of-Color-Blindness: Notes on the Afterlife of Slavery." *Social Text* 28, no. 2 (2010): 31–56.

Sexton, Jared. "Response." Syndicate Symposium on *Ontological Terror*, by Calvin Warren Convened and introduced by Andrew Santana Kaplan. *Syndicate*, 2021. https://syndicate.network/symposia/theology/ontological-terror/.

Sexton, Jared. "The Social Life of Social Death: On Afro-Pessimism and Black Optimism." *InTensions* 5 (2011): 1–47.

Sexton, Jared, and Sora Han. "The Devil's Choice: Slavery and the Logic of the *Vel*." In *Esoteric Lacan*, edited by Philipp Valentini and Mahdi Tourage. Rowman and Littlefield, 2020.

Sharpe, Christina. *In the Wake: On Blackness and Being.* Duke University Press, 2016.

Simpson, Audra. "The Sovereignty of Critique." *South Atlantic Quarterly* 119, no. 4 (2020): 685–99.

Simpson, Leanne Betasamoske. "The Place Where We All Live and Work Together: A Gendered Analysis of Sovereignty." In *Native Studies Keywords*, edited by Stephanie Nohelani Teves, Andrea Smith, and Michelle Rehaja. University of Arizona Press, 2015.

Smith, Barbara. "Black Feminism Divorced from Black Feminist Organizing." *Black Scholar* 14, no. 1 (1983): 38–45.

Smith, Barbara. "The Boston Murders." In *Life Notes: Personal Writings by Contemporary Black Women*, edited by Patricia Bell-Scott. W. W. Norton, 1994.

Smith, Barbara. "Toward a Black Feminist Criticism." *Conditions* 1, no. 2 (1977): 25–44.

Smith, Barbara. "Toward a Black Feminist Criticism." In *In the Memory and Spirit of Frances, Zora, and Lorraine: Essays and Interviews on Black Women and Writing*, edited by Juliette Bowles. Institute for the Arts and Humanities, Howard University, 1979.

Smith, Beverly. "Diane." *Common Lives/Lesbian Lives* 1 (1981): 59–67.

Smith, Beverly. "The Wedding." *Conditions* 2, no. 2 (1979): 103–8.

Smith, Marquard. "On the State of Cultural Studies: An Interview with Paul Gilroy." *Third Text* 49 (1999–2000): 15–26.

Smith, Pamela A. "Green Lap, Brown Embrace, Blue Body: The Ecospirituality of Alice Walker." *CrossCurrents* 48, no. 4 (1998): 471–87.

Snediker, Michael D. *Queer Optimism: Lyric Personhood and Other Felicitous Persuasions.* University of Minnesota Press, 2009.

Soler, Colette. "The Paradoxes of the Symptom in Psychoanalysis." In *The Cambridge Companion to Lacan*, edited by Jean-Michel Rabaté. Cambridge University Press, 2003.

Solow, Barbara. "Capitalism and Slavery in the Exceedingly Long Run." *Journal of Interdisciplinary History* 17, no. 4 (1987): 711–37.

Sorentino, Sara-Maria. "The Abstract Slave: Anti-Blackness and Marx's Method." *International Labor and Working-Class History* 96 (2019): 17–37.

Soto, Sandra K. "Where in the Transnational World Are U.S. Women of Color?" In *Women's Studies for the Future: Foundations, Interrogations, Politics*, edited by Elizabeth Lapovsky Kennedy and Agatha Beins. Rutgers University Press, 2005.

Spigner, Nicole A. "All the Things You Could Be by Now if Hortense Spillers Was Your Mentor." In *The Flesh of the Matter: A Critical Forum on Hortense Spillers*, edited by Margo Crawford and C. Riley Snorton. Vanderbilt University Press, 2024.

Spillers, Hortense. "Afterword: Cross-Currents, Discontinuities: Black Women's Fiction." In *Conjuring: Black Women, Fiction, and Literary Tradition*, edited by Marjorie Pryse and Hortense Spillers. Indiana University Press, 1985.

Spillers, Hortense. *Black, White, and in Color: Essays on American Literature and Culture.* University of Chicago Press, 2003.

Spillers, Hortense. "A Hateful Passion, a Lost Love." *Feminist Studies* 9, no. 2 (1983): 293–323.

Spillers, Hortense. "Mama's Baby, Papa's Maybe: An American Grammar Book." *Diacritics* 17, no. 2 (1987): 64–81.

Spillers, Hortense. "Quarrels into Ploughshares: Feminism and Race." In *True Confessions: Feminist Professors Tell Stories Out of School*, edited by Susan Gubar. W. W. Norton, 2011.

Spillers, Hortense, Saidiya Hartman, Farah Jasmine Griffin, Shelly Eversley, and Jennifer L. Morgan. "'Whatcha Gonna Do?' Revisiting 'Mama's Baby, Papa's Maybe: An American Grammar Book.'" *Women's Studies Quarterly* 35, no. 1–2 (2007): 299–309.

Spivak, Gayatri Chakravorty. *A Critique of Postcolonial Reason: Toward a History of the Vanishing Present*. Harvard University Press, 1999.

Sweet, James. "The Iberian Roots of American Racist Thought." *William and Mary Quarterly* 54, no. 1 (1997): 143–66.

Telling, Kathryn. "Quite Contrary: Mary Daly Within and Without Women's Studies." *Journal of International Women's Studies* 13, no. 6 (2012): 32–43.

Terada, Rei. "The Frailty of the Ontic." *South Atlantic Quarterly* 110, no. 1 (2011): 37–55.

Terada, Rei. *Metaracial: Hegel, Antiblackness, and Political Identity*. University of Chicago Press, 2023.

Terada, Rei. "The Racial Grammar of Kantian Time." *European Romantic Review* 28, no. 3 (2017): 267–78.

Terada, Rei. "Scruples, or, Faith in Derrida." *South Atlantic Quarterly* 106, no. 2 (2007): 237–64.

Tompkins, Kyla Wazana. *Racial Indigestion: Eating Bodies in the 19th Century*. New York University Press, 2012.

Vance, Carole S., ed. *Pleasure and Danger: Exploring Female Sexuality*. Routledge and Kegan Paul, 1984.

Vaziri, Parisa. "On 'Saidiya': Indian Ocean World Slavery and Blackness Beyond Horizon." *Qui Parle* 28, no. 2 (2019): 241–80.

Veracini, Lorenzo. *Settler Colonialism: A Theoretical Overview*. Palgrave Macmillan, 2010.

Visperas, Cristina. *Skin Theory: Visual Culture and the Postwar Prison Laboratory*. New York University Press, 2022.

Wacquant, Loïc. "From Slavery to Mass Incarceration: Rethinking the 'Race Question' in the US." *New Left Review* 13 (2002): 41–60.

Wacquant, Loïc. "The Great Penal Leap Backward: Incarceration in America from Nixon to Clinton." In *The New Punitiveness: Theories, Trends, Perspectives*, edited by John Pratt, David Brown, Mark Brown, Simon Hallsworth, and Wayne Morrison. Routledge, 2005.

Wagner, Bryan. *Disturbing the Peace: Black Culture and the Police Power After Slavery*. Harvard University Press, 2009.

Walker, Alice. *The Cushion in the Road: Meditation and Wandering as the Whole World Awakens to Being in Harm's Way*. New Press, 2013.

Walker, Alice, and Pratibha Parmar. *Warrior Marks: Female Genital Mutilation and the Sexual Blinding of Women*. Harcourt, Brace, 1993.

Wang, Jackie. *Carceral Capitalism*. Semiotext(e), 2018.

Webster, Jamieson. "The Psychopharmacology of Everyday Life." *New York Review of Books*, 19 November 2018. https://www.nybooks.com/online/2018/11/19/the-psychopharmacology-of-everyday-life/.

Weizman, Eyal. *Hollow Land: Israel's Architecture of Occupation*. Verso, 2007.

West, Cornel. "Reconstructing the American Left: The Challenge of Jesse Jackson." *Social Text* 11 (1984–85): 3–19.

Wiegman, Robyn. "Academic Feminism Against Itself." *NWSA Journal* 14, no. 2 (2002): 18–34.

Wiegman, Robyn. "Feminism, Institutionalism, and the Idiom of Failure." *differences* 11, no. 3 (1999): 107–36.

Wiegman, Robyn. *Object Lessons*. Duke University Press, 2012.

Wilderson, Frank B., III. "Biko and the Problematic of Presence." In *Biko Lives! Contesting the Legacies of Steve Biko*, edited by Andile Mngxitama, Amanda Alexander, and Nigel C. Gibson. Palgrave, 2008.

Wilderson, Frank B., III. "Gramsci's Black Marx: Whither the Slave in Civil Society?" *Social Identities* 9, no. 2 (2003): 225–40.

Wilderson, Frank B., III. *Red, White and Black: Cinema and the Structure of US Antagonisms*. Duke University Press, 2010.

Williamson, Terrion L. *Scandalize My Name: Black Feminist Practice and the Making of Black Social Life*. Fordham University Press, 2017.

Woodard, Vincent. *The Delectable Negro: Human Consumption and Homoeroticism Within US Slave Culture*. New York University Press, 2014.

Žižek, Slavoj. "Holding the Place." In *Contingency, Hegemony, Universality: Contemporary Dialogues on the Left*, by Judith Butler, Ernesto Laclau, and Slavoj Žižek. Verso, 2000.

Žižek, Slavoj. *In Defense of Lost Causes*. Verso, 2008.

Žižek, Slavoj. *The Sublime Object of Ideology*. 2nd ed. Verso, 2008.

Index

www.ingramcontent.com/pod-product-compliance
Lightning Source LLC
LaVergne TN
LVHW090922190926
848399LV00031B/239